An Introduction to
Ethnic Conflict

An Introduction to Ethnic Conflict

Milton J. Esman

polity

First published in 2004 by Polity Press Ltd.

Polity Press
65 Bridge Street
Cambridge CB2 1UR, UK

Polity Press
350 Main Street
Malden, MA 02148, USA

ISBN: 0-7456-3116-9
ISBN: 0-7456-3117-7 (pb)

A catalogue record for this book is available from the British Library and has been applied for from the Library of Congress.

Typeset in 10½ on 12pt Sabon
by SNP Best-set Typesetter Ltd., Hong Kong
Printed and bound in Great Britain by TJ International Ltd, Padstow, Cornwall.

For further information on Polity, visit our website: www.polity.co.uk

Foreword

The subject of this book is ethnic conflict.

The purposes of this book are to help readers appreciate the origins of ethnic conflict, to recognize and account for its many and varied manifestations, and to gain an awareness of alternative approaches to mitigating the intensity of such conflicts and enabling competitive ethnic communities to coexist in peace. Basically, the goal is better understanding of a pervasive and many-faceted global phenomenon.

The subject is presented in ten chapters. Chapter 1 lays out the scope of ethnic pluralism and the varieties and complexity of ethnic conflict in the contemporary world. In chapter 2 we define the principal terms and concepts that appear in this book and evaluate the main approaches in the literature to understanding ethnicity, ethnic solidarity, and ethnic conflict. Chapter 3 explores the sources of ethnic pluralism and the processes, peaceful and violent, by which ethnic communities are mobilized to protect and promote their collective interests. Chapter 4 examines the circumstances that precipitate conflict among ethnic communities and the stakes for which they contend. Chapter 5 discusses the various roles that governments play in generating and managing ethnic conflict, and the transnational and international forces that impinge on interethnic encounters. Chapters 6, 7, and 8 describe, analyze, and evaluate the main patterns of interethnic relations, which are domination, power-sharing, and integration. Chapter 9 deals with the various processes by which ethnic conflicts can be managed, with emphasis on the peaceful regulation of disputes. In chapter 10 we project the dynamics of ethnic pluralism into the future and speculate cautiously on what lies ahead.

As we go to press, all eyes are on Iraq. Here is the site of some of the world's oldest civilizations, while containing the world's second largest petroleum reserves. Its population of 25 million includes several ethnic communities, of which the most populous are Kurds in the north, Sunni Arabs in the center, and Shia Arabs in the south, the latter the apparent majority. There is considerable suspicion and some hostility between these communities and within their many factions, which greatly complicate the problem of organizing and operating a democratic government. Neighboring Iran promotes the interests of their fellow Shia, while neighbor Turkey frowns on any significant autonomy for Iraqi Kurds, fearing this would stir up their own restive Kurdish minority.

Why do Iraqis cling to these separate identities? What do they disagree about and what do they fight over? Why can't they relax and learn to live and let live, to be simply Iraqis and concentrate on making a living, practicing their religious faith, raising their families, and enjoying an abundant life? But if they persist in retaining these separate communal identities, what methods are available to help them coexist and settle their differences in peace, rather than endure the horrors visited on other ethnic communities in such places as Northern Ireland, Bosnia, Sri Lanka, Rwanda, and Sudan?

These are some of the problems we address in the ten chapters of this book.

Contents

1
Incidence and Scope of Ethnic Conflict

Ethnic pluralism

Ethnic conflict is a consequence of ethnic pluralism. Ethnic pluralism occurs when two or more ethnic communities are present in the same political space. Political space normally refers to the area under the jurisdiction of the same political authority – in modern times, a territorial state with an effective government.[1] When ethnic communities encounter one another, their contact provides the necessary condition for conflict. Relations among them or between them and governments may be amicable, but often they are hostile and hostility may degenerate into organized violence.

Ethnic conflict may occur at any level of social interaction, from localities and neighborhoods to the central government. Violent clashes between French gangs and North African gangs over access to public swimming pools in the slums of Lyons may be settled locally without any involvement of the government in Paris; likewise, an election contest for mayor in Los Angeles in which a Hispanic candidate is opposed by a White candidate supported also by leaders of the African-American community may have little effect on national politics. Indian cities with civic associations in which Muslims and Hindus jointly participate experience far fewer violent disturbances than those cities where they live entirely separate lives.[2] But when riots broke out in Malaysia's capital city,

Kuala Lumpur, in May 1969, the security forces of the national government immediately intervened, followed by constitutional amendments and new economic policies that drastically affected relations between Malays and non-Malays. Initiatives from the central government may have decisive effects on local affairs. The Voting Rights Act enacted by the Congress in Washington in 1965 resulted in the election of several African-American mayors, city councilmen, and members of Congress from districts previously represented only by Whites.

Though ethnic conflict may occur and be managed at all levels of society, from local communities to the state (the central government), our emphasis in this book is at the state level, because this is the point at which rules are made and enforced that set the standard for regulating ethnic conflict throughout the society.

Contemporary scope of ethnic conflict

Hardly a day passes without newspaper or TV headlines reporting violent encounters in which one or both contestants identify themselves and are identified by others as ethnic communities. The genocide of Tutsi by Hutu in Rwanda, the Chechen revolt against the Russian state, the two decade-long civil war between Tamil insurgents and the Sinhalese government in Sri Lanka, the Bosnian war involving Serbs, Croats, and Muslims followed by the ethnic cleansing of the Kosovar Albanian majority by their Serbian overlords, lethal encounters between Muslims and Christians in the Indonesian Maluku province and between Muslims and Hindus in the Indian state of Gujerat – these have become the principal sources of organized violence since the termination of the Cold War between the United States and Soviet superpowers. The Security Council of the United Nations, which was established to prevent or limit organized violence between states, now confronts mainly intra-state conflicts involving ethnic communities. In 1994 Professor Gurr counted no fewer than 50 currently active ethnic-based conflicts, of which 13 had resulted in 100,000 or more fatalities.[3] Contrary to some journalistic accounts, ethnic conflicts did not suddenly burst forth at the end of the Cold War. Many occurred prior to and during the Cold War and had no relevance to the Cold War or to its termination.

Though the states that comprise the United Nations are conventionally designated as "nation-states," the great majority are, in fact, multiethnic. Very few, such as Korea and Portugal, can claim to be ethnically homogeneous. The great majority contain one or more ethnic minorities of significant size. Using 1990 census figures, Gurr identified 223 politically salient minorities, a fair approximation of the global phenomenon we analyze in this book.[4] Minorities that are large enough to be politically significant are found on all continents, in rich countries (e.g., France and Canada), and poor countries (e.g., India and Ethiopia); in large countries (e.g., Russia and Nigeria), and small countries (e.g., Trinidad and Belgium); in old states (e.g., Spain and China), and new states (e.g., Malaysia and Sudan). Not all intra-state violence is ethnically related. The persistent violence in Colombia can be traced to peasant protest re-enforced by predatory drug cartels. US action against the Saddam regime in Iraq in 2002–3 was not related to ethnic concerns, but the subsequent effort to reconstruct post-war Iraq soon became embroiled in ethnic complexity, notably tensions between Kurds, Sunni Arabs, and Shiite Arabs. At the dawn of the twenty-first century groups defined as ethnic have become the principal contestants in violent organized conflict.

Ethnic conflict is not a function of relative numbers. India's major ethnic communities, several of which number in excess of 50 million, have, with the exception of Kashmir, learned to coexist peacefully in a federal state. Though they comprise only 7 percent of its population, China's non-Han peoples occupy 64 percent of its territory, much of it bordering such states as India and Russia which the Beijing elites regard as chronic security problems. Because of these security concerns, these areas and their populations are closely supervised by China's army and police services. Large numbers of Han colonists have been moved onto these lands, while relatively low levels of economic development and low per capita incomes further aggravate relations with the central government. The central government is accused of attempting to sinicize these societies and destroy their cultures. In Europe, Muslim immigrants from the Mediterranean basin comprise between 2 and 5 percent of the population. But because they are visible (dark-skinned), culturally exotic, resistant to assimilation, and compete with native workers for unskilled jobs and housing, they have become the objects of widespread hostility, charged with criminal behavior, as unsanitary carriers of diseases such as AIDS, and as malingerers who prefer to exploit Europe's generous tax-financed welfare provisions to support their large families. Violent clashes between natives and immigrant gangs have become commonplace; hostility to these immigrants has become a major political issue in most western and central European countries and a rallying point for demands to deport illegal immigrants and block further immigration. Large relative numbers do not portend conflict, nor do small numbers prevent it.

Conflicts, peaceful and violent

Yet at this point an important caution is in order. Ethnic identity does not imply ethnic conflict and ethnic conflict is not necessarily violent. An analysis of civil wars between 1945 and 1999 revealed that ethnic or religious diversity do not make a country more prone to large-scale violence.[5] Most relations among ethnic communities and between them and governments have been historically and are at present conducted peacefully. Even as they harbor grievances, the members and leaders of ethnic communities prefer to accommodate to one another and to governments peacefully; and governments normally manage to preserve peace even among mutually unfriendly ethnic constituencies. Tensions between Catalans and the Spanish government have been adjusted peacefully, while those involving Basque separatists in the same country have been punctuated by sporadic episodes of deadly violence and have implicated Basque communities across the border in France.

When political scientists speak of conflict they refer to competition among groups for power, resources, opportunities, status, or respect, competition that is usually pursued and adjusted by peaceful means, but may under some circumstances turn violent. Organized violence attracts attention from mass media, from governments, and from international organizations because it threatens the lives, the security, and the livelihoods of large numbers of innocent persons, may produce massive floods of refugees, and may spread lethal conflicts across international borders. It was the assassination of the Austrian crown prince by Serbian nationalists in the Bosnian capital, Sarajevo, in 1914 that precipitated the enormous cost and destruction of World War I. More recently the bloody conflict in Rwanda between Hutu and Tutsi has spread to neighboring Congo and drawn armed forces from Uganda, Angola, Burundi, and Zimbabwe into the fray.

Though ethnic nationalism has become the dominant political ideology in the modern era, contrary to some writers, ethnic awareness and solidarity have deep roots in human history.[6] The ancient world gave birth to a number of societies that regarded themselves and were regarded by others as distinctive peoples with their own lands, languages, laws, religious and political institutions, and myths of common origin. Many of these ancient peoples – Picts in Scotland, Minoans in Crete, and Chams in Vietnam, for example – have passed into history; but others including Persians (Iranians), Hebrews, Chinese, and Armenians survive to this day as nations. Ethnic solidarity expresses a profound human need to belong, a source of physical and psychological security, of fictive kinship that expands the boundaries of family relationships to an extended network of individuals that share the same culture and the same historical myths and collective memories. This enables the mortal individual to enhance his precarious self-esteem by identifying with a great and meaningful tradition that will endure into the future after he or she has long departed this world.

The opportunity to identify with a great people and to participate in their struggles appeals especially to people who have achieved limited success and enjoyed only marginal status in this life. This is why, despite Marx's prediction of international proletarian (working-class) solidarity, persons whose economic prospects and social status are at risk are often among the most stalwart supporters of extreme ethnonationalism and other ethnic-based movements. Though the leadership of the Palestinian independence movement comes mainly from elite families, most of the fighters and suicide bombers are recruited from young inmates of squalid refugee settlements with no discernable future prospects. The same applies to the Tamil fighters for an independent Tamil Eelam in Sri Lanka and to Hindu mobs that attack Muslims in India.

The awareness of distinctive people-hood is re-enforced by early socialization, as children learn in their family circle and among neighbors to cherish the proud traditions and folkways of their people as their own, how they are linked to their people by common origin, a common destiny, and common interests, and how they differ from the outsiders they are likely to encounter. Outsiders may be friendly or they may be hostile, but in either case they are different, they are the "other."

Collective identities

Ethnic awareness is a form of collective identity or membership in a group that shares certain common attributes. Most individuals share a number of collective identities. An individual may at the same time be a woman, a Catholic, a Scot, a Britisher, a physician, an environmentalist, a member of the Scottish National Party, and an alumna of the University of Aberdeen. A man in Kuala Lumpur may be a Malaysian citizen, a Tamil, a Hindu, a member of the Malayan Indian Congress, a trade unionist, an avid golfer, and a war veteran. Which of these multiple memberships and loyalties influence her or his behavior at any particular time depends on the circumstances. For many of life's choices her Scottish or his Tamil affinity may be of little or no significance, for example when selecting what kind of automobile to buy or where to spend next year's vacation. For others, such as who to marry or how to vote, it may be crucial. In some instances the individual may be cross-pressured, pulled in opposite directions. As a Scottish patriot, she may favor independence for her homeland; as a physician she values and would prefer to continue participation in the British Medical Society. First, she will try to find a way to reconcile these competing pressures; at some stage, however, she may have to decide which of these collective identities should take precedence. During the colonial era, the Nigerian trade union movement included members of all Nigeria's ethnic communities (often referred to in Africa as "tribes"). After independence, politics in Nigeria became organized along contentious ethnic lines and the trade union movement split into its ethnic components. Ethnic solidarity became more critical to Nigerian workers than occupational or class solidarity.[7]

Like all human associations, ethnic identities and solidarities are not fixed for all time. If ethnic solidarities are to survive, they must adapt to often unpredictable, changing conditions. Failure to adapt means that they lose their relevance and usefulness, and their members drift away. Through the ages many peoples such as Khoikhoi in South Africa, Babylonians in the Middle East, and Visigoths in Europe failed to survive as distinct ethnic communities and passed into history. Some were conquered, others simply absorbed by more powerful neighboring peoples.

On the other hand, French-speaking Québécois in Canada are a classic, contemporary example of successful adaptation.[8] French-Canadians in Quebec long regarded themselves and were regarded by others as an undereducated, Catholic minority attempting to survive, under the watchful tutelage of their conservative clergy in a hostile Anglo-Protestant environment as a peasant people (*habitants*) outside the modern commercial economy. Large numbers of French-Canadians, unable to earn a living in their homeland, were forced to migrate to other Canadian provinces or to New England where most of their offsprings assimilated into the dominant English-speaking society; their French-Canadian origins became little more than nostalgic memories.

With the onset of industrialization and urbanization, it became evident to a new generation of lay leadership that the traditional strategy of peasant survival would condemn their people to permanent backwardness and subordination. In a short time, beginning in 1960, their "Quiet Revolution" succeeded in redefining their community in secular terms as Québécois, the French-speaking majority in their provincial homeland. It harnessed the resources of Quebec's provincial government to promote the participation of French-speakers in the modern sectors of the economy. It fortified the role of French as the primary language of work, education, and government, expanded higher education in the French language, especially in engineering and business management. It reduced the role of the previously dominant Catholic clergy to their pastoral functions.

In a single generation they completed a radical adaptation to a threatening set of circumstances. In the process of adaptation, ethnic groups may revise their boundaries to include fresh recruits, may change their designation, may revise the content and purpose of their peoplehood. The necessity of dealing with fresh challenges underlines the fragility of ethnic solidarity that fails to adapt, and the robustness of those that succeed. Pressures to adapt are one source of the internal divisions that beset all ethnic groups as factions disagree on how much and what kinds of changes should be accepted. Catholics in Northern Ireland are sharply divided on the use of violent tactics to promote their collective interests. The problem of internal factions will be explored in some depth in chapter 2.

Relations among ethnic communities and between them and the state may take many forms and, as discussed in chapter 5, occur under a great variety of circumstances. Some ethnic communities claim homeland status, that they and their ancestors have occupied their homeland for generations and centuries, have stamped their distinctive culture on its settlements, cities, religious structures, and burial grounds to the point that the land is believed to be their unique and sacred inheritance, never mind that they may have been relatively recent arrivals, displacing other peoples who were there before them. Though they displaced and subordinated aboriginal peoples who still survive, and many are relatively recent arrivals from Indonesia, Malays claim peninsular Malaysia as their homeland vis-à-vis more recent Chinese and Indian immigrants. By virtue of their indigenous status, they believe they are entitled to greater rights and to enjoy a superior moral claim on government than more recent arrivals. Some homeland peoples constitute the majority or have achieved a dominant position in their country. Others are minorities, but because they are territorially concentrated in their homeland, they may claim the right to self-determination either as an autonomous self-governing unit within a federal state or as an independent nation. The Tamil minority claim a large swath of Sri Lanka's northern and eastern region as their homeland; some would be satisfied with regional autonomy within a federalized state; others have waged a civil war demanding independent statehood.

Who have the better claim to homeland legitimacy and what these claims entail is being played out in the Finger Lakes region of upstate New York. There, the Cayuga Indian nation claims large tracts of land, 64,000 acres, as its rightful heritage, resulting from an illegal seizure of Cayuga land by the State of New York in violation of a 1790 law enacted by the United States government. In the intervening two centuries, thousands of White settlers occupied, cultivated, built homes and churches, operated businesses, and organized local governments on this land. Their descendants believe they are the rightful owners, holding valid titles to the property, and that their rights are being threatened by capricious, latter-day claims inspired by unscrupulous White lawyers. The Cayugas argue that the land was stolen from their ancestors in violation of Federal law and demand that it be restored to them or that they receive financial compensation of $1.7 billion from New York state. This dispute has generated rancorous charges and countercharges and public demonstrations, but has not resulted in physical violence. In 2001 a Federal jury awarded $247.9 million in damages to the Cayugas. New York has appealed this judgment to a higher court. Meanwhile, the two branches of the tribe, one now based in Oklahoma, are disputing their relative entitlements to shares of the financial award.

Many ethnic communities consist of recent immigrants, having left their original homeland to escape religious or political persecution, or as economic migrants seeking a better life for themselves and their families. Without rejecting their inherited culture, they must necessarily find ways of adjusting to their adopted country where they may be welcome for their labor, but rejected or discriminated against socially and politically. They may adopt different strategies to gain acceptance by the host society or to assert their right to be different, depending on the opportunities available to them by the laws and practices of their host society. Polish immigrants who settled in France between the two world wars adapted willingly to French society and culture and were readily accepted. By contrast, the 5 million Muslim North Africans who have moved to France during the past half century are needed for their labor, performing menial and low-paid tasks that most Frenchmen disdain. Many of them are reluctant to assimilate to French secular culture, demanding the right to perpetuate their North African Muslim way of life, including the controversial right of female students to wear headscarves at school. Their status has become a major issue of contention in French politics. The National Front, the political movement that regards North African immigrants as unassimilable, charges them with undermining French culture, causing crime, AIDS, and unemployment, and supporting their numerous children by tax-funded welfare payments. It urges their exclusion and deportation. The National Front garnered more than 18 percent of the vote in the first round of the 2002 presidential election. Hostility to visible minorities, especially to Muslim immigrants, has become a conspicuous feature of recent politics throughout western and central Europe.

Ethnicity and class

The conjunction of ethnicity and class is a rough indicator of the relative status of ethnic communities. In some cases these relationships are highly stratified. Throughout eastern and central Europe the Roma people (formerly known as Gypsies) occupy the lowest rungs of the social and economic hierarchy, roughly similar to the status of dalits (untouchables) in India. They are politically powerless, undereducated, confined to marginal and menial occupations, widely believed to be engaged in petty crime, socially despised, and their culture is treated with contempt. In such situations as this, ethnicity becomes coterminous with social and economic class. By contrast, French-speaking Walloons and Dutch-speaking Flemings in Belgium are distributed in more or less similar proportions among owners and managers of enterprises, the professions, and skilled workers. They are equally active and effective politically. This situation of approximate socioeconomic equality provides opportunities for the emergence of cross-cutting identities; members of both communities may discover common interests as environmentalists, agronomists, lawyers, golfers, or Catholics that facilitate, though they cannot guarantee, cooperation across ethnic lines of cleavage.

Between these two extremes of class stratification and rough equality, sometimes referred to as ranked and unranked status, there may be many variations and these may change over time. During the apartheid era in South Africa, rigid racial stratification was enforced. Though there was a class hierarchy among Whites, any White person enjoyed status and opportunities in every phase of life from which Blacks were systematically excluded. With the collapse of the apartheid regime, the Black majority elected a government dominated by the African National Congress, which had waged a long campaign for a non-racial democracy. Though political power has passed to the Black majority, Whites remain free to participate as voters, office-seekers, office-holders, and government employees. The economy, however, continues to be stratified. Most industrial and commercial enterprises and most productive agricultural lands are owned and operated by Whites. Most Whites are well educated and continue to enjoy comfortable middle-class lifestyles, while most Blacks remain ill-educated, occupy the lowest rungs of the economic ladder, and continue to subsist in poverty. Yet, a significant Black middle class has emerged as government-sponsored programs open fresh opportunities for Blacks in education, employment, the professions, and skilled labor. Without directly threatening the inherited educational rights and economic stakes of the White minority, the Black-controlled government will continue to use its powers to elevate the economic and social status and opportunities of its majority Black constituents and gradually modify the economic stratification inherited from the apartheid era.

Many situations are characterized by a cultural division of labor, where each ethnic community occupies a separate role in the economy. Often this is a form of social and economic stratification, one group monopolizing elite roles, while others are relegated to inferior positions. This was the case in Quebec prior to the Quiet Revolution of 1960. There, senior and middle management positions in the corporate world were the domain of Protestant English-speakers, while foremen and workers on the factory floor were almost entirely Catholic French-speakers. One eventually successful goal of the Quiet Revolution was the elimination of this pattern of employment. The cultural division of labor may occur under more benign conditions when an ethnic group manages to establish an economic niche for its members, as when Koreans in New York and other East Coast cities gained a dominant position in the retail fruit and vegetable business. In the New York City civil service, for many years the Irish dominated the police department, Italians the sanitation services, and Jews the social service agencies. Ethnic networks applying informal preferences and sanctions succeed in perpetuating opportunities for the in-group and excluding outsiders. The economic roles occupied by middleman minorities in many countries (see chapter 6) constitute another expression of the cultural (ethnic) division of labor.

Strategies and opportunities

The ability of immigrant (diaspora) communities to assert their rights and promote their collective interests depends, in part, on the strategies they pursue and in part on opportunities provided by host governments and societies. Some immigrants strive mightily to learn the local language and acculturate rapidly to the local way of life. Others choose to retain important elements of their inherited culture and adapt slowly and selectively to their new environment. In some countries legal immigrants acquire some rights and protections immediately upon arrival and are encouraged to opt for citizenship and acculturate to the indigenous society. This has been the practice in countries that have been built by recent immigration, among them the United States, Australia, and Brazil. Others, such as Japan, are committed to maintaining what their opinion leaders believe to be their racial and cultural purity. Though they are urgently in need of additional labor as their population ages and their birth rate continues to decline below replacement levels, Japanese government leaders, with the apparent support of public opinion, do not welcome immigrants. They tolerate them for their labor, but make it difficult, if not impossible, for immigrants to acquire a status other than as tolerated foreigners in their midst. Some immigrants may be more welcome than others. Persons of Japanese ethnic origin, though third-generation Brazilians or Peruvians, are granted full citizenship when they "return," while Chinese, Pakistanis, and Vietnamese resident workers are held at arm's length indefinitely.[9] For nearly a half century before 1965, the United States welcomed immigrants from northern and western Europe, while strictly limiting immigration from eastern and southern Europe and barring Chinese and Japanese entirely. *Ius sanguinis*, the policy practiced by Japan, is the principle that citizenship and allegiance should be determined by ethnic origin; *ius soli*, the policy practiced by the United States, holds that citizenship and loyalty are determined by residence and commitment to the institutions of the state.

Some ethnic groups attempt to achieve and maintain a dominant position in government; others struggle for autonomy in the form of regional self-government, minority rights, or secession and independent statehood. Still others, particularly immigrant communities, attempt to achieve full inclusion for their members and equal status in government, education, and the economy. Modern governments play an important part in the lives of their citizens and subjects. The rules they make, the policies they enforce, and the resources they allocate can have a critical impact on the status, opportunities, and well-being of members of ethnic communities. Much of the organizational energies and resources of ethnic communities may be expended to influence the policies and behaviors of governments. Mexican-Americans in California mobilized politically in 1998 to defeat Republican Party candidates for the governorship and state assembly because Republicans had sponsored measures that would have excluded illegal immigrants, mostly Mexican, and their children from education, welfare, and other state-provided services. The state thus becomes an important actor in ethnic politics, a major arena of ethnic conflict, and a major target of ethnic competition, a theme that we explore in greater depth in chapter 5.

In many instances, ethnic politics can be understood as a challenge and response relationship between representatives of ethnic communities and governments. Normally, the initiative originates with ethnic communities whose spokespersons assert demand on government to which the latter must respond. Policies and practices adopted by governments may, however, be perceived by ethnic communities as beneficial or harmful, and elicit favorable or hostile responses. Invitations by the Ecuadorian and Bolivian governments to foreign corporations to exploit their natural resources have been perceived by the Indian peoples of the Andean highlands as unwelcome give-aways of their patrimony from which they receive few if any benefits and which threaten to encroach on their traditional way of life.

Sinhalese applauded, but Tamils greeted as demeaning to their dignity and hostile to their interests a Sri Lankan government policy that all university entrance and civil service exams would henceforth be administered only in the Sinhalese language. Governments have been known to abandon any pretense of impartiality in the face of ethnic disputes. Under President Milosevic, the Serbian government launched its state-sponsored campaign of ethnic cleansing against Albanian Kosovars. Pogroms, government-sponsored attacks by ethnic mobs against their ethnic enemies in which the police stand by without protecting the victims, occur from time to time. Recently, in the Indian state of Gujerat, the state government provoked Hindu mobs to attack Muslims, causing hundreds of deaths, the burning of thousands of homes, and looting of businesses as the police looked on. Prior to the civil rights movement in the American South, state governments systematically disfranchised their African-American minority, provided inferior public services, practiced rigid segregation in education, housing, and public transportation, and excluded them from all but the most menial occupations.

The importance of the state in establishing and enforcing the terms for interethnic relations does not tell the whole story. Through voluntary organizations in what has come to be known as civil society, representatives of ethnic groups, especially at the local level, may without any involvement by government attempt to achieve and maintain friendly relations with counterparts from other groups, negotiating agreements and dampening incipient conflicts before they become destabilizing. Tamil and Sinhalese water-users' associations continued to coordinate their activities in operating and maintaining the Gal Oya irrigation system in Sri Lanka and to head off conflicts between them even as a vicious ethnic civil war raged in their country. Where governments are weak and unable to exercise effective authority, differences that arise between ethnic communities are prone to erupt into violence unless they can be mediated by local or other non-government organizations. With the collapse of the authoritarian Suharto dictatorship in Indonesia, disputes between Muslims and Christians have led to orgies of mutual slaughter, as the weak successor governments have been unable or unwilling to intervene.

Theories and equities

Because of the great variety and combinations of circumstances surrounding relations among ethnic communities and factions of these communities, as hinted in the previous paragraphs, efforts to incorporate these relationships into general theory are likely to fail. Inspired by the physical sciences, social scientists often strive to explain what appear to be varieties of experience by parsimonious general theory.[10] Many have attempted to generalize from a few cases to the entire realm of ethnic encounters, only to see their hypotheses falsified by their inability to explain or predict other cases. An influential school of American social scientists, for example, drawing on their understanding of American experience with recent immigrants and the oppression of African-Americans, attempted to explain ethnic tensions as prejudiced attitudes leading to discrimination, to be overcome by education, more enlightened attitudes, and civil rights legislation.[11] This theory proved unable to explain genuine clashes of interest between organized ethnic communities, such as the incompatible claims of Israelis and Palestinians to the lands between the Jordan River and the Mediterranean. Students of modernization confidently predicted that with industrialization, urbanization, bureaucratization, and secularization, local, parochial, ethnic, and other "traditional" identities would become increasingly irrelevant and would be succeeded by more "rational" loyalties and associations such as state nationalism, economic class, and cultural and recreational interests. They were stunned when in the 1960s in some of the most modernized countries such as Great Britain, Canada, the United States, and Belgium ethnic grievances and demands became important political issues.[12]

One author has recently propounded the interesting hypothesis that inclusive civic, non-governmental associations are the key to preventing ethnic violence.[13] Based on data from several Indian cities, he found that where such ethnically inclusive associations existed, violence between Hindus and Muslims had been averted; cities where such associations were absent, where Hindus and Muslims led entirely separate institutional lives, have witnessed some of the most savage and lethal communal conflicts. This author believes that this proposition may have wider applicability and may even be generalizable to all ethnic conflicts. Having reasoned from a limited set of experiences, he appears to be unaware of cases that would falsify this proposition as a general statement. The city of Sarajevo was long hailed as an outstanding example of harmonious ethnic coexistence, where Muslims, Croats, Serbs, and other communities participated in a common civic life and were active in the same sets of local institutions. Yet, when Bosnia split into warring ethnic enclaves, the people of Sarajevo were unable to resist this pressure. They too broke apart into separate, hostile camps as Sarajevo turned into an ethnic battleground. Earlier in this chapter we noted the participation of Nigerian workers in the same ethnically inclusive labor unions during the colonial period, and that these unions broke apart into ethnically separate associations as national politics crystallized along ethnic lines.

In order that this optimistic proposition may remain viable, it would be necessary for the author to recognize that it cannot apply to all violent ethnic conflicts and to specify under what limiting conditions it retains its explanatory value. There is also the related problem of actionability: under what conditions can it help policymakers. Where, for example, hostility and distrust have become as intense as between Israelis and Palestinians, between Hutu and Tutsi in Rwanda, or Serbs and Albanians in Kosovo, it is unlikely that members of these communities can function in common civic associations. In such cases the proposition cannot be useful as a guide to action. Other means must be introduced to forestall violence when inclusive institutions of civil society are not available. Like so many attempts to construct general theory about ethnic conflict, this one too is defeated by the complexity of the phenomenon it attempts to explain and for which it attempts to prescribe. The vastly different geographic distribution of ethnic populations, some territorially concentrated, others located in ethnically mixed areas, is another factor that limits the possibility of general theory.

But, though general theory is likely to be unobtainable, it is possible to formulate and test statements about limited ranges of similar cases. In this book the reader will encounter a number of such examples of partial or middle-level theory, efforts to explain and attempt to predict with a high degree of probability what is likely to occur under generally similar circumstances. Examples are the likely fate of middleman minorities (chapter 6), the process of outbidding by zealots to thwart compromise adjustments of ethnic disputes (chapter 9), and claims of homeland peoples to control the national culture (chapter 6). In every instance, however, it is important to be sensitive to the particular context, the unique set of circumstances that imparts a distinctive character to every situation of ethnic conflict.

Readers who expect to find general explanations or simple policies or cook book formulas to prevent or resolve ethnic conflicts will not find them in this book. Though it does not add up to a general theory, what readers will find as they move through this book is an approach to this subject that regards most ethnic communities as enduring historical entities and ethnic conflict as grounded in real disputes over political power, economic resources, or cultural values. They will find only limited support for constructionism (chapter 2) or explanations of conflict based on psychology or economic differences (chapter 4). What they may expect and what they should be looking for are: (1) enhanced sensitivity to the ethnic dimensions of politics wherever it occurs; (2) understandings that help to explain or predict behavior or outcomes under limited ranges of similar situations; and (3) policies that may contribute to the prevention or mitigation of ethnic-based violence and the achievement of peaceful coexistence, again under more or less similar circumstances.

As with all human relationships, it is impossible to exclude moral judgments, the evaluation of rights and wrongs when ethnic communities collide. When units of the Indonesian army ran amok in East Timor, killing and pillaging a people who in a recent referendum had expressed a nearly unanimous desire for independence; when the Chinese military, claiming the right to suppress rebellion in a secessionist province, systematically destroys the institutions of traditional Tibetan culture and moves thousands of Chinese colonists into the Tibetan heartland, it is impossible to avoid judgments about which side is right, which is wrong, and which deserves the sympathy and support of persons of good will. The same was true in South Africa during the apartheid era where the Black majority was ruthlessly disfranchised, despoiled, impoverished, and humiliated by a minority racist regime.

When ethnic groups come into conflict, spokespersons for both sides are likely to develop elaborate arguments to rationalize their behavior, both to sustain the morale of their followers and to impress external audiences. Kosovar Albanians claim that as the 90 percent majority in Kosovo they are entitled to self-determination, to decide whether they prefer to remain a province of Serbia, to opt for independence, or even to join Albania. If all peaceful efforts to assert this right are thwarted, they consider themselves entitled to the ultimate right to rebel. Just as Serbs exercised that right in the nineteenth century to take up arms and secede from the Ottoman Empire, so Kosovars claim the same right to secede from Serbia. Serbs, however, claim that Kosovo is the cradle of Serbian civilization, the center of the great medieval Christian Serbian empire, that its monasteries have continued over the centuries as centers of Serbian Orthodox culture, that after Serbia was overcome by the Turks in the year 1389, the Turks colonized their country with Albanian Muslims. Kosovo, they argue, has been recognized since the Treaty of Berlin in 1878 as an integral part of Serbia, and the Serbian army has merely been suppressing a terrorist rebellion. In this dispute the European Union decided, and the United States eventually concurred, that the government of Serbia had flagrantly violated the basic human rights of Kosovar Albanians. They intervened militarily through NATO to halt the ethnic cleansing and enable Kosovar refugees to return to their homes. The majority of Serbs believe that as a small nation they have been victims of illegitimate international interference in their domestic affairs in contrast to the failure of NATO to intervene, for example in the ruthless Russian operations in Chechnya.[14] Most observers have concluded that the weight of moral equities strongly favors the Kosovars and that the NATO intervention was fully justified.

However, in many instances of ethnic conflict the equities are so confused and uncertain that observers should be careful not to rush to judgment. France has long operated a rigidly secular system of public education, reflecting its republican traditions that emphasize the equality of all citizens. Schools have served as a means of socializing students of all backgrounds to their common status as French citizens. The display of religious symbols by school authorities or by students is forbidden, as these manifest the sectarian differences among students. In recent years, Muslim girls have insisted on their right to wear headscarves at school, as prescribed by their religious practices. School authorities, they argue, should respect the social and cultural diversity in their student body. The Ministry of Education has denied that request, holding that headscarves in public schools are religious symbols forbidden both by the letter and the spirit of France's republican and egalitarian tradition. Which side is right?

Malays consider themselves to be the indigenous people in Malaysia, by virtue of which they are entitled to control its government and to establish their faith, Islam, as the state religion and their vernacular as the national language. They further believe that their colonial experience left them undereducated and ill-prepared to compete in the modern sectors of the economy against immigrant people who were admitted to their country by the former colonial authorities.

They insist on affirmative action or special rights for Malays in education, employment, and access to ownership and managerial roles in the modern sectors of the economy, until Malays are able to compete on equal terms with their non-Malay compatriots. In the absence of such measures, they would be unequipped to compete, the more prestigious professions and productive sectors of the economy would be monopolized by non-Malays, and Malays would be reduced to the pitiful status of "red Indians in the United States." Non-Malays, nearly half the population, argue that as patriotic citizens, locally born, they are entitled to equality of status and equal participation in government and the economy based on individual initiative, skill, merit, and performance. They therefore favor a "Malaysian Malaysia," in which all citizens regardless of "race" should enjoy equal opportunity in education, government, and the economy – equal rights for all, special privileges for none.[15] While this brief account simplifies a more complex debate, it outlines the core of the divergent perceptions between Malays and non-Malays. Which side occupies the moral high ground?

In coping with ethnic conflict, national strategists may face painful dilemmas. The government of Azerbaijan demands that the invading Armenian army withdraw from the enclave of Nagorny Karabakh, despite its ethnic Armenian majority, because that area is clearly within the internationally recognized borders of Azerbaijan. At the same time it is tempted to claim a swath of northwestern Iran which is home to an Azeri majority, even though this territory is clearly within the internationally recognized borders of Iran. While, as Emerson observed, "a foolish consistency is the hobgoblin of little minds," a blatant inconsistency in this matter might undermine Azerbaijan's moral claim to jurisdiction over Nagorny Karabakh. Which principle should take precedence: the right of an ethnic minority to self-determination, or the inviolability of international borders?[16] Or, perhaps, the rule of the stronger?

In moving through this text, the reader will encounter many similar cases where the moral equities are not as obvious as they were in the Kosovo dispute and in apartheid South Africa. It is inevitable, indeed desirable, that outside observers, attentive publics as well as governments and international organizations should evaluate and act on the moral equities in ethnic-based conflicts. It would, however, be prudent on their part not to rush to conclusions, but to suspend judgment until they are confident they comprehend and have fully weighed the competing moral claims.

Globalization and ethnic solidarities

The late twentieth and early twenty-first centuries are believed by many to herald the onset of a new era of globalization. Propelled by technological developments in transportation, communications, and information, the ideology of globalization visualizes a borderless world in which goods, investments, information, and people move freely anywhere in the world in pursuit of economic efficiency and a better life. Governments are expected to decline in importance, as more of the world's affairs will be regulated by market processes. As people everywhere come to share the same information and similar lifestyles, differences among them will become increasingly irrelevant and are destined eventually to disappear. How, then, can one account for the simultaneous eruption of ethnic awareness and ethnic solidarity, which seems to negate the promise of an emergent common humanity?[17] Why, at this juncture, should we be witnessing two such apparently contradictory developments?

There is no simple solution to this enigma. One approach is to minimize the effective reach of globalization, to demonstrate that the great majority of the world's people have not (yet?) been touched by globalization; and that many who have been affected, in rich and poor countries alike, believe themselves to have been harmed by the effects of globalization, rather than helped, by loss of jobs, incomes, security, or infringements on their ways of life. As the world about them changes unpredictably, as they encounter greater uncertainty in their lives, ethnic solidarity provides a bastion of security and meaning for individuals, enabling them to cope more confidently with threats to their livelihoods, their dignity, and their way of life.

At the same time, the idea of democratic entitlements and human rights has spread world-wide. As imperial and colonial regimes have been abandoned, ethnic communities that had previously been repressed have gained the opportunity to assert rights previously denied them. Meanwhile the nineteenth century principle that each state should constitute the homeland of a single homogeneous nation, that state officials should actively sponsor nation-building, and that minorities are obligated to assimilate into the national mainstream – all residents of France must become French, all residents of Turkey must become Turks, all residents of Burma must become Burmans – has yielded to new international norms: ethnic pluralism, multiculturalism, minority rights. International organizations, including the United Nations and the Organization for European Security and Cooperation (OSCE), recognize that human rights now apply to ethnic groups as well as to individuals and that governments are obligated to accommodate the reasonable needs of ethnic communities, as long as they are advocated by peaceful means. Though many governments continue to ignore and repress their ethnic minorities, they are swimming against the tide of a growing global consensus that ethnic minorities have rights that deserve to be recognized and respected. The Turkish government's repression of the demands of its large Kurdish minority for political and cultural autonomy has been given as one reason for the European Union's refusal to entertain Turkey's application for membership.

What this brief discussion demonstrates is that economic and informational globalism have thus far had little impact on the collective identities of most people, even in countries that have most experienced its benefits. In fact, they have strengthened these sentiments against the uncertainties that the marketization of economic relationships brings in its wake. The global ascendancy of democratic thought has legitimated ethnic solidarities and induced more governments to accommodate them. While the Franco dictatorship in Spain (1939–74) had severely repressed all expressions of Basque and Catalan identity, the successor democratic regime has granted them regional autonomy. So far as ethnic communities are concerned, the opportunities afforded by democratization have outweighed the threat of globalization to their survival.

Globalization has the effect of strengthening separatist sentiments among homeland peoples. By reducing barriers to the transnational flows of trade and investment, globalization reduces the dependence of regions on national markets and sources of capital in favor of much larger international markets and more diversified sources of investment. This is especially true of regions that can look forward to participating in multinational economic unions or free-trade areas. Thus, separatists in Quebec have enthusiastically embraced the North Atlantic Free Trade Area (NAFTA) since they find the vast US market (plus Mexico) far more interesting than the much smaller market of English-speaking Canada. The net economic costs of separation from Canada are greatly reduced, if not eliminated, while Quebec's security would continue to benefit from the defensive shield provided by the US for all of North America.

Similarly, Scottish nationalists have become enthusiastic supporters of the European Union which affords much wider opportunities for the export of Scottish manufactures and services than the much smaller, slow-growing English market.[18] The same considerations applied to Slovenia and Croatia which separated from the Serbian-dominated Yugoslav federation and, as independent states, became immediate candidates for membership in the European Union. Some promoters of the European Union idea visualize the future as a "Europe of (ethnic) regions," while national states (Spain, France, Britain) become less relevant to the economic and security needs of their peripheral regions. The Achinese people at the northern tip of the Indonesian island of Sumatra have waged an insurrection against the Java-centered government of Indonesia. They believe that in a globalizing economy they would be much better off as an independent state than as a province of Indonesia, whose government monopolizes the royalties from Aceh's rich petroleum deposits and returns little of it to the local economy.

There has been a lively debate in the literature about the effects of economic and informational globalization on economic development in less developed countries. Does globalization enhance or retard their economic growth? One side argues that increasing ethnic awareness resulting from informational globalization increases the likelihood of ethnic conflict, which retards economic development.[19] The other holds that despite increased ethnic awareness, domestic political institutions and government policies determine whether ethnic mobilization is channeled toward civic behavior or toward violence. Thus, it is not globalization per se, but the effectiveness of government and the policies it pursues that determine the impact of globalization on economic development.[20] I believe the weight of evidence supports this latter position.

Conclusion

In this chapter we have introduced the complex reality of communities based on collective ethnic identity and of interactions among them when two or more such communities are present in the same political space. While these interactions are normally peaceful, often they lead to conflicts that turn out to be violent and disruptive to the lives of large numbers of people. Ethnic conflict is a world-wide phenomenon that has become the leading source of lethal violence in international affairs.

We are skeptical of the possibility of general theory to explain the variety and the many circumstances that produce ethnic conflict or to reveal methods for their peaceful resolution. This book presents an approach to the subject that (1) regards most ethnic communities as rooted in historical experience, and (2) considers disputes involving ethnic communities as real differences over political power, economic resources, or cultural values. In some disputes the moral equities seem clear; in others the question of right and wrong between the parties may be hard to evaluate.

2
Ethnic Sentiments and Solidarities: Collective Identities

Ethnic sentiment is an expression of who I am, how I identify myself, to what group of people I belong. As a member of that group this becomes for me a collective identity. When a collective identity becomes an interest group, the result is known as identity politics. Normally, ethnic identity is a matter of inheritance rather than of voluntary choice, and is reinforced by intensive socialization from early childhood. In some instances, however, ethnicity may be thrust on people by outside forces, as when individuals who had never considered themselves to be Jews were nevertheless so classified by the Nazi regime and compelled to wear the yellow star. Ethnic solidarity is my sense that I share the same common attributes, a valuable common culture, a notable historical experience, and a common fate with my fellow ethnics; that these distinguish us from outsiders; that I feel more comfortable and more secure among my own people than among outsiders; and that I may be asked and even prepared to invest my energies, my material resources, and risk my life in its defense.

As we noted in chapter 1, ethnic identity is only one of several collective identities that endow an individual's life with meaning. As Aristotle informed us, humans are political animals, craving human association to help meet their most basic physical and emotional needs. The need for belonging, to be anchored to a group for security, economic survival, social fellowship, and the fulfillment of spiritual aspirations is what motivates group affiliation and gives rise to collective identities. But ethnic identities usually draw on deeper layers of emotional sensitivity than those based on more pragmatic interests such as professional associations, recreational activities, or political parties. Individuals often internalize as their own the successes experienced by members of their ethnic community, as many African-Americans rejoiced in the victories of Mohammed Ali and the successes of Jackie Robinson; and many Muslims world-wide sympathize with what they believe have been the injustices visited on their Palestinian fellow Muslims. On the negative side, many Muslims refuse to believe that fellow Muslims could have committed the atrocities of September 11, 2001, many Catholics in Northern Ireland are embarrassed by the crimes committed in their name by the Irish Republican Army, and Italian-Americans protest the identification of Italians with organized crime (the Mafia).

For such reasons, when persons are forced to choose between ethnic and other loyalties (collective identities), the ethnic normally prevails. Prior to World War I, leaders of the Socialist International Party from the major European countries pledged that they would never again fight in capitalist wars. But when war broke out, that pledge was quickly set aside and all of them fell in behind their bourgeois governments. Ethnic solidarity, in this instance ethnonationalism – German, French, English – overwhelmed working-class solidarity and the ideology of proletarian internationalism.

Our working definition of ethnicity encompasses solidarities based on common culture, common belief systems and practices (religions), and common racial features, all of which are inheritable attributes.[1] Though culture, race, and religion are analytically distinguishable, the behaviors evoked by these forms of communal identity are so similar that they cannot readily be distinguished or disentangled.[2] Often the categories overlap and which group fits which category is often impossible to fathom. Are brown-skinned Hispanic-Americans a racial or cultural category? Or both? How has their behavior as an immigrant community differed from that of Chinese immigrants (a racial group), of European immigrants (cultural groups), or of Jews or Armenians (cultural or religious communities)? Are Bosnian Muslims an ethnic or religious community? Are Malaysian Chinese a racial, religious, or ethnic minority? While we shall take note of these differences as we encounter them, we shall otherwise encompass cultural, racial, and religious solidarities under the common ethnic rubric.

The particular contours or expressions of ethnic identity may be shaped by circumstances. In Africa where all persons are dark-skinned, ethnic (tribal) identity and ethnic differentiation are based on cultural distinctiveness and identification with a territorial homeland. In America, slavery obliterated these cultural distinctions and the lines of cleavage were sharply drawn between Black and White. So persons of African descent became, in the United States, a community based primarily on color, their ethnic origins largely forgotten, their culture shaped by the common legacy of slavery and socio-economic marginalization.

Ethnicity has no meaning except in relational terms. There must always be an "other." Where there is no other, identities and conflicts focus on kinship groups, regional differences, or economic interests. In medieval China, where everyone was Chinese and there were no outsiders except for vague reports of distant "barbarians," ethnicity had no relevance to the everyday experiences of political elites, intellectuals, the man on the farm or on the street. Differences that arose and conflicting loyalties that emerged were based on kinship rivalries, economic interests, social class, ideologies, personal ambitions, or combinations of these factors. But, when Chinese merchants ventured to the south seas and encountered Javanese, Hindus, Malay Muslims, Thai Buddhists, and other strange peoples and their civilizations, their Chinese distinctiveness became apparent and previously felt differences among fellow Chinese such as regional dialects faded in importance as all became identified simply as Chinese. Those that later emigrated and settled in Southeast Asia, Overseas Chinese, became separate ethnic communities in their own eyes and in those of surrounding communities.

Persons of mixed descent often encounter complex and ambiguous problems of adjustment, depending on the choices allowed them by those who make the rules for their society. In the United States persons of mixed African and Caucasian descent, until recently, were rejected by White society and classified, often against their will, as Negro or Black. In many colonial and post-colonial societies, such as India, persons of mixed European and indigenous origins were marginalized both by colonial European society with which they aspired to identify and by the indigenous society. They formed separate Eurasian communities (mulatto in Africa and the Caribbean, mestizo in Latin America). In Vietnam, Korea, and Japan the offsprings of Black American soldiers and local women are cruelly ostracized by these Asian societies. In some countries ethnic boundaries are rigidly maintained, the products of mixed unions are excluded, though different rules may apply to persons of different social backgrounds. In other situations they are free to choose their ethnic identity (a French-Canadian prime minister of Quebec was named Daniel Johnson). In the United States the mainstream now includes people of mixed European ethnic origins, Irish and Italian for example, and increasingly of mixed European-Asian and European-Hispanic backgrounds.

The awareness of differences, even the existence of separate communities (social pluralism) need not result in mutual hostility. Ethnic groups may adopt strategies of mutual avoidance; they may evolve mutually beneficial divisions of labor and mutually respectful cooperation. Friendly interchange among individuals or groups may lead to intermarriage and the eventual absorption of one community by the other. But competition for economic resources such as land, hunting and grazing rights, or trading opportunities, and for political power may generate mutual suspicion and antipathy that provide, as we shall see, the raw material for ethnic conflict.

The three persuasions

Social scientists have produced three competing conceptions or images of the meaning of ethnic identity and ethnic solidarity. I shall refer to these as persuasions or schools of thought.

Those associated with what, for a better term, is referred to as the *primordialist* school look upon ethnic identities as historically rooted, deeply embedded in a people's culture, reinforced by collective myths and memories, social institutions and practices, perpetuated intergenerationally by early socialization and therefore likely to persist over time.[3] Though their detractors charge them with "essentializing" ethnicity, that is investing it with a mythic unchanging essence emerging full-blown from the misty past and transferred from generation to generation, this is, in fact, a debater's straw man. Those of the primordialist persuasion recognize that ethnic communities originated from historical circumstances that drew individuals, families, and extended kinship groups together in response to common threats or opportunities; over time they developed common beliefs, practices, and institutions to which their members became attached; and as they evolved they faced fresh challenges and changing environments to which they needed to adapt. Historical evidence demonstrates that many adapt successfully, while those that cannot are unlikely to survive. Normally, however, ethnic communities that manage to persist over time as distinctive communities, along with the changes they have adopted, retain some of the cultural properties that link them to a remembered past, most prominently a distinctive language, a literature oral or written, religious beliefs and practices, cuisine, and modes of dress. The primordialist conception of ethnic solidarity is rooted in late eighteenth and early nineteenth-century historicist ideas and is regarded today as orthodox theory, similar to the status of classical economics in that discipline.[4]

The collective memory of ethnic communities may convert historical triumphs or rankling victimhood into living realities from generation to generation. Each July, Northern Ireland Protestants of the Orange Order celebrate the victory in 1690 of their hero, King Billy (William III of Orange) over the Catholic ruler, James II, by marching in uniform with banners aloft through Catholic neighborhoods of the leading cities. This victory consolidated the Protestant ascendancy in Ireland which the Orange Order intends to perpetuate in Northern Ireland, a "Protestant state for a Protestant people," the Catholic minority of 45 percent notwithstanding. Armenian-Americans, a well-established community in California, one of whose sons recently served two terms as the state's governor, "remember" the massacres visited on their ancestors nearly a century ago. They vigorously lobby the US Congress to deny military and economic assistance to Turkey, a NATO ally, until such time as Turkey's government acknowledges and apologizes for these atrocities. Historical events may be exaggerated or even invented, heroes and heroic achievements mythologized, or setbacks at the hands of enemies ascribed to their treachery in order to buttress the collectivity's self-esteem or demonize the traditional ethnic enemy.

The biological version of primordialism argues that the historical longevity of collective identities and solidarities stems from mankind's primal instinct for genetic continuity, an urge to extend and perpetuate one's genetic inheritance into future generations, thereby confounding the individual's mortality by insuring the intergenerational survival of the blood line. By analogy, the same logic extends to the individual's community, the culture, values, and traditions that the individual prizes and incorporates into his personality, that he wishes to safeguard, and regards as his responsibility to extend into the future. Thus, the primal desire for survival of the species becomes fused with the need to insure the survival of a culture that has endowed life with meaning and that should be available to serve the needs of generations of offsprings. There are several variants of the biological explanation for ethnic solidarity, all of them based on the individual's drive to insure genetic continuity.[5]

Instrumentalists (some versions of which are referred to as circumstantialists or ethnoskeptics) regard ethnicity either as a surrogate for more basic social forces such as class or colonial domination, or as a fraud perpetrated by persons with self-serving objectives to exploit mass publics in pursuit of their political or economic ambitions. Some instrumentalists conceive the world as composed of rationally calculating individuals seeking to maximize their security, economic welfare, social position, or power over others.[6] Groups and associations are formed and function primarily to help individuals pursue these goals. Ethnicity is mainly a myth propagated and exploited by ambitious and unscrupulous political entrepreneurs to build political followings for themselves and help them to attain and secure political power. To the extent that ordinary people allow themselves to be lured and manipulated by ethnic appeals, they become hapless victims of false consciousness. This is a term used by Marxist intellectuals to describe the use of ethnic sentiments by members of the bourgeois ruling class to mislead and undermine the solidarity of the working class and divide them by spurious "ethnic" differences. Colonial powers are accused of inventing or exaggerating ethnic categories to classify and more easily rule their colonial subjects. Ethnoskeptics argue that ethnic sentiments frequently have little basis in historical reality, while their alleged traditions are recent inventions either of literary nostalgics or of persons with more tangible self-regarding interests.[7] What instrumentalists of all shades share is a deep distrust of claims made in the name of ethnic solidarity and a rejection of ethnicity as an authentic category for political or social action.

Instrumentalists deny that the mayhem in Bosnia during the 1990s, in which the participants defined themselves and their struggles in ethnic terms, had anything to do with competing ethnic interests or mutual hostility, such as historical animosity between Serbs and Croats or Serbs and Muslims. Instead, they believe the Bosnian war was precipitated by scheming politicians and carried out by gangs of thugs who appropriated ethnic symbols to legitimatize what amounted to protection rackets, and that many in whose name these military operations were conducted regarded them without enthusiasm or were even opposed to them.[8]

This cynical and opportunistic view of ethnic solidarity has difficulty explaining how and why people who presumably behave rationally would allow themselves to be so deceived and manipulated, unless they harbor some underlying sentiments of group identity and solidarity to which unscrupulous manipulators can appeal. It is like arguing that German national sentiment was created, rather than exploited, by Hitler and that because some Germans opposed the Nazi regime, Germans who elected Hitler as their president and in whose name Hitler functioned had no responsibility for World War II. Ethnic solidarity, in fact, is seldom based on rational calculations of benefits and costs, but on intrinsic values such as dignity and collective self-esteem. Individuals like suicide bombers willingly sacrifice their lives in ways that defy calculations of material benefits and costs. Individuals can be manipulated by self-serving elites, but only if such manipulation appeals to and draws on a priori sentiments of collective identity and group solidarity.[9]

As we shall see, the instrumentalist position is closer to the constructionist than to the primordialist persuasion.

Social constructionists regard ethnic solidarity as an invention of the human imagination, an intellectual construct, not an objective reality. Though it has no basis in nature, it can nevertheless be regarded as real to the extent that people treat it as a reality and behave accordingly. But because it is imagined, it can also be unimagined.[10] Thus, ethnic communities are likely to be transitory, as individuals "negotiate" their identity and may find it beneficial to be affiliated with more than a single ethnic group and to move easily among them. They are likely also to be contingent, depending on changing circumstances, manipulated by governments and others who wield power, subject to sudden and abrupt changes as peoples' needs and aspirations change. Far from being historically rooted, constructionists argue that most contemporary ethnic communities are of relatively recent origin, serving practical and changing needs, continuously passing from history while new ones are born.

Social constructionism is closely linked to post-modernist beliefs that the world we experience is composed mostly of intellectually invented symbols and that notions of objective reality are false and illusory. A version of post-modernist thought that commands a large following among contemporary humanists and social scientists holds that ethnic categories are recent inventions of power elites or competitors for power, bent on consolidating their position in society.[11] Because of their control over educational institutions and the news media and their ability to allocate governmental resources in ways that re-enforce these categories, they are able to propound "narratives" about the origins and distinctive attributes of these imagined communities which members of society come to believe and accept as central to their social orientation and their interests. This process endows them with allegiances that may persist for long periods of time. This is held to be especially the case with colonial societies and to explain the intensity of ethnic conflicts among recently constructed communities in many post-colonial systems. Social constructionism has become the dominant belief system among younger academic social scientists and humanists who write about ethnic encounters and ethnic conflict.

Though the partisans of these three persuasions continue to contend, often dogmatically, neither of them succeeds in fully explaining the complex and multifaceted manifestations of ethnic solidarity. The orthodox primordialist position is supported by the evident fact that many ethnic communities, self-defined and recognized by outsiders, have persisted for generations and centuries, some for millennia. Some have been patronized by state authorities, others have survived without state support. Members may have drifted away, while new members are recruited; elements of the culture may be de-emphasized, reinterpreted, even discarded and new ones borrowed and incorporated from the surrounding environment. All have continuously adapted to changing environments, but their communities and cultures have successfully maintained their collective identities and collective memories over time.

There are conspicuous examples of the exploitation and manipulation of ethnic sentiments by unscrupulous politicians, notably the recent exploitation of Serbian ethnicity by former Yugoslav president, Slobodan Milosevic which led to behavior bordering on genocide in Bosnia and Kosovo during the 1990s. At the time of writing, Milosevic is being tried for crimes against humanity by a special UN war crimes tribunal in the Netherlands. Conservatives tend to look favorably on ethnonational sentiments because they stress group cohesion and the common interests of persons of all social classes, thus diminishing prospects for social conflict. German capitalists helped finance Hitler's rise to power in Germany in the early 1930s to forestall what they believed to be a threatened communist revolution. Liberals, on the other hand, tend to be suspicious of ethnic solidarity because they believe it subordinates individual autonomy to group membership and collective discipline. Many of the apostles of the instrumentalist and constructionist persuasions come from the left side of the political spectrum.

In most instances of ethnic conflict there are some instrumental goals, some practical benefits that are promised, or threatening deprivations averted for members of ethnic communities, if their struggle should succeed. But this does not demonstrate that ethnicity is a myth or that its principal function is to endow ambitious candidates for leadership with a platform to mobilize support for their greater glory. Populations can be mesmerized and led by demagogues, at least for short periods of time, often with disastrous results for them and for outsiders, but the ethnic sentiments to which demagogues appeal are not created from whole cloth. Milosevic did not create Serbian nationalism. Ethnic appeals are effective for mobilization precisely because they draw on layers of sentiment and feelings of group solidarity that are powerful enough to evoke popular support and induce some even to risk their lives in what they believe is its defense. The suicide bombers who attacked the World Trade Center in New York City on September 11, 2001, sincerely trusted that they were defending Islam against hostile infidels.

Ethnic groups may pass from history and new solidarities may be created by new circumstances. Burgundians and Gascons who once figured prominently in western European history have been absorbed into the French nation. Bengali nationalism, which fueled the 1971 war that led to the dismemberment of Pakistan and the launching of the new state of Bangladesh, threatened a large number of non-Bengali Muslim residents who supported Pakistan, the losing side, during the Bangladeshi war of independence. As a result, these non-Bengali Muslims fled to Pakistan, joining an earlier group of Muslim refugees from the Indian state of Gujerat and establishing themselves in the Karachi metropolitan area. There, as refugees, they encountered an unwelcoming native Sindhi population that regarded them as foreign interlopers, competitive threats to their already difficult economic situation. In order to promote and defend their common interests in this new environment that rejected them, these refugees found it necessary to organize. Thus, a new ethnic community, the Mohajirs, was born.

Social constructionists are right when they observe that unlike gender and age, ethnic categories do not exist in nature. In this respect, however, ethnicity is like all other human aggregates such as class, religious associations, political parties, and business corporations. To say, for example, that the Catholic Church is an imagined community would hardly be helpful in understanding its role in the lives of the faithful or its influence in public affairs. It is similarly unhelpful to hold that Armenians or Khmers or Croats, who have built and sustained political institutions, languages, literatures, and social practices over many centuries and are recognized by outsiders as distinct peoples, are only imagined communities – artificial, transient, contingent. Though they do not exist in nature and are not immortal, such ethnic solidarities continue to be valued and maintained by their members; they have been and remain realities in their lives and among outsiders who are touched by their activities.

Writers of the constructionist persuasion are at pains to remind their readers that "ancient hatreds," as they call them, have nothing to do with contemporary ethnic conflict or ethnic-based violence. They are asserting, in effect, that history and collective memories play little or no role in human behavior. It is clear that some ethnic solidarities have no discernible historical antecedents and can be traced to recent events. The "colored" or "mixed race" identity was the late nineteenth-century invention of the South African government, which mandated separate residential neighborhoods and separate institutions for this population, including a university outside Cape Town. Though the ending of apartheid raised their hopes, these were soon dashed as they discovered that their marginalization and discrimination continued in a different form. "In the old system, we weren't White enough; now we aren't Black enough."[12] Since this identity was imposed on them and they have no incentive to retain it, it may gradually die out if South Africa evolves into a truly non-racial democracy. But most ethnic solidarities are combinations of material and emotional bonds, of daily experiences and historical memories that are not easily broken or readily forgotten and that account for the longevity of so many ethnic communities. The transient and opportunistic quality that constructionists find in all ethnic identities represents the triumph of academic dogmatism over visible evidence.

Ethnic communities do not contend over history as such. What engages them are disputes over political, economic, or cultural values and resources such as those that are elaborated in chapter 4. But historical animosities and collective memories greatly facilitate the process of mobilization, of persuading members of ethnic community A that their counterparts in community B harbor hostile intentions toward them as did their ancestors, and that these must be resisted by force, if necessary. Serbs have been taught that their great medieval Christian empire centered in Kosovo was ravaged by Ottoman Turks who then proceeded to subject the Serbian nation to five centuries of Muslim domination before Serbia was able to throw off their yoke and regain its independence in 1878. Many Serbs choose to believe that the Muslim Albanian majority in present-day Kosovo are descendants of the medieval Ottoman Turks and frequently refer to them disparagingly as "Turks." The Serbian campaign of ethnic cleansing in Kosovo was not caused by ancient hatreds, but those antagonistic collective memories had the effect of dehumanizing their Albanian victims and justifying the brutal treatment that was meted out to them by the Serbian military.

Nor is it possible to appreciate the intense suspicion and mutual hostility between Protestants and Catholics in Northern Ireland without reference to the oft-repeated Protestant narrative of the heroic performance of the outnumbered Protestant forces that defeated the Catholic hordes in 1690; and to the Catholic memories of centuries of suffering, impoverishment, and humiliation under Protestant British rule which justifies their struggle by any means, fair or foul, including terror, for complete freedom from Britain ("Brits Out") and for a united republican Ireland. Much of the emotional thrust associated with ethnic conflict is the consequence of victories reenacted or of grievances stored up and magnified in collective memories, grievances that have yet to be avenged or atoned for and that cannot be allowed to be forgotten. Americans, with their ahistorical perspective, have difficulty appreciating the tenacity of historical memories and their influence on contemporary behavior.

Many social scientists during the twentieth century had difficulty coming to terms with ethnic solidarities. The two leading social philosophies of that era, liberal individualism and Marxism, for different reasons rejected ethnicity as a legitimate basis for social organization. To liberals, the individual is the sole legitimate unit of value in human society; any presumed social collectivity, such as ethnicity, that compromises the sacred autonomy of the individual is suspect. Modernization theory, an offshoot of liberal individualism, held that ethnic solidarity is a form of enforced status that constrains individual autonomy and freedom of choice. It predicted that with the inevitable global onset of industrialism, urbanization, and secularization, ethnic sentiments, residues of an earlier stage of human development, were destined to lose their social utility and gradually disappear, the sooner the better.[13] Marxists regarded economic class as the sole objective cleavage in the capitalist phase of socioeconomic development. Thus, ethnic solidarity was either a surrogate for underlying class divisions, or more likely an expression of "false consciousness" provoked and perpetuated by the capitalist ruling class in order to split and weaken the proletariat by dividing it into mutually hostile ethnic groups.

For such reasons many social scientists have been disinclined to accord ethnic solidarities the status of free-standing social realities and collective identities as independent variables that can initiate and sustain political behavior. They refuse to accept the definition of their members as social collectivities based on subjective belief in common origins, interests, and destinies with which they identify and in which they invest their loyalties. Having refused to regard the Bosnian war as an ethnic conflict, many western social scientists clung to the notion, despite compelling evidence to the contrary, that post-conflict Bosnia could be organized as a community of individuals without regard to ethnic considerations.[14] Until observers and practitioners, as well as scholars, are prepared to respect ethnic identities as important in the lives of their members and to regard ethnic communities as legitimate actors in public affairs rather than platonic surrogates for deeper realities such as class or hapless victims of elite manipulation, until they are prepared to grant to ethnic solidarities the same legitimacy as religious organizations, political parties, or business corporations and study them accordingly, they will continue to sow confusion among students and readers.

The truth is that partisans of each of the three persuasions can find contemporary cases that illustrate their preferred explanation of collective ethnic identity. For example, the constructionist explanation seems especially relevant to ethnic formation in sub-Saharan Africa. The question of origins will continue to engage many social scientists. But origins notwithstanding, ethnic communities become political actors. The goals they pursue bring them into contact with other ethnic communities and with governments. These contacts often become the seeds of ethnic conflict, some peaceful, others violent, which is the focus of this book. The premises of this book are straightforward: (1) ethnic communities are authentic and important social collectivities; (2) conflicts among them and between them and governments are critical realities that cannot be wished away; therefore (3) they must be carefully examined and analyzed so that the dynamics of ethnic-based conflict can be better understood, that violence resulting from such conflicts can be prevented or moderated, and that outcomes can respect the legitimate rights of ethnic communities and of their individual members.

Without dilating further on the three persuasions, it may be noted that the differences between them often reflect different interpretations of the world around us. A respected scholar, for example, asserts that "nationalism can and should be understood without invoking nations as substantial entities. Instead of focusing on nations as real groups, we should focus . . . on nation as practical category, institutionalized form, and contingent event."[15] By contrast, this author regards nations – Japanese, Mexican, Swedish, Thai – as very real entities to their members and to outsiders with very real impacts on the lives of their members and on international affairs and not at all as "contingent events."

Ethnicity and nationalism

We should be clear about the relationship between ethnicity and nationalism in the current era, recognizing that nationalism has been the world's reigning political ideology during the past two centuries. It has garnered whole libraries of scholarship.[16] Along with its sibling doctrine, the right of all peoples to self-determination, nationalism has spread to all continents, spawning revolutionary anti-colonial movements and serving as a useful instrument for consolidating the rule of state elites. Despite the emergence of economic and informational globalism, there is little evidence that its power as a political ideology has diminished.

The core of nationalist ideology is the conviction that the nation and the state that represents that nation embody a people's deepest and most abiding values and virtues, that the destiny of individuals is indissolubly linked to the fate of their nation, and that consequently they owe the nation their undivided loyalty and devotion. In its more extreme and aggressive expression, nationalism implies the superiority of a people over others and even the moral right or duty to dominate and subordinate them. Thus, the French proclaimed their "civilizing mission" to justify colonial ventures in Africa and Asia during the nineteenth century, and Hitler taught the German people that they were a "master race" entitled and destined to rule over their inferior neighbors.

As with all ideologies that attract widespread followings, nationalism has given birth to three different versions, each implying a different structure of the state to which it corresponds. The first is *ethnonationalism*, the belief that any people that aspires to political self-determination and self-rule is a nation and as such is entitled to independent statehood. Such a state should reflect and promote the culture and interests of its titular people, of the nation it embodies, though it may tolerate minorities in its midst. Thus, Zionism or Jewish nationalism is the constitutive ideology of the state of Israel. Its national symbols – flag, anthem, language, heroes, holidays, and festivals – are derived from Jewish experience and celebrate Jewish nationalism. Jews, world-wide, enjoy the right to "return" to their ancient homeland where they are received immediately as full and equal citizens. Its substantial Palestinian minority enjoys basic civil and cultural rights, including citizenship; they may accept the state as a practical reality and conform to its laws, but they lack any basis for emotional attachment to Israel. Similarly, Malay nationalism is the official ideology of the state of Malaysia (literally, land of the Malays). As the state embodies their interests and aspirations, all the symbols of statehood reflect exclusively Malay culture; the state constitution entrenches the special position of the Malays and authorizes their preferential treatment by government. Chinese and Indian minorities possess important civil rights, including citizenship, but their traditions and cultures are absent from the official ideology and from the symbols of the state.

The second version of nationalism, *civic nationalism*, is a territorial concept, defining the nation as all persons regardless of ethnic provenance who accept the duties and responsibilities of citizenship. What binds them together as a political community is not their ethnic origin, but rather their commitment to a common set of political institutions, political values, and way of life. The United States is an example of a nation motivated by the ideology of civic nationalism. In the language of its constitution, "all persons born or naturalized in the United States are citizens of the United States . . ."; "equal protection of the laws" applies to all of them, "regardless of race, religion, or previous condition of servitude." This polyglot nation is united by a powerful nationalist sentiment undergirding an active foreign policy that is global in scope. For some of its citizens America is the bearer of a national mission to make the world safe for democracy. The depth and intensity of American nationalism and sense of national unity were demonstrated in the popular response to the terrorist attacks of September 11, 2001. Ethnic communities in the United States are free to foster and maintain their own cultural institutions on a voluntary basis, but none are patronized by government. They may also compete as interest groups for representation in government, for shares of government offices and resources, and for influence on public policy, but what they advocate for themselves must be justified as benefiting the nation as a whole and as fully consistent with its principles and traditions.

In multinational states that include two or more nations, *syncretic nationalism* is an ideology that attempts to construct a new, inclusive national sentiment that will subordinate and eventually supplant the original national sentiments of its component peoples. Bi-national or multinational states encompass within their boundaries two or more peoples who consider themselves to be distinct nations, but choose voluntarily or are compelled to function as components of a larger state. The United Kingdom (Great Britain) is a multinational state composed of English, Welsh, Scottish, and Northern Irish peoples; prior to 1922 it also included the Irish. For more than two centuries its political elites have attempted, and with some success, to cultivate an overarching British identity that would coexist with and gradually supersede the national sentiments of its component peoples. Yet, at the moment of its greatest peril during the early years of World War II, the tune that reflected the abiding hope and determination of its embattled people, "There'll always be an England," appealed directly to the national sentiments of its majority population, not to the more formal British connection.

The efforts of the Soviet and Yugoslav leadership to engender Soviet and Yugoslav national sentiments and identities among the component peoples of their multinational states experienced little success and eventually collapsed. Their successor states embody the ethnonationalism of their titular people, among them Russians, Ukrainians, Georgians, Uzbeks, Latvians, Serbs, Croats, Slovenes. In the victory celebration of the Soviet triumph over their German invaders, Stalin, the Soviet prime minister and himself a Georgian, toasted the Russian, not the Soviet people.

Within some nations there is an ongoing struggle to define the character of their nationhood. French-speaking Québécois regard themselves as a distinct nation. They dispute among themselves whether their national interest is best served by remaining a semi-autonomous province of the Canadian state, or by opting for independent statehood. A recent controversy has centered on the structure of Quebec nationality. While there is no disputing the primacy of the French language, there are those who advocate that first-class membership in the national community be restricted to descendants of the charter people, Catholics of French origin who were the original European settlers of the St Lawrence valley. Later arrivals of alien stock would be excluded from full membership in the Quebec nation, lacking as they must the necessary emotional attachment to French Catholic culture. Their opponents, advocating civic nationalism, argue that all who choose to make their lives in Quebec and abide by its laws, including the official status of the French language, should, regardless of ethnic origin, be welcome to equal membership in the Quebec nation. The contrast is between advocates of ethnically exclusive and territorially inclusive concepts of citizenship and nationality.

Ethnic conflict can occur in states that practice any of these patterns of nationalism. Japan's traditional state ideology regards the Japanese people as a large extended family under the emperor who stems from an unbroken line of rulers descended from the Sun Goddess. This version of ethnonationalism makes it virtually impossible for ethnic outsiders ever to qualify for membership in the Japanese polity, while ethnic Japanese born abroad of parents who were born abroad may "return" to Japan and be accepted as citizens. Japan harbors a substantial minority of Koreans who, despite Japan's democratic constitution, are effectively excluded from membership in the Japanese nation and are marginalized politically, socially, and economically. With its declining population, Japan's current demographic dilemma is that it urgently needs to recruit immigrants to replenish its diminishing labor force, but denies prospective immigrants the opportunity to aspire to Japanese nationality, because this would dilute the ethnic purity of the Yamato race.

The United States which practices civic nationalism has encountered ethnic conflict, some of it violent, at national, regional, and local levels. From the earliest years of European settlement, there was bloody conflict with native peoples (Indians) resisting the encroachment of Europeans on their homelands. As far back as the 1840s violent attacks were aimed at Irish Catholic immigrants charged with undermining American labor standards and subverting the institutions of American democracy by their loyalty to a foreign potentate, the Roman Pope. An anti-immigrant, anti-Catholic political party won several local and state elections. The long struggle of African-Americans for basic civil rights against stubborn White opposition, especially in the southern states, led to the enactment in 1965 of federal civil rights and voting rights legislation. The enforcement of these laws plus the earlier court-mandated desegregation of public schools and desegregation of the armed forces were major steps in reducing racial barriers to equal protection of the laws. In the New

York City mayoralty election of 2001, the Democratic candidate for mayor was defeated because Puerto Rican and other Hispanic voters believed he had insulted one of their respected political leaders and had failed to offer an apology. Though they normally vote Democrat, they chose to punish the offending Democratic candidate by staying away from the polls or by voting for his Republican opponent in sufficient numbers to enable the Republican to win the election.

Nigeria is a multinational state in which the three largest peoples, Hausa-Fulani in the north, Yoruba in the southwest, and Ibo in the southeast compete for power and political influence. In 1966 the leadership of the Ibo people, convinced that they were being victimized by a central government controlled by hostile Hausa-Fulani politicians and army personnel, attempted to secede and form an independent Ibo state, Biafra. A bloody civil war ensued, and after four years of fighting and nearly a million casualties, the Ibo rebellion was suppressed. Though ethnic conflicts dominate its politics, some Nigerian intellectuals continue to believe that their society is evolving into a nation that will subsume its many ethnic communities.

Divisions and factions

Ethnic politics cannot be understood without reference to the inevitability of divisions and factions *within* ethnic communities. Ethnic communities are seldom, if ever, monolithic. Though we speak of ethnic communities – Palestinians and Israelis, Sinhalese and Tamils, Flemings and Walloons – as collectivities, what we really refer to are those who at a particular point in time represent and act in the name of their ethnic community. Members are likely to agree on certain bottom-line interests of their community, but to divide on important issues of strategy and tactics. Palestinians, for example, are united in wanting Israeli settlements and the Israeli military out of the West Bank and Gaza; they differ on whether a future Palestinian state should be a secular democracy or an Islamic polity; and whether it should be achieved by armed violence, including terrorist tactics, or by negotiation and compromise; and whether what is now the territory of the state of Israel should remain a Jewish state, or eventually be incorporated into a united, Arab-controlled Palestine. Israelis agree that Israel must remain a Jewish state and for that reason the numerous descendants of Palestinians who once claimed to live in pre-independence Israel cannot be allowed to "return." They are, however, divided on many issues involving relations with Palestinians, including the future of the West Bank and its settlements, and whether it is possible or even desirable to negotiate a territorial settlement with the present Palestinian leadership. They also disagree on whether Israel should remain a secular democracy or be governed by a rabbinate enforcing religious law.

After World War II, the overseas Chinese communities in Southeast Asia were embroiled in bitter and sometimes violent controversies between partisans of the new communist regime in China and the defeated nationalists based in Taiwan. Both sides dispatched political agents, propagandists, and teachers to work among the overseas communities to vie for their political and financial support. Competing newspapers, schools, recreational associations, and even financial intermediaries were set up by local partisans of these warring regimes. Governments in Southeast Asia, depending on their own orientation to affairs in China, sometimes intervened to favor one party or the other among their Chinese minority.

The contemporary Islamic world is witnessing a struggle among three factions to determine what is the most effective strategy for rescuing Islamic societies from their current political weakness, economic and scientific backwardness, and cultural stagnation. All of them justify their preferred strategy by reference to the same sacred texts. One faction, represented by former Malaysian prime minister, Mahathir Mohamad, advocates secular modernization and engagement with non-Islamic societies. The second, conservative fundamentalism, represented by the Saudi regime, argues that Muslims can benefit from economic interchange with infidels, but must respect the leadership of established Islamic regimes and find their inspiration in traditional Islamic experience and practices. The third faction, revolutionary fundamentalism, represented by the current Iranian government and such offsprings as Hezbollah in Lebanon and Hamas in Palestine, preaches the need for militant jihad (struggle) to overthrow corrupt imposter governments in Muslim countries and seek renewal from within by returning to the pure teachings of the Prophet and his immediate disciples. In their vigorous competition for influence among the faithful, these factions advocate not only different strategies, but also different tactics to achieve their goals. The modernists seek to benefit from trade, investment, and informational exchanges with non-Muslim societies and practice religious tolerance; the conservatives participate in economic exchanges, but are wary of informational exchanges that may be subversive to their culture and have no interest in religious toleration; the revolutionaries prefer to isolate themselves from infidel contacts and are prepared to use violence, including terrorist tactics, in pursuit of their goals.

Divisions and factions arise in all ethnic communities. They may be based on kinship attachments, on social and economic class, on personal ambitions, on ideology, or on combinations of these factors. Factions compete for influence and support among members of their community, for the right to control its institutions and collective resources, to speak authoritatively on its behalf, and to represent it to outsiders. They may even choose to promote their objectives by working with like-minded groups across the ethnic divide, as Catholic and Protestant women in Northern Ireland, who had lost close relatives in the fighting, formed associations to foster inter-group understanding and campaign for a peaceful settlement. Divisions may turn on questions of basic strategy. Scots are split on whether their collective interests would best be served by remaining a semi-autonomous entity while continuing to participate in the institutions of the United Kingdom; or whether they would be better off as an independent state with membership in the European Union. They agree, however, that whatever their goal, it should be pursued by peaceful, democratic means.

As circumstances change, cleavages within ethnic communities change in response. Prior to the Holocaust, the reformed branch of Judaism, arguing that Judaism is a religious, not a national community, opposed Zionism and the project to establish a Jewish state. After the slaughter of 6 million of their co-religionists, the destruction of Jewish life in central and eastern Europe, and the urgent need of a refuge for the survivors, they reversed their position and became active supporters of the state of Israel. During the apartheid era in South Africa, the National Party was the principal political vehicle of the dominant Afrikaner people, committed to rigid racial segregation and separate development. After the collapse of apartheid and the introduction of non-racial democracy, the leadership of the National Party recognized that under the changed circumstances it would have to expand its membership base if it was to compete for political power. It broke with its past policies and began to recruit membership among non-Whites.

At any point in time, one faction or another may control the institutions and collective resources of an ethnic community, may be empowered to speak in its name and represent it to outsiders. But in all likelihood there will be dissenting factions committed to gaining support among their fellow ethnics, influencing the community's goals, strategies, and tactics, and eventually taking over the leadership. Politics, the competition for power and influence, is seldom absent from the affairs of any human collectivity. For a time it may slumber, but it seldom sleeps. Scholars and other observers must be sensitive to this reality. While persons who speak and act for an ethnic community purport to represent the true interests of a united people, such unity is likely to be ephemeral and to conceal internal cleavages of which the spokespersons themselves are quite aware.

Conclusion

This chapter has defined some of the terms and concepts that will reappear throughout this book (they are further elaborated in the glossary). Not surprisingly, a phenomenon as many-faceted as ethnic solidarity has generated several explanations reflecting the ways different individuals perceive the world around them. Though their partisans debate vigorously among themselves, and this author reveals his own preference that tilts in favor of the primordialist explanation, each of them has some merit and most convincingly explain some situations.

We emphasize the importance of internal factions in all ethnic communities and the danger of treating them as monolithic entities. Internal politics are never absent from an ethnic community as competitors struggle to define its interests, control its resources and institutions, and represent it to outsiders. The strategies and policies that their leaders and spokespersons adopt at any particular time toward both friendly and hostile outsiders may represent compromises between various factions, while internal opponents may oppose and even do their best to undermine these policies.

3
Origins of Ethnic Pluralism

Ethnic pluralism – the presence of two or more peoples within the same political space – is a necessary condition for ethnic conflict. When they were joined in the state of Czechoslovakia, there were continuous and often bitter tensions and disputes between spokespersons for the Czech and Slovak nations over the distribution of the costs and benefits of government policies. When in 1993 these disputes appeared to be irreconcilable, their leaders concluded that cohabitation was no longer viable. The result was the "velvet divorce"; two new states, the Czech Republic and the Republic of Slovakia were born. Contrast this with the bloody and exhausting two decades of warfare before Ethiopia finally conceded independence for Eritrea; and the violent suppression of the Chechen separatist rebellion by the Russian government. Now that Czechs and Slovaks are governed by two separate authorities, relations between the two nations are no longer matters of ethnic politics. Instead they are mediated by the provisions and processes of international law. Within Slovakia, however, relations between the Slovak majority and the substantial Magyar minority, two ethnic communities under the same political authority, continue to be the subject of ethnic politics and the source of ethnic tensions. The activities of neighboring Hungary on behalf of their fellow Magyars in Slovakia further complicate this relationship.

Under stable conditions, a community with a single culture and a single common collective identity may occupy a particular territory for an extended period of time. But human societies tend to be restless and in flux. Individuals, groups, and sometimes entire peoples find occasions to move, fleeing drought or famine, seeking improved economic opportunities, escaping persecution, determined to extend their political dominion or to impress their superior culture or belief system on heathens or infidels. For combinations of such reasons, people migrate to new lands and there they encounter different peoples. These encounters in the same political space result in ethnic pluralism and create the preconditions for ethnic conflict.

Those who are acquainted with the Hebrew scriptures will recall the migration of the children of Israel under their patriarch, Jacob, who fled the drought and famine in their homeland and settled in Egypt where, fearful of their growing numbers and their unwillingness to assimilate into Egyptian society, the pharaohs enslaved them and subjected them to hard labor. Finally, they mobilized under their leader, Moses, and with divine protection and guidance made their way out of Egypt and, after numerous trials and hardships, eventually reached their promised land. There they encountered other peoples who had to be dealt with, mainly by warfare. After the "discovery" of the vast western hemisphere, European migrants of many ethnic backgrounds ventured and settled in the Americas, eliminating some of the native peoples, subjugating others, imposing their religions, forcing still others to abandon their homelands and move to strange, less desirable, and less fertile lands, and importing African slaves to perform labor that the natives refused to accept. The European occupation and settlement of the Americas created complex and changing patterns of ethnic conflict whose many consequences persist to the present.

Sources of ethnic pluralism

Analytically, it is possible to identify five principal sources of ethnic pluralism.

Perhaps the most common is simply *conquest*, as one people invades, defeats the original inhabitants, takes over, and settles a territory that had been the homeland of another people whom they kill, drive out, or subjugate. In rare cases they evolve patterns of coexistence, sharing the territory on equitable terms with the original inhabitants. The Roman conquest of Britain resulted in the subjugation of the original Celtic inhabitants, followed by the Saxon and Danish invasions after the departure of the Roman legions, and finally the Norman conquest, which resulted in the subjugation of the Saxons and Danes. It required four centuries for Normans, Saxons, and Danes to evolve an English collective identity. Similar patterns of large-scale population movements and encounters between invaders and native peoples can be traced in virtually every country and every area of the world. For example, the tsarist expansion during the eighteenth and nineteenth centuries into Siberia, eastern Europe, central Asia, and the Caucasus created a vast multiethnic empire of restive peoples ruled by the repressive apparatus of the Russian state. The main theme in world history is the chronicle of such large-scale invasions and conquests. For our purposes, the most significant consequences are the ethnic encounters, the ethnic pluralism, and the resultant ethnic conflict or coexistence that follow from these population movements.

Annexation is a less common but significant source of ethnic pluralism. This occurred not infrequently as a consequence of dynastic marriages in which populations along with territories were transferred from one ruling family to another to seal the bargain and complete the negotiations. Much of the expansion of the multiethnic Habsburg Empire over the centuries occurred in this manner. In 1532 the Breton people came under the French crown when Anne, princess of Brittany, was wed to the French king, François I. A distinctive Breton identity persists to this day within metropolitan France. When Margaret, the Maid of Norway, married the Scottish ruler James III, in 1468, the Shetland and Orkney islands were annexed, along with their Danish-speaking peoples, to the Scottish crown. In more recent times, treaty arrangements have resulted in annexations that produce ethnic pluralism as when in 1803 Emperor Napoleon I sold the Louisiana Territories including the French-speaking people in and around New Orleans to the English-speaking United States.

Most of the 53 states of Africa are multiethnic. Many ethnic groups in Africa find themselves in different countries, separated by international borders drawn by colonial map-makers, mainly during the nineteenth century, at the heyday of European colonial expansion. These borders that were inherited at the time of independence after World War II were originally drawn in European capitals to regulate disputes among the European powers without, of course, consulting the peoples directly affected or manifesting much concern for the integrity of ethnic communities. There are similar inher-itances in Asia, among them the border between Pakistan and Afghanistan which follows the Durand Line drawn by a British colonial administrator in 1893. This line divides the Pushtun people, 18 million strong, equally between the two countries. For this reason, that international border is porous and routinely disregarded as Pushtuns move and conduct business and family affairs with fellow ethnics across the border. Occasional demands for a united Pushtunistan have proved a nightmare for the governments of these two un-stable neighbors. In their pursuit of Al Quaeda's high command, American forces have been thwarted by the ability of Osama bin Laden and his Taliban allies to move freely across the border and secure protection among sympathizers in Pakistan's Pushtun community.

Aside from conquest and annexation, there are three kinds of population movements that contribute to ethnic pluralism. The first can be classified as *settler migrations*, organized group movements into a territory with the intention of estab-lishing permanent residences and assuming control of the area. The settlers may persuade themselves that the territory they occupy is void of any significant population or is so sparsely settled that their presence will not disturb and may even benefit the original inhabitants. This was the view of the early Dutch and Huguenot settlers in the Cape region of South Africa and of the early Zionist settlers in Palestine, who convinced themselves that this was "a land without people for a people without a land." Once this illusion was no longer tenable, they argued that their presence would benefit the

local Arabs by helping them to modernize, improve their
health conditions and living standards, and resist the traditional ruling families, many of them absentee landlords, who
exploited the local peasantry. This view is invariably mistaken, as any desirable area of settlement is already claimed
by another people, no matter how sparse and dispersed their
presence. They will eventually mobilize to resist the settler
incursions, as the South African Dutch and later English
settlers, the Zionists, and the European colonists in the
Americas soon discovered. Thus, settlers often evolve into
conquerors.

The most common process of migration, especially in
recent years, is the *voluntary movement* of individuals or
small groups in search of economic opportunities or political
freedom, or as refugees from persecution into areas that may
already be rather densely populated. These migrants have no
intention of challenging the prevailing political or social
order. Some such migrants are professionally trained and
highly skilled, for example the Indian software engineers
who settle in California's Silicon Valley. However, the
majority who leave their homeland tend to be unskilled
and ill-educated, and when they reach their destinations
they occupy, at least at the beginning, the lowest and least
remunerative rungs of the socio-economic ladder in their
adopted countries. This has been the experience of the Irish,
Italian, and Polish immigrants to the United States in the
nineteenth century and of Mexican and other Hispanic immigrants in the current era, of Turkish "guest workers" in
Germany and the Netherlands, North Africans in France,
West Indians in Britain. Wherever there appear to be employment opportunities, these act as magnets for labor from
impoverished, overpopulated areas with few economic
prospects. So desperate is their need for employment and
income that many will risk great hardships and illegal status
to reach a country where employment may be available.
Smuggling Chinese laborers into the United States has
become a lucrative criminal industry. Recently 20 Chinese
were found starved and suffocated to death in a shipping con-
tainer in San Francisco.

The new arrivals will not immediately acculturate to their
new environment. They will congregate together for mutual

assistance, fellowship, and sometimes for security, forming their own diaspora residential communities, organizing their own institutions for religious, recreational, and cultural activities usually in their ancestral language, and promoting their common interests in local and, where need be, in national political forums. Unless they are blocked by racial markers, successive generations tend to acculturate and finally assimilate into the indigenous society.

In the present era, especially in Europe and North America where prosperity has created large markets for unskilled labor, this is the most dynamic source of ethnic pluralism and ethnic conflict and is likely to persist into the future. In every western and central European country, immigration has become a central political issue, featuring a notable political backlash against visible minorities – those of dark-skinned, non-European backgrounds. As in North America, many European employers favor a liberal immigration policy, as it provides abundant pools of low-wage labor, while others impute elevated crime rates, rampant disease, depressed wage rates, and inflated welfare expenses to immigrants and their children. Above all, they resent the prominence in their midst of exotic foreigners speaking strange languages who are believed to be poor candidates for assimilation into their nation.

The third category of population movements that generate ethnic pluralism is *coerced migration*. The African diaspora to the western hemisphere is the legacy of chattel slavery, an institution that survived in the United States until 1863 and in Brazil until 1889 and whose consequences endure to this day. Though the United States has been peopled by waves of voluntary immigration that continues to the present, the most intractable, sensitive, and ongoing source of ethnic conflict remains the relationship between White America and its large African-American communities. While much has been accomplished in the wake of the civil rights movement and the civil rights legislation of the 1960s, much remains to be done before the promise of equal justice and equality of treatment has been realized. Reacting against the gap between American ideals and their experience with discrimination and rejection, a minority of alienated African-Americans have adopted separatist and often hostile postures toward

American institutions, embracing Islam or Pan-Africanism as their ideology.

Less prominent, but of great importance, was the movement of indentured labor within the far-flung British Empire during the nineteenth century, particularly the transportation under contract of workers from the Indian subcontinent to destinations as dispersed as Fiji, Trinidad, Ceylon, Malaya, and Guyana. Indians were assigned to work the rubber plantations, sugar estates, railways, and other enterprises where local labor was unavailable or unwilling. In each of these locations, once their contracts were fulfilled, many remained as wageworkers. They and their descendants have constituted distinct societies, there has been little mixing with indigenous peoples, and Indians have participated as electoral blocs in the politics of these countries. The indentured working classes should be distinguished from voluntary migrants from the subcontinent, Hindus as well as Muslims, to the countries of eastern and southern Africa where they constitute relatively small but prominent and economically important communities of commercial entrepreneurs. One such minority in Uganda, 45,000 strong, was expelled and deported in the 1960s by the populist dictator, Idi Amin, with devastating effects on Uganda's economy. The role of such middleman minorities is discussed in chapter 6.

A third type of coerced migration is the mass movement of refugees across international borders resulting from warfare or forced deportations (ethnic cleansing).[1] The war in Bosnia drove an estimated 900,000, mostly Croatian and Muslim, refugees across international borders, some to other former Yugoslav republics, others to Germany, Austria, Hungary, Switzerland, and Sweden where most are expected to remain permanently. The Soviet invasion of Afghanistan and its aftermath drove 5 million people, 20 percent of its population, into neighboring countries, mainly Pakistan and Iran. Burma's war against its ethnic minorities has resulted in 300,000 refugees in Thailand.

Ethnic cleansing has deep historical roots. In 1492 Spain expelled its large Jewish population. In 1758 the British deported Acadians from Nova Scotia. After World War II, Czechoslovakia expelled its entire German minority. Aside from the suffering visited on these displaced persons by the loss of homes and livelihoods, these communities become burdens on other countries and international relief agencies, such as the UN High Commission for Refugees. Coerced migrations then result in the creation of diasporas in countries that accept them. In some instances, these entail unwelcome political consequences. The events of 1948 and 1967 brought an estimated 750,000 Palestinians to Jordan; these recent arrivals and their progeny have become the majority of Jordan's population. During the 1980s, Malaysia refused to accept any Sino-Vietnamese refugees, "boat people," whose flimsy craft were hovering precariously off their shores, fearing that the additional ethnic Chinese would adversely affect the delicate ethnic proportions in their country.

Self-determination of peoples

Under the influence of eighteenth-century British and French philosophers, lawyers, and publicists, democratic thought gradually became the dominant intellectual current and principle of governance during the modern era, a historical trend that shows no sign of abating. Democratic logic mandated that legitimate public authority requires the consent of the governed – in Lincoln's phrase, government of, by, and for the people. Even authoritarian regimes often feel compelled to clothe themselves in democratic garb, such as the rhetoric of the "People's Republic of China," and former European Soviet satellites, such as the "German Democratic Republic." A corollary to the consent of the governed is the principle, however violated in practice, of popular sovereignty.

As rule by the people became the basis for legitimate government, rule by foreigners became illegitimate, even by foreigners who might be more advanced in the arts of civilization and more benevolent than local elites. The British White Man's Burden, the French Civilizing Mission, not to mention the rule of the stronger became morally suspect as they denied peoples what came to be regarded as a basic human right. People who had previously acquiesced in rule by foreigners, first in Europe then world-wide, became aware of their nationhood, mobilized for struggle, and claimed the right of all nations to self-determination. During World War I, the American president Woodrow Wilson, proclaimed the right of all nations to self-determination as a principal war aim of the United States. The moral basis of European colonialism was thus undermined well before the institution itself collapsed.

The post-World War I settlement imposed by the victorious allies applied the principle of self-determination very selectively, only to territories of the defeated European powers, the Habsburg, German, tsarist, and Ottoman empires. From these defeated empires new nation-states emerged, among them Poland, Czechoslovakia, and Lithuania; Croatia and Slovenia combined with Serbia to become constituent republics of the new kingdom of Yugoslavia. The victorious Bolsheviks, aware of Lenin's description of the tsarist regime as the "prison house of nations," paid lip service to the principle of self-determination by creating a series of ethnic-based "republics" that composed the Soviet Union, with theoretical but not practical autonomy, including the right to secede. In addition, the new League of Nations required several of the defeated and the newly independent states to sign treaties that conferred autonomous cultural privileges on a number of their ethnic minorities, this status to be supervised and enforced by a section of the League's secretariat. This was to implement two corollaries of the principle of self-determination: (1) that it did not require political sovereignty, but could be satisfied by various degrees of autonomy in a multinational polity, as long as this status was voluntarily arrived at; and (2) that under some circumstances where independent statehood is impractical (because the population is too small or is entirely entangled with the majority and thus not separable territorially), collective cultural or political rights guaranteed by the state to its minority populations complies with the requirements of self-determination.

At the Versailles settlement and its aftermath, it became clear to President Wilson and his supporters that America's allies intended to limit the application of self-determination to Europe and only to the territories of their defeated enemies. It was not to apply to the Irish, who were in revolt against British rule, nor to the Flemish minority in Belgium. Nor was it to apply to the vast British and French colonial empires in Asia, the Caribbean, and Africa whose (non-White) inhabitants were held to be unqualified or insufficiently "evolved" to be candidates for self-rule. Though the moral basis for colonialism had been fatally compromised, the interests of the victorious powers were able to maintain their increasingly discredited institution for another generation. During this interval, the well-publicized campaign of the Indian National Congress under Mahatma Gandhi in this most important and bellwether European holding inspired indigenous forces in the Dutch East Indies (Indonesia), French Indochina (notably Vietnam), the Gold Coast (Ghana), Algeria, Morocco, Burma, and other colonial territories, as well as opponents of empire in the home bases of the colonial powers, to press their campaigns to end colonial rule. In 1936 the United States formally promised independence to its Philippine colony after a transition period of ten years.

World War II ushered in the end of European colonialism and the realization on a global scale of self-determination. The Japanese conquest of Southeast Asia demolished the myth of the White man's invulnerability. The Japanese promoted independence sentiment – under Japanese tutelage in a "Greater East Asia Co-prosperity Sphere" – for Indonesia, Indochina, Malaya, and Burma and organized an Indian National Army to threaten British rule in the subcontinent. When in 1947 Britain, exhausted financially and militarily by its long struggle for survival, conferred independence on India and Pakistan, followed soon by Burma and Ceylon, colonial rule elsewhere was doomed. By 1976 all the significant British, French, Dutch, and Portuguese territories had gained political independence, though elements of economic colonialism persisted. Finally, in 1990 the collapse of the Soviet Union, the last of the European imperial regimes, resulted in the independence of European, Caucasian, and central Asian republics that had been ruled originally by the tsars and then by the Russian-based Soviet state. The membership of the United Nations which stood at 51 in 1945, mostly European and American states, a half century later numbered 189.

So compelling and so normative has become the doctrine of self-determination that violations have become conspicuous and subject to international opprobrium. Having annexed East Timor following the collapse of Portugal's colonial regime, after a quarter century of repression, Indonesia finally conceded independence to this rebellious people. Among the most conspicuous violators of self-determination is the People's Republic of China, which, in the face of manifest hostility by its inhabitants, persists in the subjugation and occupation of Tibet and its program of colonizing Tibet with ethnic Han (Chinese) settlers. Other instances where a people has been forcibly denied this basic right are the Indian control of predominantly Muslim Kashmir, Russian suppression of the Chechen revolt, Iraqi domination of the Kurdish people, and the Israeli occupation and colonization of the West Bank. Each of these situations has provoked resistance, frequently violent, from people opposed to foreign rule and convinced that their basic human rights have been transgressed.

The end of colonialism does not, however, signal the end of ethnic pluralism and ethnic conflict, for the newly independent entities are likely to include more than one ethnic community. Very few contemporary states are ethnically homogeneous. In independent India, for example, each of 24 distinct languages is spoken by more than a million persons. The largest ethnic communities have become the titular people and achieved a considerable measure of self-government in each of the 28 states that comprise the Indian federal union. Bengali are the titular people of the state of West Bengal whose population is 66 million, as are Tamils in Tamil Nadu with 62 million – larger than most of the member states of the United Nations. Each of these states contains minority peoples who demand respect for their culture and especially their language and religious rights, and this is separate from the very sensitive and conflict-prone relationship between the majority Hindus and the large Muslim minority. As every African state includes more than one ethnic community, the management of this pluralism has become a continuing preoccupation of African political leaders. Several have resulted in violent action, notably in Sudan, Chad, Nigeria, Ethiopia, and Rwanda. Having achieved the goal of self-determination, the successor states of the former Soviet Union now confront the demands of their ethnic minorities.

Ukraine must cope with the needs of the Russian majority in its province of Crimea; Georgia has been unable to satisfy its restive Abkhazian, Ajarian and South Ossetian minorities; independent Azerbaijan inherited a large, irredentist enclave of Armenians who aspire to unite with their fellow ethnics in neighboring Armenia. The unresolved outcome of that controversy has been the occupation of Azerbaijani territory by the Armenian army.

In most such situations, self-determination need not entail independent statehood. For a variety of reasons, independence may appear to be impractical, unwanted, or to involve a degree of conflict that does not warrant the probable costs. In such cases minorities find it prudent to settle for less, for federal arrangements that guarantee a substantial measure of self-government, or for minority rights which provide some autonomy including the means to perpetuate their distinctive culture. Minority rights may be readily conceded, for example the language and education rights granted by Finland to its Swedish minority. By contrast, the achievement of self-determination may involve long years of struggle. After decades of attempted Arabization and violent incidents as recently as April 2001, the Government of Algeria recently agreed to accord official status to Tamazight, the language of its large Berber minority, and to provide education at public expense in that medium. One of the leading issues dividing factions within ethnic communities is precisely this question of strategy: what degree and form of self-determination would best serve the community. Should the Kurdish nation, 25 million strong, now split between Turkey, Iraq, Iran, and Syria, struggle for a united, independent Kurdistan, or be willing to settle for autonomy or minority rights in each of these four countries? Should the embattled peoples of southern Sudan settle for nothing short of independence, or be satisfied to strike a deal with the Khartoum government that would grant them regional self-rule?

Self-determination was originally conceived to apply to people who could claim a territorial homeland. But, as we have noted, the dynamic that is producing ethnic pluralism these days results from large-scale cross-border migration. Where peoples of different ethnic provenance are intermixed to the point that independence or regional self-rule are unfeasible, what they are likely to claim under the rubric of minority rights are versions of *cultural autonomy* that enable them to sustain their distinctive community and perpetuate elements of their ancestral culture, while participating in the economic opportunities and political life of their larger society on a non-discriminatory basis. This formula is an aspect of multiculturalism. Examples are the availability in Spanish of signs, official forms, ballots, and licenses, and of bilingual public education (Hispanic immigrants in the United States); the right to carry ceremonial daggers and wear turbans in the military and police forces (Sikhs in Britain); and the right to elementary school education in the Mandarin and Tamil languages (Malaysia). In this way, the right to self-determination, originally a territorial concept intended for homeland peoples, has been extended to incorporate fresh patterns of pluralism created by immigration and the resultant diaspora communities.

Pluralism, competition, and mobilization

Ethnic pluralism is a necessary condition for interethnic contact, but not a sufficient condition for competition or conflict. As indicated in chapter 2, peaceful coexistence is possible based on complementary divisions of labor, mutual respect for the others' customs and vital interests, and in some cases cautious mutual avoidance. In some instances economic intercourse may result over time in the amalgamation of communities or the eventual absorption of one people by their erstwhile neighbors. More commonly, even under conditions of friendly coexistence, ethnic communities tend to perpetuate their boundaries and to maintain awareness of their distinctiveness. They may be helpful and respectful on the surface, but at least mildly disparaging in private of the customs and behavior of their otherwise friendly neighbors.

Some observers expressed dismay at the unexpected emergence of vicious and deadly ethnic conflict in Sarajevo, a city where on the surface Serbs, Croats, and Muslims appeared for generations to have lived together peacefully, a textbook example of harmonious inter-group relations. More perceptive observers, however, would have noticed that the boundaries between the communities tended, nevertheless, to be maintained and that relatively few had intermarried or adopted an overarching Bosnian or Yugoslav identity, though this was encouraged by government. Thus, as the breakup of the Yugoslav federation loosened the restraints on interethnic suspicions and the communities in Bosnia began to mobilize for defense, Sarajevo too began to break up into its ethnic components. Some surprised observers ascribed this process of ethnic fission to the machinations of unscrupulous political extremists and their brutal gangs of enforcers who intimidated a reluctant majority into sullen conformity – the instrumentalist explanation for ethnic conflict. They failed to understand that unless there is continuous, widespread, and deeply rooted adherence to collective ethnic identities, the appeals of these political entrepreneurs would have fallen on deaf ears and failed to elicit a response. Though many individuals in Sarajevo and elsewhere in Bosnia deplored the degeneration of their once friendly city into communal warfare, there was little they could do to prevent or reverse the rupture of the frail links that bound these communities into patterns of respectful coexistence, once their vital interests appeared to be threatened and the logic of collective survival took over.

As issues emerge that appear to challenge the vital interests of an ethnic community or to provide fresh opportunities to redefine and assert its collective interests – what these issues are will be analyzed in chapter 4 – communities mobilize for the defense and promotion of their common interests. Aggrieved communities may require decades or more before they develop the means and the will to resist. Effective mobilization for political action, civic or violent as the case may be, must be sustained over time and this entails organization. The various components required for the organization of a political movement are outlined below.

(1) *Leadership* is essential to define and articulate a set of goals, strategies, and tactics to guide the struggle, to inspire its membership to support and participate, and to settle conflicts that arise among the factions in these movements. The performance of Dr Martin Luther King in inspiring the

mobilization of African-Americans in the civil rights movement of the 1950s and 1960s is one example of outstanding leadership. At the same time Yasser Arafat was mobilizing a demoralized Palestinian people for a long, uncertain, and often violent struggle. The leadership that succeeds in the process of mobilization must often first challenge, then displace an earlier leadership that is more conservative, often self-serving, and less inclined to bold action.

The African National Congress (ANC) was founded in 1912 by members of the upper crust of native South African society. They hoped that by exemplary behavior, as Africans became more "civilized" (embraced Christianity and spoke English), they would qualify and be admitted to citizenship. Three decades later, their membership totaled a mere 5,600 and their efforts had been entirely fruitless. In 1944 a group of educated young men led by Nelson Mandela organized the Congress Youth League, committed to a militant strategy of non-violent confrontation and resistance to apartheid, inspired by the successful example of the Indian National Congress under Mahatma Gandhi. In 1949 they assumed the leadership of the ANC and converted it into a mass organization committed to struggle for a democratic, non-racial South Africa. The ANC was outlawed as a subversive conspiracy by the apartheid government in 1960, but thirty years later, after a generation of defiance and persecution, the apartheid regime collapsed and Mandela, who had languished in prison for 26 years, was elected president of a democratic, non-racial South Africa. The youthful leaders of the Quiet Revolution in Quebec in the late 1950s, with their bold vision of a progressive and assertive Quebecois people, outmaneuvered and displaced a reactionary, corrupt, and backward-looking ruling clique. Upon gaining control of the provincial government, they undertook to use the resources of the provincial state to launch the vigorous modernization of French-Canadian society and to confront the Ottawa government with unprecedented demands for provincial autonomy.

(2)   Successful mobilization requires a group of *intellectuals* who are thinkers and publicists rather than activists. Their function is to provide the body of ideas or ideology that

serves to motivate and chart a coherent set of purposes and strategies to unite the many and diverse individuals who are prepared to invest their energies in the movement. These are the core ideas that maintain internal morale and explain and justify the movement's objectives to the outside world. Their ideas are frequently embodied in journalism, literature, and the performing arts as writers and artists are recruited into the struggle; their work serves as vehicles for spreading and popularizing the message.

(3) Next come the *activists* who form the core of the movement's *organization* and are dispersed among the ethnic population. Through division of labor, they introduce efficiency, predictability, and robustness into the common effort. It is they who implement the strategies and carry out the programs of action determined by the top leadership. It is they who actually mobilize and deploy the resources, financial, physical, informational, and human that are available for the struggle. They are responsible for getting out the vote where votes matter, or for managing and running the risks of violence and encountering the enemy where violence is the tactic of necessity or choice. Clashes between factions are frequently engineered by competing groups of activists, for example between the Islamist Hamas and the secularist Fatah among Palestinians.

The particular circumstances or context surrounding the mobilization of ethnic communities for political action differ in every case. There can be no standard formulas to account for this process. The mobilization of Malays in 1946 behind the new United Malays' National Organization (UMNO) had little in common with the mobilization of Palestinians a generation later. Leadership among Malays was assumed by their established aristocrats, with Malay school teachers as the principle activists and grass roots organizers. Their goals were to maintain the prevailing structures of Malay society and to fortify the special position of Malays vis-à-vis the other "races" in their country. Their tactics involved pressures directed at the British colonial authorities in Malaya and in London, and negotiation with conservative representatives of the Chinese and Indian communities. Leadership among the Palestinians, by contrast, was assumed by young, educated men of middle-class origins rebelling against traditional figures who had been co-opted by the Jordanian occupying authorities in the West Bank prior to the 1967 war. The latter were charged with timid and ineffectual opposition to the illegitimate Israeli presence on Palestinian soil. Their ideology of secular nationalism was shaped by educated Palestinians, many working in exile, following the prevailing line in Pan-Arabist circles under the influence of Nasserite thinking in Egypt and Baathists in Iraq and Syria. Their goal was to establish Palestinian dominion over all of Palestine, expelling both Israelis and Jordanians. Their tactics focused on securing recognition and financial and military assistance from Arab and other sympathetic governments such as the Soviet Union and the employment of violence to weaken, demoralize, and destabilize the Zionist entity.

The circumstances that they confront condition the process of mobilization, the strategies they adopt, the tactics they employ. The large Chinese minority in Malaya prior to World War II was divided into two major factions: those who accepted the leadership of their economic elites and the communists. During the Japanese occupation, while Chinese were treated as enemy aliens, the communists organized and conducted a guerrilla campaign aimed at harassing the Japanese authorities, then expelling the British colonialists, and achieving a social revolution. After the defeat and withdrawal of the Japanese, the returning British, who had aided the Chinese guerillas during the war, mounted a military campaign that succeeded after several years in isolating and defeating the communists. During these military operations, the British herded large numbers of rurally based Chinese into "new villages" to deny logistical help to the communists. The conservative Chinese organized lotteries and other activities to provide food, medicines, and other assistance to the inmates of these new villages. As Malays organized for political action behind the UMNO, the Chinese felt the need for parallel or competitive mobilization, lest their needs and interests be unrecognized and overlooked in negotiations leading to Malaya's independence. The result was a conservative political coalition brokered by the leaders of UMNO and the new Malayan Chinese Association (MCA). In these negotiations, Chinese accepted the role of junior partners and Malay control of government in the new interethnic Alliance Party, in return for the conferral of citizenship on locally born non-Malays and economic freedom for Chinese business interests. This ethnic coalition, renamed the National Front, notwithstanding inevitable internal strains and opposition elements in both communities, has governed Malaya, and its successor, Malaysia, continuously since 1954.

One contextual factor that is likely to influence the shape of ethnic mobilization is the posture of government. The role of government in ethnic politics is explored in depth in chapter 5. Here it should be noted that the hostility or permissiveness of government, as the case may be, goes a long way toward explaining the process of mobilization and the behavior of mobilized communities. The hostility of government virtually insures that ethnic leadership will embrace revolutionary strategies and sooner or later resort to violent tactics. The hostility of the Turkish government, which proscribed any expression of organized dissent among the large Kurdish minority, discredited moderate leadership among the Kurd and paved the way for militants committed to revolutionary violence. The discriminatory treatment provoked by military enforcement of the Arabization and Islamization policies of the Khartoum government provoked armed resistance among the southern Christian and animist peoples in Sudan. Though committed in principle to non-violence, the brutal repression meted out by the apartheid regime left the African National Congress (ANC) with little choice but to organize a military wing and embark on violent operations directed against agencies of the apartheid state. On the other hand, the permissiveness of the post-Franco democratic state in Spain enabled the Catalan autonomist movement to operate peacefully and control a regional government in Catalonia that fulfills their requirements for self-determination. Yet with the same opportunity for regional autonomy, a fragment of the Basque people, ETA, unwilling to accept any status short of total independence, continues to pursue that goal by terrorist tactics, identical with those it employed against the repressive Franco dictatorship.

Confrontation between ethnic groups or between an ethnic community and government may be carried out by peaceful means, by legal, political, or polemical methods according to rules and practices sanctioned by the state. Such civic confrontations are common in democratic systems where dissidents are free to organize politically and express their grievances, and where differences can be debated and compromises negotiated. Scottish demands for greater autonomy have been pursued through propaganda, electoral, and parliamentary means within the rules of the British parliamentary system, culminating after a quarter century of pressure in a Scottish parliament and Scottish executive with broad legislative and taxation powers. Those for whom these autonomous arrangements are insufficient provide the main opposition in the Scottish parliament and continue their campaign, using entirely civic tactics, for Scottish national independence.

In authoritarian states where opposition is treated as subversion, discontented ethnic communities may seek redress by respectful petition or by bribery, recognizing that any perception by the authorities of pressure may invite repression, imprisonment of leaders, or the outlawing of the organization. This was the fate of Basque and Catalan ethnic movements in Franco's Spain. Even democratic states may sometimes make it difficult for the concerns of dissidents to gain a place on the agenda of government. They may be ignored until violent protest compels government to address their concerns and attempt to resolve them. The grievances of African and Caribbean immigrants in Britain were overlooked until riots on the streets of several cities forced government to take steps to act on these grievances. Since there are divisions in all ethnic communities, factions that advocate direct action and militant tactics may disregard the advice of more cautious leaders and precipitate violent incidents. These, in turn, may provoke violent responses by the security forces of government, the effect of which is to radicalize the community and overwhelm the influence of those who continue to favor political and other non-violent methods of articulating and promoting their community's grievances. This was the dynamic in Sri Lanka where the Tamil Tigers, resentful of the discriminatory policies of the Sinhalese-dominated government and committed uncompromisingly to independent statehood by revolutionary violence, displaced the more cautious leaders of the Tamil community and unleashed the civil war that has raged for the past two decades.

Conclusion

The global expansion of European power in the form of colonization from the sixteenth century until well into the twentieth resulted in conquests, population movements, settlements, and boundary changes that produced ethnic pluralism in the same political space on an unprecedented scale in the Americas, Asia, and Africa. The encroachment of foreigners on their territory sowed the seeds of ethnic conflict. In the latter stage of European expansion the spread of democratic doctrine and of the principle of self-determination emboldened previously quiescent peoples to demand and struggle for their liberation. As colonial powers relaxed their hold on native societies, latent tensions between indigenous communities often erupted into conflicts that successor governments were unable to control.

Members of the human species are a restless lot, prone to move from place to place in search of conquest, greater freedom, or economic opportunities. With the development of rapid, reliable, and cheap transportation after World War II, international migration has reached record-setting proportions and shows no sign of abating. Some of this migration consists of refugees from war zones, but by far the greater number are persons from poor labor-surplus countries seeking employment in the prosperous economies of Europe, North America, and Japan. These migrants form diaspora communities whose demands and often mere presence excite resentment among elements of the indigenous society, providing the mass base for anti-immigrant politics. At the outset of the twenty-first century large-scale migration has become an important source of ethnic conflict.

4

For What Do They Contend?

Types of ethnic conflict

In chapter 1 we identified ethnic conflicts that are pursued by civic or peaceful methods, through such means as propaganda, negotiation, elections, litigation, and attempts to influence government administrators and legislators by persuasion, including campaign contributions and similar financial incentives. At the other extreme are large-scale violent conflicts that involve central governments, extend over many months and even years, and may eventuate in civil wars with extensive casualties, property damage, refugee flows, and disruption of the normal routines of life.

A third type is ethnic riots, generally localized, explosive, short-lived, but often extremely brutal. Some ethnic riots result from accumulated anger against governments which are accused of neglect of just grievances or persistent discriminatory treatment and disrespect. One purpose of this class of ethnic riots is to draw public attention to these grievances in the hope that this will compel government to act. Violent outbreaks by young Afro-Caribbeans in several British cities, targeted often at the police, are examples of this type of ethnic riot, as were similar episodes in Los Angeles protesting police brutality against young African-Americans.

The more common type of ethnic riots, those directed against other ethnic groups, has been analyzed by Professor

Horowitz.[1] Such explosive outbreaks of violence are often accompanied by extensive brutality, including bodily mutilation and targeted destruction of homes and businesses. Accumulated suspicion and anger, plus rumors of atrocities and threats provoked by the ethnic enemy, whip up the fury of the mob composed mostly of ordinary men who, as individuals, would never contemplate such uncivilized behavior. The ethnic "other," often a long-standing enemy, is charged with such atrocities and with such criminal intentions as to justify indiscriminate brutality against any member of that community (for example, "the only good Indian is a dead Indian"). Whatever inhibitions might restrain the mob are neutralized by a sense that there will be no price to pay, government will not interfere because it is too weak or because it sympathizes with the mob. Ethnic conflict may persist long after a particular explosive riot has spent its force, the mob has dispersed, and the victims have been buried. Antagonism and ethnic conflict between Hindus and Muslims will long outlast the lethal 2002 riots in Gujerat, and the same can be said of hostility between Christian Ibo and Muslim Hausa three decades after the massacre of Ibo in several northern Nigerian cities in 1965–6.

What precipitates conflicts?

We have noted that ethnic communities may function in close proximity or under the jurisdiction of the same political authority, yet coexist peacefully. What then precipitates conflicts or causes them to break out among ethnic communities or between them and governments?

The first such cause of ethnic conflicts is *perceived affronts to a community's honor or dignity,* bearing in mind that collectivities even more than individuals place a high value on their self-esteem and are likely to respond aggressively when their dignity has been impugned or offended by others. Often it is difficult to separate tangible from emotional sources of conflict, but it is certain that men do not live by bread alone, that they expect to be treated respectfully by neighbors and by those in authority, and that when that respect is denied they look for ways to retaliate. We noted in chapter 2 how a perceived insult by the Democratic Party candidate for mayor of New York City to a prominent Hispanic political figure prompted Hispanic voters, normally Democratic, to punish the offending Democrat by abstaining from voting, thus contributing to his defeat.

The attempt by the government in Khartoum to impose the Arabic language and apply the Islamic penal code to the non-Muslim, non-Arabic peoples of southern Sudan was perceived as an insult to their culture that justified violent resistance. When the Sinhalese-dominated government of Sri Lanka decreed that henceforth all tests for university entrance and exams for civil service positions were to be conducted only in the Sinhalese language, members of the Tamil minority interpreted this not only as an assault on their employment opportunities, but also as a sign that their culture would be accorded no respect by a government committed to Sinhalese nationalism. This proved to be the policy that triggered Tamil demand for a separate state and the ensuing civil war. The headscarf controversy in France is perceived by its growing Muslim minority as their demand that government agencies demonstrate respect for the requirements of their religion. (Many of the young women who insisted on wearing headscarves were, like the majority of North Africans born in France, not observant Muslims.) A community may be too weak to respond aggressively to deprivation or humiliation, but may seek relief in humor, passive resistance, or similar means of soothing their injured self-esteem.[2]

The most common precipitator of ethnic conflict is *tangible threats to the vital interests of an ethnic community* by another ethnic group or by a government. The encroachment of Jewish settlements sponsored by the Israeli occupation authorities and protected by the Israeli army on lands in the West Bank and Gaza, which Palestinians regard as theirs by right, is perceived by Palestinians as an imminent threat of dispossession and permanent Israeli rule. The result has been the current (2004) intifada and wave of suicide bombings. In western Europe the influx of dark-skinned, non-European, labor immigrants has been viewed by many working-class natives as a hostile invasion, a threat to their jobs, their pay rates, their neighborhoods, their schools, and the safety of their families. Though others object to these immigrants as socially and culturally unassimilable to their national community, the most vigorous demands for curtailing and rolling back immigration stems from working-class Europeans who feel most directly impacted.

The threat of permanent disfranchisement, dispossession, and powerlessness led the Congress Youth League to mobilize resistance to the apartheid system and demand equal rights and opportunities for Blacks in South Africa. Malays, who had been rather passive politically, mobilized rapidly and formed the United Malays' National Organization (UMNO) in 1946 in response to the British-sponsored Malayan Union project which threatened to strip traditional Malay rulers of their prerogatives and eliminate the special rights of Malays, while conferring equal citizenship on resident non-Malays – in effect threatening Malay control over what they believed to be their homeland, their just inheritance. Once the Malay mobilization succeeded in scuppering the Malayan Union proposal, non-Malays, in turn, were threatened with neglect of their interests unless they, too, organized for political action.

There are, of course, occasions when there is no evident response to perceived threats, when an ethnic community considers itself too weak or too poorly organized to challenge the hostile actions of government. Such was the case in the former Confederate states after the US Civil War when the withdrawal of federal troops allowed the White state governments to disfranchise the emancipated former slaves, impose racial segregation in inferior facilities including substandard schools, and confine Negroes, as they were then called, to the most menial and dependent means of livelihood. Three-quarters of a century were to pass before it seemed possible for Blacks in the US South to mobilize to demand rights that had been illegally denied them by law and intimidation. Jews in tsarist Russia were too weak to offer resistance to the pogroms incited by the tsarist regime.

This leads to the third precipitator of ethnic conflicts: *fresh opportunities to gain advantages or redress grievances*, to upset an unsatisfactory status quo that had previously been considered impervious to change. What changes in circumstances enabled southern Blacks in the US after two centuries of slavery and three-quarters of a century of subsequent oppression to finally mobilize to demand equal protection of the laws? Service in the US army and in defense industries during World War II, desegregation of the armed forces by President Truman, the landmark, unanimous Supreme Court ruling in 1954 requiring desegregation of public schools, the deployment of US marshals and the US military by President Eisenhower to enforce the Supreme Court ruling, evidence that the government in Washington was prepared at long last to intervene to protect Blacks in the peaceful exercise of their constitutional rights – these, combined with inspired leadership by Martin Luther King, persuaded Black activists and their mass following that progress was finally possible, sufficient to justify the risks involved in participating in the civil rights movement.

The collapse of the Soviet Union followed by the independence of its former constituent republics, including the Muslim peoples of central Asia and the Caucasus, emboldened the Chechens, a Muslim people, to demand independence for themselves, though they were legally a component of the Russian Federated Republic. Their determined rebellion was repressed by the Russian military at very great cost to both sides. At the eastern and western extremes of the vast Indonesian archipelago, the restive Papuan and Achinese peoples had been contained during the long Suharto dictatorship by a heavy-handed military presence. The fall of Suharto and the unpopularity of the military under a fledgling democratic regime induced the Jakarta government to concede independence to the embattled people of East Timor. To militants in Aceh and Papua/West Irian, what was impossible during the Suharto era now seemed within reach under the new set of circumstances with a weakened central government and a discredited military. Circumstances had changed, and what proved possible for East Timor might be possible also for them, might warrant the risks of armed rebellion.

The bones of contention

When ethnic communities confront one another or when they face off against governments, what are the issues that divide them, what are the different outcomes they seek? Are the conflicts basically irrational and easily avoidable if only the parties would be sensible; or are they struggles over matters of importance that can make significant differences to members of the contending communities whether the tactics they employ are peaceful or violent?

The issues that divide the contending parties can be conveniently classified as political, economic, and cultural.

Political

Control of territory is the rawest and most fundamental of political issues. It is most obviously at stake in the century-long clash between Palestinian and Jewish nationalisms, both claiming exclusive rights to Palestine, the ancient land between the River Jordan and the Mediterranean. Religious Zionists believe this to be the land promised by God to the children of Israel; secular Zionists argue that this land was promised as a homeland for the Jewish people by the British in the 1917 Balfour Declaration and confirmed by the League of Nations in the mandate awarded to Britain in 1922. Palestinians are convinced that they are the indigenous people and rightful owners of this territory, and that Zionist settlers are instruments of a discredited, latter-day European colonialism. All efforts to resolve this controversy by dividing the land between the two peoples in separate neighboring states, beginning with the UN Partition Resolution in 1947, have failed to win acceptance; moderates in both camps who favor a territorial compromise have been overridden by militants. Palestinian militants insist on "the right of return" of descendants of those who fled or were expelled during Israel's War of Independence in 1948 (which Palestinians call "the catastrophe"). Israelis fear this would signify the end of Israel as a Jewish state. Israeli zealots insist on their right to build settlements anywhere in biblical Israel and be protected by the Israeli armed forces, which Palestinians fear would strip them of their remaining land and condemn them to permanent dependency and military occupation. Palestinian militants resort to sporadic terrorist violence, Israel responds with military incursions into suspected centers of Palestinian violence and the cycle of violence and reprisals continues.

The status of territory is at the heart of many instances of ethnic conflict. The Beijing government considers Tibet an integral part of China and consolidates its political and military control by sponsoring the colonization of Tibet by ethnic Chinese. Tibetans assert their right to self-determination, to govern the country either as an independent state or as an autonomous province of the People's Republic. Serbs believe that Kosovo is part of the patrimony of the Serbian people even though Serbs at present are a small minority of its inhabitants; Albanians believe that as the overwhelming majority, they should determine the status of Kosovo, preferably as an independent state. The inability of Serbs and Albanians to settle this issue resulted in the Serbian campaign of ethnic cleansing, followed by the NATO military intervention, and, for the time being, a UN Protectorate.

Within the territory of a multinational state, what should be the status of its various ethnic minorities? Should Quebec opt for sovereignty or continue as a semi-autonomous unit of the Canadian confederation? What should be the status and rights of Quebec's English-speaking minority and of the Cree, Mohawk, and other Indian communities that inhabit large tracts of Quebec's territory? What should be the status of the large Kurdish minority in northern Iraq, of the Basques in Spain, of South Ossetians and Abkhazians in Georgia? Wherever there is a homeland people within a multiethnic state – Scots in Britain, Flemings and Walloons in Belgium, Tatars in Russia, Achinese in Indonesia, Puerto Ricans in the United States – the status of the homeland and the claim of homeland people to self-determination may at any time become a critical political issue. In many such cases there are sharp divisions within these communities over which status and which arrangements would best serve their common interests, and in some cases whether these interests are best served by resort to violence or by peaceful political pressure. The delicate balance in Belgium between Flemings and Walloons has been negotiated peacefully, though not without considerable tensions; elements of the Kurdish minority in Turkey, having resorted to terrorist tactics in their campaign for provincial autonomy, have invited severe reprisals by the Turkish military.

In many instances a single ethnic community has gained control of state institutions and used that control to channel the benefits available from government to members of its own ethnic group. This has occurred in Malaysia, where Malays have entrenched themselves in government and operate a regime of Malay preferences in access to higher education, government employment (civil and military), government contracts, credit for business enterprises, and employment in managerial positions in private firms. In Kenya, as in much of Africa, government has been regarded as a source of spoils for members of the politically dominant ethnic coalition. There, the political game is not a matter of changing state boundaries or of seeking autonomy or minority rights, but rather of gaining control of the state apparatus. In the early years of independence, the Kikuyu community under its leader, the redoubtable Jomo Kenyatta, controlled the government and distributed the spoils primarily among its (ethnic) supporters. Later an ethnic coalition under President Daniel Arap Moi won an election and began to channel government largesse to its supporters, especially to President Moi's Kalinga minority. The abuses became so brazen that foreign aid donors threatened to withhold further assistance unless the government undertook to distribute overseas scholarships, health clinics, schools, and other donor-financed facilities more equitably among the country's several ethnic communities.

In Afghanistan, after the ouster of the Taliban regime, the interim government was dominated by members of the Tadjik minority, because they constituted the core of the Northern Alliance which had provided indispensable ground troops in support of the US military effort. Their disproportionate prominence in government created great concern among Afghanistan's other ethnic communities, notably among Pushtuns, the country's largest, fearing that Tadjiks would freeze them out of government employment, the new national army, and the substantial financial aid promised by donor governments. Though non-Malays have no expectation of dominating the state, the "Malaysian Malaysia" slogan epitomizes their aspiration for more equitable participation and a fairer share of benefits flowing from government. The question in such cases is not a matter of revising borders, but of which ethnic community should be in charge and to whom the fruits of statehood should be distributed.

Ethnic communities that cannot claim homeland status and who believe their members have been victims of unequal treatment are likely to demand equitable inclusion in the polity. This applies especially to recent immigrant diasporas whose members often experience various forms of discrimination and exclusion. They demand for themselves all the rights of participation by voting and office-holding, as well as equitable access to the outputs of government such as housing, employment, education, and community facilities. This has been the strategy of nearly all immigrant communities in the United States and Canada as well as of the African-American civil rights movement. These minorities may also ask for evidence of official respect for their community and for their distinctive identity, for example, by the appointment of leading members to prestigious positions in government, or more controversially, recognition of their culture in ways that depart from mainstream norms, such as headscarves in French schools and kosher slaughter in New York state. The US political culture is responsive to demands for equitable inclusion, but finds questionable such claims for special treatment as bilingual education for children of Hispanic immigrants, which generated a political backlash in the form of a movement for English only.

Economic

A number of observers and commentators have argued that ethnic conflicts are, at their roots, economic – clashes over access to, control over, and the enjoyment of, economic resources. Disputes over what appear to be political power, so runs the argument of economic determinists, at a deeper level involve power over economic resources. Those who gain political power will always use it to secure economic advantages for themselves and their followers at the expense of their adversaries. Those whose grievances are expressed in political language are really protesting their disadvantageous economic situation. Once their economic grievances have been eliminated, mainly by economic growth, their political discontents will fade away. Apartheid in South Africa, they would insist, was really a matter of stripping Africans of ownership of valuable land, excluding them from access to capital, and reducing them to a mass of unorganized, exploitable wage laborers. Similarly, they argue that if the economies of the West Bank and Gaza could be developed to insure opportunities for Palestinian businessmen and good jobs for Palestinian workers, their hostility to Israel would dissipate and a peaceful settlement could be negotiated between the two peoples. Such thinking is based on the premise that man is an economic animal, motivated primarily by the quest for livelihoods, economic security, and wealth.[3]

This is not the place to pursue the question whether humans are such unidimensional creatures, except to assert the author's position that human behavior is normally characterized by mixed motives, of which economic advantage is one of several. Malays, for example, are interested in increased participation in modern economic activities, but far more important to most of them is maintaining firm control of government and insuring the paramountcy of the Islamic faith and Malay culture. In some ethnic conflicts, for example in the struggle between Serbs and Albanians over the status of Kosovo, economic issues may be relatively unimportant, even absent. This is not to deny the importance of economic factors in many disputes between ethnic communities, or, stated more positively, there are likely to be economic dimensions in most ethnic conflicts.

Among the economic issues that may be in dispute are employment in government agencies and public corporations, and employment rights in private enterprises that may be regulated by rules imposed by the state. Under affirmative action legislation in the United States, companies doing business with government were required to demonstrate honest efforts to achieve minority representation in their workforce in proportion to their share in the local population; discrimination in personnel management, including promotions, could be litigated in the courts. Minority controlled companies demanded fair shares of government contracts, prompting protests from White-owned firms that this subjected them to reverse discrimination. Access to and control of economic assets, such as land, capital, and commercial credits may be contested. In some countries this has been accomplished by compulsory transfers of ownership, as when President Idi Amin expelled all Asians from Uganda and handed over their property to his followers. Under Malaysia's New Economic Policy initiated in 1970 with the express purpose of "eliminating the identification of race with economic function," Malays were guaranteed preference in acquiring ownership shares of companies owned or acquired by government, with the objective of insuring that Malays would increase their participation in share ownership and in management positions from 1 percent in 1970 to 30 percent over a period of twenty years. This policy was protested by non-Malays as blatant government-sponsored discrimination against them even though, unlike government practice in some countries, there was no confiscation of their property and few practical limitations on the ability of non-Malay businesses to prosper and to expand. Non Malay businessmen were as much offended by discrimination against them in a government-sponsored program and the inference of second class citizenship, as by the practical effects of the New Economic Policy.

Access to higher education as the pathway to more prestigious and lucrative careers is a common source of ethnic conflict. Governments, as in Malaysia and Sri Lanka, arrange for their ethnic constituents to gain preferential admission to universities, often at the expense of better qualified (by scores on entrance exams or secondary school performance) applicants from other backgrounds. This pattern of discrimination is deeply resented, since it is perceived as penalizing and even blocking the legitimate aspirations of deserving youngsters, precisely those who are most likely to provide the corps of activists for ethnic protest movements. Much of the leadership of the Tamil Tigers in Sri Lanka was drawn from young men whose university admission was blocked by the requirement that entrance exams be administered only in the Sinhalese language.

Affirmative action in the United States as a government-enforced policy has granted preferential entry, in some cases the equivalent of quota protection, to members of designated minorities who had suffered previous discrimination and were underrepresented in the student body. The beneficiaries have been African-Americans, Hispanic-Americans, in some places Asian-Americans, and women. The purpose has been to give members of these underrepresented minorities a helping hand in gaining university admission and to achieve the presumed benefits of greater diversity in the student body. This has led inevitably to resentment among some White males who believe they have been unfairly excluded, despite superior qualifications, from professional education in the fields of law and medicine. Affirmative action in higher education has been challenged in the courts as reverse discrimination, denial of equal protection of the laws. It has also been challenged politically in state legislatures and in popular referenda. A number of White politicians have attempted to promote their electoral fortunes by championing White "victims" both in university admissions and government employment.

This raises the general question of fair and appropriate criteria for the allocation of scarce benefits, such as university admissions, government jobs, civil and military, government contracts, access to capital and credit, health facilities, and public infrastructure such as roads, electric power, and water supplies. In some countries these benefits are awarded politically to supporters or clients of the regime in power, including preferred ethnic communities, with inevitable resentment among those that have been excluded, such as Hutu in Burundi and Kurds in Iraq. The criterion in most democratic countries has been individual competition: the "merit" system for government employment and university admissions, market competition in the business world. This is believed to contribute to efficiency for society and fairness among individuals. But what if its effect is to exclude members of ethnic communities who, because of historical experiences of deprivation or cultural disabilities, are handicapped in individual competition? What if individual competition for admission to the Medical Faculty of the University of Malaya yields only Chinese and Indian doctors, most of whom speak Malay haltingly and are unfamiliar with Malay culture, while a majority of their prospective patients and clients will be Malay. Is this an acceptable situation? Was it acceptable in Quebec, 80 percent French-Canadian, that

French-Canadians should be virtually absent fom the ranks of owners and managers of major economic enterprises where business was conducted entirely in English ("English in the board room, French on the factory floor")?

Where the processes of individual competition produce such unbalanced results, the rules governing allocations can be changed. Governments can intervene to channel resources and opportunities to members of the less favored community.[4] One method is the application of proportionality that guarantees to members of each ethnic community fair shares of the benefits of economic participation. The negative consequences may be some loss in instrumental efficiency, resentment among some that despite superior formal qualifications they are penalized by reverse discrimination, and complaints that the benefits often accrue to persons who are already privileged members of their ethnic community, for example whose families have been able to provide them with a good basic education. These negatives are to be weighed against the political gains, including increased legitimacy of the political system among those now participating for the first time in educational experiences, professions, and business activities in which they had previously been unrepresented. Do such changes in the rules of allocation reduce the likelihood of ethnic conflict?

Cultural

The principal cultural issues that generate ethnic conflicts are language and religion. Both are at the core of an individual's sense of identity and the collective dignity and honor of ethnic communities.

Language has both symbolic and instrumental value. It symbolizes which of two or more ethnic communities is strong enough and prestigious enough that its language should be honored as the official language of government and education, while the languages of other ethnic communities are reduced to vernacular status, to the family and marketplace. It is instrumentally important because those whose familial language is the language of instruction in school, the language of university entrance and civil service exams, of command in the military and of communication in government enjoy a distinct advantage, practical as well as psychological, over those who are required to perform in a second language. Thus, language becomes a common subject of interethnic contention.[5] Malays have insisted that theirs must be the national language of Malaysia, the exclusive medium of education, the mass media, and government communication; Mandarin and Tamil are allowed to be languages of instruction only in elementary schools.

Canada has evolved a complex language regime. To provide French-speaking Québécois with an incentive to remain in Canada, in 1969 both French and English were designated official languages of the Government of Canada. All government services were to be available anywhere in Canada in either official language. A language ombudsman was appointed to monitor the implementation of this policy. But since most public services under Canada's federal system are provided by the provinces, the language of activities under provincial control is determined by their governments. Quebec's government proceeded to designate French as the sole official language of that province, though services including education would be available in English to persons of English-speaking backgrounds. To insure a French cultural ambiance throughout the province, French was to become the predominant language of work in government, in industry and commerce, and on commercial signs. The provincial government of New Brunswick declared itself bilingual in the two official languages. The other provinces remained officially English-speaking. Many persons of non-English-, non-French-speaking backgrounds, whose ancestral languages were accorded no official status, resented the official status conferred by the Government of Canada on French, in what they considered an English-speaking country. When in 1982 Canada incorporated a Charter of Rights and Freedoms into its constitution, the English-speaking provinces committed themselves as a constitutional requirement to provide public education in French, where there was sufficient demand.

To appease its many ethnic communities whose ancestral languages are ignored by its language policy, the Government of Canada has implemented a version of "multiculturalism" which honors all these ethnic communities by subsidizing their cultural institutions – schools, performing arts, publications – encouraging them to perpetuate their cultures in what Canadians refer to as their "mosaic." Canada has also conceded considerable territorial and cultural autonomy to its many aboriginal communities, Indians and Inuit (Eskimos), designating them as "First Canadians."

The complex language regime in Canada illustrates how meticulously language policy may have to be worked out to satisfy the often conflicting aspirations of its ethnic communities. When language policy fails, as we have seen in Sri Lanka and Sudan, violence, even civil war may ensue. The Berber areas in Algeria were in revolt until the government finally yielded to their demand for education and public services in the Berber tongue. In its post-apartheid constitution of 1994, South Africa designated 11 "national" languages, including English, Afrikaans, and the languages of all its major tribes. Where there is sufficient demand, government is committed to providing elementary and secondary education in all these languages. English, however, is expected to be the national *lingua franca*, the working language of government and business and the principal medium of instruction at all levels of schooling. To finesse the thorny language issue, several countries, especially in Africa, have adopted a "neutral" language, usually that of their former colonial rulers, as the official medium of government and education: English in Kenya and Ghana, French in Senegal and the Ivory Coast, for example. This avoids potentially dangerous conflicts over the status of language among their component ethnic communities. But it has the unfortunate effect of alienating a small elite, well educated in the official neutral language, from the mass of citizens with little formal education who continue to live and work in their indigenous medium. Under some circumstances individuals may find it necessary in their daily routines to operate in several languages, one at home, another on the job, a third at the market.

An even more sensitive topic than language is religion. As well as reflecting collective identity, it involves systems of belief about the basic nature and destiny of humankind, of their place in the universe and the institutions that embody and defend these beliefs. For most individuals their religion is an ascriptive status, a given in their lives, an identity not of choice but of birth. Is it the duty of the state to promote and defend the one true system of belief, proscribing all others, heretics and infidels; or to patronize one religion but tolerate others; or to maintain a neutral stance, relegating religious belief and practice to the domain of private choice?

When groups mobilize around their religious identities and clash with their adversaries, in modern times at least, they are not disputing theological issues, they are fighting over raw power. Compromise, splitting the difference, or mutual toleration are hard to achieve, since live-and-let-live might imply betrayal of the true faith and toleration of heresy or falsehood. Thus, when "Catholics" and "Protestants" face off in Northern Ireland, they are not disputing questions of theology or dogma, but of power between partisans of Irish nationalism (Catholics) and of union with Britain (Protestants).

Independent India was established as a secular state, in deference to Gandhi's principle of universal tolerance and as a means of fostering peaceful coexistence among the many religious communities on the subcontinent. The large Muslim community, 12 percent of the population, was granted its own educational system and the right to regulate family affairs and inheritance matters according to Islamic law (sharia). This secular policy was never acceptable to Hindu nationalists who argue that the state should promote the doctrine and practice of its 85 percent Hindu majority and circumscribe the rights of its Muslim minority whom they regard as enemies of Hinduism, subversive of the state, and a potential fifth column in support of India's Muslim adversary, Pakistan (Indian Muslims were observed publicly cheering the victory of Pakistan over India in an international soccer match). It was a Hindu extremist who assassinated Gandhi in 1948. A Hindu nationalist political party, the Bharatiya Janata Paksh, emerged whose leaders inflamed a Hindu mob to attack and destroy the Muslim Babri mosque that, they were told, had usurped the site of a former important Hindu temple located at the birthplace of the god Ram. That party eventually led a coalition that took over the government of India. In contrast to India where the Muslim minority is made to feel insecure, several Muslim dominated states in northern Nigeria, disregarding protests from their Christian minorities, have adopted and begun to enforce Islamic criminal law including such punishments as stoning adulterers to death and severing the limbs of thieves. In the Maluku region of Indonesia, Christian and Muslim mobs have engaged in mutual mayhem, resulting in thousands of deaths and enormous damage to property.

Since independence from France in 1943, politics in Lebanon have been organized around confessional communities, Christian (Maronites Orthodox), Muslim (Sunni, Shia), and Druse. To preclude sectarian violence, which has plagued so much of Lebanon's history, each community was awarded designated senior positions in government and a fixed proportion of seats in parliament and civil service jobs. This regime of rigid proportionality exacted some costs in efficiency, but kept Lebanon at unaccustomed peace until two unanticipated factors intervened: as demographic proportions appeared to shift over time, some communities felt underrepresented, thus cheated by the existing proportions (there had been no census since 1932 for fear of upsetting these proportions); and a new force, armed Palestinians, had occupied part of the country and disturbed the delicate balance among the established confessional communities. Though the armed Palestinians were eventually expelled by the Syrian army which has since occupied the country, the Lebanese have not found a mutually satisfactory substitute for the regime of proportions which, despite its rigidities and its many faults, had allowed for peaceful coexistence and economic well-being among the contentious religious communities in this divided country.

Numbers games

Population censuses would appear, at first glance, to be a technical, apolitical activity, counting the people of a country, where they reside, their age, sex, and ethnic distribution, their economic pursuits, and other activities, the purpose being to establish an accurate and complete demographic account of a nation's human resources. Normally, censuses are conducted every ten years. Yet, it is not uncommon for periodic censuses to ignite intense ethnic-based disputes.[6]

As we have noted, the last census in Lebanon was held in 1932 under French colonial rule. Independent Lebanon was governed by a National Pact between the leaders of its several confessional communities. Positions in government and government expenditures were allocated by a formula of six Christians to five Muslims and Druse, which was presumed to be the correct ratio at the time of independence during World War II. But, what if a subsequent census were to reveal that these proportions no longer held, that the majority had shifted in favor of the Muslims, as many observers believed was actually the case? To avoid the destabilizing effects of that possibility, the Lebanese elites simply declined to hold subsequent censuses.

Nigerian public affairs have been roiled by intense and sometimes violent competition between Muslims in the north and Christians in the south and between the largest of its many ethnic communities, Hausa-Fulani in the north, Yoruba in the southwest, and Ibo in the southeast. Every census since independence in 1960 has precipitated intense political struggles over numbers, accompanied by charges and countercharges of manipulation of data, deliberate under-counting or inflation of results, and falsification of figures. Why have censuses in Nigeria become so politicized? Because representation in parliament is based on the territorial distribution of populations, each ethnic group attempting to magnify its numbers at the expense of its competitors. Moreover, public services such as schools, health clinics, hospitals, and public works are allocated according to relative population and each ethnic group struggles for its piece of the budgetary pie. As a result, "political acceptability rather than statistical accuracy or demographic reliability clearly remains the most important determinant of the fate of the census in Nigeria."[7]

In a less-developed country such as Nigeria, part of the disputes over census outcomes may be attributed to a poorly trained, under-financed, and inexperienced statistical agency. But the same cannot be said of the US Census Bureau, a professionally competent, sophisticated, and universally respected institution. Yet, the US decennial census of the year

2000 was marked by a bitter political struggle. The issue was whether the final results should be based entirely on physical counts by census enumerators, or whether these should be supplemented by statistical sampling to account for persons, especially in the larger cities, who may not have been located, therefore not counted, by the enumerators. Most of those who were likely to be overlooked were low-income African-Americans and Hispanic-Americans, both groups inclined to vote for candidates supporting the Democratic Party.

If they were to be included in the revised figures, this might affect the allocation of seats in the US House of Representatives and in state legislatures to the benefit of Democrats and would increase the flow of Federal funds to districts that include large numbers of African- and Hispanic-Americans. The Democratic administration of President Clinton favored the use of statistical sampling, as did most professional demographers. But Republican politicians who controlled both houses of Congress opposed this procedure for the same reason that Democrats favored it, arguing that the language of the Constitution providing for decennial censuses and the laws that implement it authorize only physical enumeration of the population. They refused to appropriate funds to finance the census unless statistical sampling was excluded. After a prolonged controversy, the Congressional Republicans prevailed, to the detriment of ethnic communities that were not part of their constituency.

Rational and non-rational interpretations of ethnic conflict

As the examples cited throughout this book demonstrate, most ethnic conflicts are genuine disputes over real and important differences between the contending parties over incompatible goals or access to and enjoyment of scarce resources. Though such conflicts normally have a rational base, once they are set in motion they are frequently aggravated by psychological mechanisms that impair the search for compromise solutions and threaten to result in violence, leading to cycles of provocation and retaliation that resist all efforts at moderation. If the disputes cannot be channeled into processes that permit them to be negotiated by political give-and-take, as normally occurs in democratic systems, each party begins to impute the most malevolent motives to the other, mistrust gradually yields to collective hatred, moderate voices are silenced, the conflict spins out of control, and violence begets more violence as extremists take control on both sides. Violence becomes self-justifying and self-perpetuating, as opponents are denigrated or demonized by negative stereotypes.[8] As the "master race," German Nazis could justify the elimination of inferior species, such as Gypsies, Slavs, and Jews. Indians in nineteenth-century America were characterized as bloodthirsty savages, justifying their dispossession, ethnic cleansing, the confinement of survivors to supervised reservations as wards of government, and even mass murder. The native population was reduced from an estimated 4 million before the arrival of Europeans to fewer than a million at the outset of the twentieth century.[9]

Violence then takes on a life of its own, displacing concern for the issues that triggered the conflict in the first place. And even after the original differences have been settled, mutual distrust and hostility may persist. Though the mayhem in Bosnia was terminated by the intervention of international organizations after years of savage violence that resulted in 100,000 casualties and a million refugees, Serbs, Croats, and Muslims remain wary of their Bosnian compatriots, prefer to live and be governed in separate enclaves, and express little confidence that, should the international peacekeepers leave, violent conflict will not erupt again.

Perversely, psychological factors have the effect of exacerbating ethnic conflicts, but seldom contribute to their mitigation. While participants and observers may become preoccupied with the violence, as many have over the years in Northern Ireland, Palestine, Sri Lanka, Rwanda, and Sudan, the violence and its psychological precipitators should not be mistaken for the root causes of their conflicts. The roots of conflicts lie always in disputes over real issues such as relative power (politics), material resources (economics), or respect (culture). This applies both to large-scale conflicts such as the Sri Lankan civil war and to local riots between French and North African gangs in the slums of Lyons. Until these underlying issues have been addressed and resolved, a conflict cannot be settled, discord will continue, and violence may reappear.

An influential school of social scientists holds that ethnic conflicts are the result of misperceptions by the contending parties of their true interests.[10] What they should be searching for are their genuine common interests in avoiding conflict, especially violent conflict which is always costly to both sides without achieving the aspirations of either. Thus, the pursuit of narrow self-interest is essentially irrational, since it is likely to leave both sides worse off. For example, both Palestinians and Israeli have paid a horrendous price and are much worse off because they have pursued their maximum self-interest than if they had pursued their common interest in a peaceful outcome. The goal should be not compromise, which may be less than satisfactory to both parties, but solutions from which both parties benefit, in effect win-win solutions. In the language of systems theory, these are called positive sum or Pareto-optimal outcomes, from which all the contending parties benefit and there are no losers. Outsiders, including social psychologists who are skilled in the art of conflict resolution, are believed to be specially useful in helping the parties to search for common ground, to transcend their fixations on conflicting self-interest, and to innovate solutions from which they mutually benefit. Anderson points to three patterns that have been successful in the past: the search for common interests, divisibility of benefits, and interdependence that rewards cooperation and discourages competitive behavior.[11]

Those who view ethnic conflicts as genuine encounters over incompatible goals or struggles for the control of scarce resources have difficulty sharing the faith that positive sum outcomes are inherent in all such conflicts. Few if any ethnic conflicts have ever been settled in this optimistic way. Because such conflicts involve clashes over genuine interests deeply held by the contending parties, these cannot be readily sacrificed or transcended by a latent common interest that has not been evident to the parties themselves. Since ethnic conflicts involve struggles over real collective interests, they usually result in the victory of the stronger party – Russian suppression of the Chechen insurrection, Hausa-Fulani defeat of the

Ibo revolt in Nigeria, European-American victory over the American Indian nations – or a series of compromises that fully satisfy neither party and certainly not their militant members, but appear to be possible to live with and less costly than continuing violence. Malays, for example, consolidated their control of government, but accepted Chinese predominance in the economy, a set of compromises that insured peace for two decades but was later upset when Chinese appeared to threaten Malay control of government and Malays retaliated by imposing on the Chinese the New Economic Policy that challenged the latter's economic predominance without risking Malay control of government.

Outstanding minds have agonized over the Israeli-Palestinian dispute without discovering a positive sum outcome. Most hope for a *modus vivendi* based on painful compromises ("sacrifices") by both sides: Israel should abandon its settlements and its occupation of the West Bank and Gaza, Palestinians should forego the use of terrorist tactics and give up their claim to a right of return to pre-1948 homes in Israel, Jerusalem should be the shared capital of both peoples. It is precisely because such standoffs have a rational base, involving real conflicts of interest, not misperceptions of a more benign reality, that consensual resolution is often so hard to achieve. Psychological factors may aggravate and prolong conflicts, contributing to cycles of violence, hatred, and mistrust, but should not be mistaken for the underlying causes of the disputes.

Conclusion

Members of the human species, as individuals and as groups, contend over things that are scarce and therefore valuable and desirable, including territory, political power, jobs, educational opportunities, capital, credit, and licenses. They also contend over matters of collective dignity and respect, such as the relative status of language and religious institutions. Often the issues become intermingled, as when a dispute over language rights proves to be, in effect, a dispute over political power.

A major argument of this book is that conflicts, whether waged peacefully or violently, reflect genuine and often incompatible demands of the contending parties. They are not misperceptions of a benign reality that the contestants have failed to grasp. Psychological factors can be responsible for intensifying conflicts, escalating distrust into collective hatred and lethal violence, compounding the task of achieving and maintaining compromise settlements. The psychological manifestations of conflicts should not, however, be confused with their real causes. It is the latter that must be addressed and resolved if any settlement is to be reached.

5
The Contemporary State and Outsider Intervention

Apportioning benefits and costs

The modern state is a central player in ethnic relations. As an expression of its sovereignty, it claims, though it may not always be able, to exercise a monopoly of legitimate force within its territory. Its constitution, its laws, its policies enact, and its administrative and judicial agencies apply rules that determine the relative status of ethnic communities and the rights of their members. Its agencies extract resources from society in the form of taxes and services which may impact on various ethnic communities differently. It regulates many of their activities and it distributes valuable facilities and services which affect the productivity, well-being, and life chances of their members.[1] Among industrialized countries the scope and scale of governments may be judged by the fact that they collect in taxes and by borrowing, and spend on public services and transfer payments between 30 and 50 percent of the national economic product.[2]

Though less affluent states spend proportionately less, they too affect ethnic communities in important ways, for example the effect of China's actions on the Tibetan people, the Sudan government's marginalization of its non-Muslim minorities, and the Ecuadorian government's encouragement of foreign investment in the homeland of the highland Indians. Numerous face-to-face encounters between members of ethnic communities at the local level may not be directly affected by the state or its activities. Non-government organizations (NGOs), both those that represent ethnic communities and those that include members from several communities, may participate in managing ethnic conflicts, often in conjunction with local authorities. One writer has recently argued that local NGOs in which members of different ethnic communities meet and associate are more important than state authorities in maintaining peaceful interethnic relations.[3] Yet, the posture and policies of the state toward ethnic communities normally sets the tone for the relative rights and status of ethnic communities throughout the country. When these relations cannot be managed locally, the state may be forced to intervene, hesitantly as with the Christian-Muslim massacres in Indonesia, forcefully as with the British government's intervention in Northern Ireland.

One function of the state is to apportion the burdens and benefits of government among its various constituencies. Some of these distinctions may be entrenched in its constitutional structure, for example the special position of Malays in the Malaysian constitution and the status of Islam as the state religion in Pakistan. Others, such as housing permits for Palestinians, are determined by politics or government policy, and these can be contested by ethnic communities and their factions in ways that are permitted by the rules of the polity: in some by open competition, in others by respectful petition, flattery of officials, or covert forms of pressure such as bribery and similar unorthodox practices; and when all else fails, by resorting to acts of violence. Except where they are not allowed to organize, ethnic communities and their factions function as interest groups, striving to influence government policy in ways that promote or defend what their leaders define as their collective interests.

In Canada all ethnic communities, homeland peoples such as Indians and Inuit as well as immigrant diasporas, are free to organize as interest groups and make demands on government at the local, provincial, and national levels. Canadian governments of both major parties have demonstrated a willingness to consider their demands and an inclination to accommodate them. There has been no significant ethnic-based violence in Canada in recent years. In Quebec French-Canadians realized that they were free to organize and promote their interests within the prevailing rules of political competition. When a small faction nevertheless resorted to violence, including kidnapping and murder, in 1970, they were disowned and lost support throughout their constituency. By contrast, after 1948 it became clear to the leadership of the African National Congress that the National Party government intended to enforce apartheid rigorously and to silence and outlaw its non-White opponents. Though they had preached and practiced non-violence, they concluded that the apartheid state left no choice for Africans except to submit or resort to violence as one method of resistance.

The state may determine what rights and opportunities are available to members both of diaspora and of homeland communities. Its laws regulate immigration and determine which persons are legally in the country, what they must do to qualify for citizenship, what public services are available to non-citizens, and what kinds of economic activities they may legally engage in. In some countries persons classified as foreigners may not own land and may not participate in certain professions and occupations. Even between homeland peoples different laws, policies, and practices may be applied by governments. Sometimes these distinctions are requested by ethnic communities in the form of minority rights that may be granted by the state.

Thus, in ethnic relations, the influence of government is powerful and pervasive. If the central government is perceived as unfriendly or neglectful, ethnic communities – for example many Quebecois, Chechens, Tibetans, Palestinians, Basques, Sri Lankan Tamils, Eritreans – may strive mightily to break away and establish sovereignty over their homeland. Their expectation is that sovereignty will enable them to become masters of their own destiny in their own homeland, so that the laws and practices mandated by government will reflect their own traditions, preferences, and collective interests.

Three postures

Toward ethnic communities the state may assume one of three postures: as the partisan of a dominant ethnic community, as a neutral mediator, or as an arena where ethnic communities exert competitive pressure on behalf of their concerns.

As partisan

The state may openly represent a single ethnic community and act in its interest, a fact that is obvious to members of the dominant community and to those who are marginalized and relegated to second-class citizenship. In Burundi the Tutsi minority, through its control of the military, operates the government in the interest of its community; its main function is to maintain control by repressing the 85 percent Hutu majority. In Israel, the government of whatever political party is in office serves what it believes is the interest of its Jewish citizens. When Northern Ireland's prime minister proclaimed in 1922 that he was heading a "Protestant state for a Protestant people," despite the Catholic minority of more than 40 percent, both sides recognized who would be in charge and whose interests would be served. Jobs in government, especially the security forces, employment in private industry, housing and public amenities, all conspicuously favored Protestants. Everywhere the aspirations of ambitious Catholics were blocked, especially for young men, many of whom migrated to England in search of employment. Catholic political parties could contest elections and raise their voices in Parliament, but they were always outvoted and excluded from the executive agencies of government. For nearly half a century Catholics endured these deprivations until, inspired by the American civil rights movement, they began to practice non-violent resistance, to which the Protestant-manned security forces responded with severe reprisals. This emboldened the clandestine Irish Republican Army (IRA), whose goal was to end the British connection and join the northern counties to the Republic of Ireland, to launch its campaign of terror against the British presence.

Many similar examples could be cited from all continents, where the state apparatus has become the instrument of a single ethnic community which awards the benefits available to government preferentially or exclusively to its members. In some instances other ethnic groups are oppressed or excluded entirely, for example Kurds in Iraq under Saddam Hussein. In others there is sufficient slack in the system that they may enjoy some opportunities for participation and self-fulfillment. This may be implemented by formal processes such as recognized minority rights, or by informal arrangements that allow members of the minority some voice and some share in the government's largesse. The various processes of ethnic domination and illustrative cases are elaborated in chapter 6.

As neutral mediator

Governments often pose as benevolent referees between contending ethnic communities, intervening where necessary to settle incipient conflicts and to maintain harmony. Where governments have achieved sufficient autonomy from society, they may attempt to serve as impartial referees on behalf of the common good, establishing conditions for interethnic coexistence and seeing that fairness is maintained among them. This was the policy enunciated by Marshal Tito, though not always implemented successfully, during his long tenure as leader of Yugoslavia. This was the intention of Emperor Franz Josef in his management of ethnic pluralism in the sprawling Austro-Hungarian Empire of the late nineteenth and early twentieth centuries. The governments of India and of Canada have claimed that they are sufficiently above the struggle that they can mediate and manage the conflicting demands of ethnic communities in ways that are fair to all parties, while protecting the integrity of their domain. Indian governments have been responsive to demands of ethnic communities for the creation of additional states within the Indian federation, but have decisively rejected any proposals for separation.

This is an ideal role for governments: to settle conflicts and maintain peace with equity among its organized constituencies. The difficulty is that what appears to the state elites to be equitable and fair may not be so regarded by the parties concerned. During the 1960s Canada's political leadership became convinced that the survival of Canada as a political entity depended on its ability to satisfy what they believed were legitimate grievances of its French-Canadian minority centered in Quebec. They organized a blue ribbon panel, the Royal Commission on Bilingualism and Biculturalism with equal membership of prestigious English- and French-speaking personalities. After several years of investigation and deliberation, the commission issued a massive six volume report.[4] This report, based on the principle of "equal partnership between the two founding races," recommended that both English and French be adopted as equal official languages of the Government of Canada and that all its services be available in both official languages anywhere in Canada. Any Canadian should feel at home in his or her official language anywhere in Canada. Where French- and English-speaking populations were intermixed, bilingual districts should be established where all services, local and provincial as well as federal, would be available in both languages. All of Quebec would become a bilingual district. But shortly after the Federal Parliament began to implement these recommendations, the Government of Quebec, rejecting the idea of bilingual districts, enacted legislation mandating that French become the province's sole official language, that French be adopted as the language of work in private enterprises as well as in government, and that public education be available in English only to persons of English-speaking backgrounds.[5]

Once Quebec rejected bilingualism, eight of the other nine provinces, including the most populous, Ontario, felt no pressure to form bilingual districts. Meanwhile, a noticeable backlash developed among members of the English-speaking majority who resented having "French stuffed down our throats" in what they believed was an English-speaking country. This attitude was especially prominent among persons of non French-, non English-speaking backgrounds who resented the preferred status of one minority language, while their ancestral languages enjoyed no official status. Many English-speaking civil servants feared that their careers would be jeopardized, even though the government offered to train them at public expense at bilingual centers, because French-Canadian competitors for government posts that require bilingual proficiency were more likely to be fluently bilingual. Three decades later, bilingualism survives in the Government of Canada, but only to a very limited extent in the activities of provincial and municipal agencies.

Illustrating the law of unintended consequences, a well-meaning effort at neutral mediation by a fair-minded government encountered unexpected resistance from both sides, especially from French-Canadians whose grievances were meant to be relieved by the proposed language regime. It can reasonably be assumed, however, that in the absence of preventive mediation in the form of Federal bilingualism, the province of Quebec would have seceded from English-speaking Canada.

As competitive arena

In many instances the state apparatus serves as the arena where ethnic communities and often factions among them contend for relative power and influence. Their goal is not to control the state apparatus, but to minimize their share of the costs and maximize their share of government-provided benefits. The stakes, as we noted in chapter 4, may be symbolic – representation in the respected institutions of the state or in the honors it confers; or instrumental – shares in the powers exercised by political office, participation in the state's security services and in government employment, in public services and amenities, or influence in the shaping of public policy, domestic or foreign. The effectiveness of ethnic communities in promoting and defending their interests depends partly on the resources they can muster in numbers and in funds, their internal unity or divisions, their political skill and determination in using these resources, and the opportunities available to them within the rules and practices of the polity.

The United States is perhaps the outstanding example of an open political system where group interest politics have an important effect on the behavior of government at all levels. Among these competitive group interests are ethnic communities who are free to organize and attempt to impress their influence on public policy. One example is the Cuban-American community concentrated in south Florida. As relatively recent refugees and exiles from communist Cuba, they are bitterly opposed to the Castro regime and seek its overthrow. As businessmen and former property owners in Cuba and as militant anti-communists, they have found a comfortable and welcoming political home in the Republican Party. In return for rigid opposition to any relaxation of US hostility toward the Castro regime and the current economic embargo, they constitute a reliable Republican voting bloc and source of financial support. Even in Republican Party circles, where business values normally prevail, they have checkmated the business enterprises who crave access to Cuba's markets and would prefer a more relaxed posture toward the Castro government.

The large African-American community is concerned primarily with domestic policy. Though divided into many factions, its most influential voice is that of the venerable National Association for the Advancement of Colored People (NAACP) to which most elected African-American office-holders belong. As voters, most African-Americans ally with the Democratic Party; of the 43 African-American members of Congress in 2002, all but one were Democrats. At all levels of government, African-Americans use their voting strength, their lobbying pressure, and litigation in the courts to insure that fellow Blacks and sympathetic Whites are elected to public office, that Black neighborhoods receive a fair share of public services, that laws against racial discrimination in relation to housing, employment, and higher education are enforced, that law enforcement does not bear down on Blacks more heavily than on others, and that Blacks are not victimized by racial profiling. In Washington, African-American legislators and lobbyists attempt to insure that civil rights laws are not attenuated by lax enforcement and that affirmative action continues to be applied in higher education, public contracting, and employment. At the symbolic level they have succeeded in having the birthday of the martyred champion of the civil rights movement, Dr Martin Luther King Jr celebrated annually as a national holiday.

Criminal and predatory exploitation of ethnic solidarities

There are numerous examples of criminal enterprises organized along ethnic lines, because common ethnicity facilitates communication, secrecy, and trust, and may provide a community that can readily be intimidated and forced to pay "protection money" to the criminal syndicate, while keeping law enforcement at bay. The Italian Mafia is a well-publicized federation of ethnic-based criminal syndicates in the United States which, having displaced the Irish and Jewish mobs, has recently been challenged by increasingly ruthless Russian, Chinese, and Hispanic racketeers whose interests range from drug trafficking to the smuggling of women for prostitution and the sale of indentured laborers to sweatshop enterprises. Law enforcement has struggled with these criminal syndicates, with indifferent results, for the past half century.

When government authority breaks down, criminal enterprises fill the vacuum and these are often constituted along ethnic lines. A special report of the US Institute of Peace details the broad scope of ethnic-based criminal syndicates in the Balkans, following the breakup of the Yugoslav federation.[6] These predatory power structures manage to control major segments of the underground economy in Bosnia, Kosovo, Macedonia, and even in Serbia under its former boss, Slobodan Milosevic. By smuggling, extortion, and strong-arm tactics, these gangs control the illegal flow of weapons, drugs, cigarettes, alcohol, stolen vehicles, and even essential items such as petroleum and certain foodstuffs. They have gained control of several state enterprises which they have stripped of assets; they shake down the local electricity and telephone suppliers. They have brokered interethnic understandings with counterpart criminal syndicates across the ethnic divide, providing the most efficient available communication among hostile ethnic communities. Until, with the help of international peacekeepers, the institutions of government can be rebuilt and the rule of law reestablished, these criminal syndicates will continue to thrive, a demonstration of the perverse use of ethnic solidarity when legitimate authority disappears.

This phenomenon in not confined to the Balkans. In multiethnic Afghanistan, the collapse of Taliban rule and the failure of the United States and its allies to extend their peacekeeping forces beyond the Kabul area have produced a power vacuum that has been occupied by ethnic-based warlords, supported by their fighters and enforcers. They finance their operations by similar criminal activities, including the pre-emption of customs duties, extortion of travelers and commercial vehicles at numerous roadblocks, and control of Afghanistan's lucrative trade in opium poppies. Here too, ethnic solidarity is a resource that has been mobilized and exploited for criminal purposes in the absence of legitimate public authority.

When ethnic conflict turns violent, non-governmental contestants must find economic resources to support their insurgency, to finance weapons purchases, and to feed, clothe, equip, and transport their fighters.[7] The methods they employ are mainly predatory – extorting "voluntary" taxes and "contributions" from the incomes and property of their fellow ethnics, soliciting remittances from members of their diaspora in foreign countries and from sympathetic governments and foreign supporters, and by looting gems, narcotics and similar high-value items and disposing of them through international criminal networks. These activities may be so profitable that they become ends in themselves for rebel cadres, reducing their incentives to settle their conflict with governmental or ethnic foes. Though these may prolong the violence, these criminal and economically parasitical activities should not be mistaken for the basic causes of ethnic-based conflict. These are likely to result from grievances that are political, cultural, or economic, as outlined in chapter 4.

External influences on ethnic conflict

The inhabited territory of the contemporary world is divided into areas whose boundaries separate them from neighboring states and denote the limits of their legitimate authority. Normally, individuals are citizens or subjects of a single state to which they owe their political allegiance, though some states now recognize dual citizenship. The political space in which most ethnic conflict occurs is usually centered within one state and its effects may be limited to that one state. But many such disputes spill over international borders and involve external intervention, either because one or more of the disputants solicits diplomatic, economic, or military support from sympathetic outsiders, or because the latter find reasons to become involved in a dispute outside their own country. External involvement may be classified as irredenta, diaspora, and strategic intervention.

Irredenta[8]

This term is Italian for "unredeemed," referring originally to the nineteenth-century territories inhabited by Italian-speakers, but ruled by foreign states. It became the sacred duty of the unifying Italian state to "redeem," that is to reunite them with the homeland by diplomatic and, if need be, by popular uprisings and military means. There are many examples of states across whose borders reside ethnic kinfolk who are a minority in their country and presumably are eager to be redeemed, along with the territory that they inhabit. This has been and remains an unending source of international mischief. Hitler exploited the alleged plight in Czechoslovakia of the German minority, mostly provoked by his Nazi agents, to justify his invasion and dismemberment of that country in 1938–9. (After World War II the Czech government retaliated by ethnic cleansing, expelling all 2.5 million ethnic Germans and confiscating their property.) The Armenian army invaded neighboring Azerbaijan at the presumed invitation of the latter's "oppressed" Armenian minority. Iraq under Saddam Hussein invaded Iran in 1979 to redeem the Arab minority in the Khuzistan area of southern Iran. In Africa, because of arbitrary state boundaries drawn by nineteenth-century European colonialists, there are numerous ethnic minorities which could serve as future irredenta. Before its own disintegration, Somalia claimed the Ethiopian province of Ogaden with its large ethnic Somali population. Hungarian politicians have made noises about the fate of Magyar minorities in Slovakia, Romania, and Serbia, but their eagerness to join NATO and the European Union has put a stop to these claims, at least for the time being.

Such situations need not, however, result in irredentist claims. The four southern provinces of Thailand bordering Malaysia contain majority Malay-Muslim populations. Despite the agitation of militants on both sides of the border, the Malaysian government has distanced itself from all such activities, refusing to allow this issue to disturb good relations with its neighbor and fellow member of ASEAN (Association of Southeast Asian Nations). The Thai government has assisted by guaranteeing complete religious freedom, authorizing the use of the Malay language in government services, including education, and fostering government and private investment to stimulate economic opportunities in these provinces.[9] Paranoid Americans fear that Mexico will one day attempt to redeem the southwestern states of the United States with their large and growing Mexican populations, especially since these lands once belonged to Mexico. To date there have been no such intimations from Mexican sources, but the Mexican government has activated a section in its Foreign Ministry to coordinate services provided by the government to the 20 million and more Mexicans living and working in the United States.

Diaspora[10]

Diasporas are the result of international migration of people fleeing political or religious repression or, more often, in search of improved economic opportunities and livelihoods. In some cases, as discussed in chapter 3, diasporas are created by forced migration in the form of slavery, indentured labor, warfare, or ethnic cleansing. Because of cheap transportation and dire poverty in many Third World countries, combined with the need for additional labor in industrialized countries, the last decades of the twentieth century witnessed unprecedentedly large flows of international migration, legal and illegal. Foreign migrants do not immediately integrate into their host societies. For the most part they form separate communities congregating together for mutual assistance, protection, and fellowship in a strange and less than friendly environment. Because of their foreign speech, exotic customs, and physical appearance, because they are believed to compete unfairly for jobs and housing, and because they are suspected of contributing to crime, delinquency, and disease, they often feel the lash of discrimination and rejection which have the effect of tightening the bonds of communal solidarity with their own kind.

For such reasons as these – discrimination, rejection, mutual assistance, and the desire to retain certain valued features of their inherited cultures – diasporas tend to maintain themselves as distinct enclave communities even as they acculturate sufficiently to function economically within their host society. Individuals may pass gradually into the mainstream at different rates, depending in large measure on the openness of the host society. In the United States, for example, the German diaspora, once the largest ethnic group with well-developed institutions, has virtually disappeared as a distinct community. By contrast, in Britain, a recent government-sponsored survey revealed that Afro-Caribbean, South Asian, and Middle Eastern immigrants, even unto the third generation, "were leading separate lives with no social or cultural contact and no sense of shared nationality" with the British mainstream. Moreover, "the country has become a breeding ground for young Islamic radicals linked to terror groups and committed to holy war against the West."[11]

For such reasons as these ethnic diasporas do not melt quickly. Individuals maintain links with family members and communities, traveling back and forth and remitting funds which often become an important source of foreign exchange for Third World governments. Members of diasporas may participate in the politics of their adopted country, deploying their voting and lobbying resources to promote or defend their collective interests. They may also intervene to affect political outcomes in their home country by lobbying their host government to influence its foreign policy, or by supplying their home government or its opponents with money, weapons, fighters, and even public officials. (The president of Estonia, for example, is a US citizen who returned to his native country only after its liberation from the Soviet Union in 1991.) At the same time, governments or political factions in the home country may call upon their diasporas for diplomatic, financial, or even military support. The cases that could be cited are legion.

The Tamil Tigers have solicited and received vital financial support for their military operations against the Sri Lankan government from Tamil diasporas in Britain, Canada, and the United States. Yet, when the United States government listed the Tigers as a terrorist organization, influential members of the diaspora threatened, successfully, to cut off support unless the Tigers abandoned terrorist methods, including suicide bombings and the recruitment of children as fighters.[12] The revolution that toppled the ancient Chinese imperial regime and installed the nationalist, republican government of Dr Sun Yat-sen in 1911 was financed by overseas Chinese, mainly from Hawaii. Members of the Sikh diaspora danced on the streets of London and Toronto when they received news of the assassination by her Sikh bodyguard of Prime Minister Indira Gandhi who had ordered the assault on their holy temple. During World War I, the imperial German government mounted an all-out effort to mobilize the large and powerful German diaspora in the United States to prevent the US from entering the war on the side of the Allies. In the US, the German and Irish diasporas – the latter opposed to helping Britain in any way – formed a coalition which worked, unsuccessfully as it turned out, to keep the US out of the European conflict. In the crucial Italian election of 1948, the US government called upon Italian-Americans to write to their families and friends in Italy urging them to vote against communist candidates. The Turkish government has accused Kurdish "guest workers" in Germany of helping to finance Kurdish terrorist organizations in Turkey and has urged the German government to block these financial transfers. In the decade following the liberation of the Chinese economy in 1978, the leading source of entrepreneurship and investment was from members of the prosperous Chinese diaspora in Southeast Asia. The Chinese government made every possible facility available to encourage these transactions. There are even ethnic airlines, such as El Al, which specialize in transporting members of the Jewish diaspora for visits to Israel, and Aer Lingus which performs a similar function for the Irish diaspora in North America.

From these few examples it is clear that ethnic diasporas can be political actors in the domestic affairs of their adopted countries, influencing their domestic policies and impacting the affairs of their ancestral country. Foreign governments may attempt to mobilize their diasporas in host countries in pursuit of their foreign policy objectives or to provide needed resources for the home country. As an incentive to its large diaspora to maintain their interest in the homeland, 10 percent of the seats in Croatia's parliament are set aside to be elected by members of the diaspora. Since transnational migration shows no sign of abating, many ethnic diasporas will continue to receive reinforcements, while new ones will be formed. Some, like the Mexican diaspora in California and Texas, will become important, even decisive political actors, while others such as the Greek-American and Polish-American diasporas may become less influential as many of their descendants intermarry and are absorbed into the national mainstream.

Strategic intervention

Irredenta and especially diaspora involve, at least in part, sympathetic sentiments, ethnic solidarity across international borders. Strategic intervention, by contrast, is motivated solely by *realpolitik*, by cold-blooded calculations of national self-interest, how actively favoring one party to an ethnic dispute will benefit the intervening government. The Israeli government provided arms and advisers to help the southerners in Sudan and the Kurds in Iraq not because of sentimental ties, but because this might weaken unfriendly Arab regimes in Khartoum and Baghdad. ("My enemy's enemy is my friend," an aphorism that was demonstrated when the royalist French government helped republican American rebels win their freedom from France's enemy, England.) During the Cold War, the Soviet Union provided assistance to the Palestine Liberation Organization (PLO) not out of particular sympathy for Palestinian nationalism, but because Israel was believed to be an outpost of the West, and especially of the United States. India provided vital assistance to the Bengali rebellion in East Pakistan, not because of particular concern for Bengali Muslims, but because the dismemberment of their enemy, Pakistan, would serve India's strategic purposes. For similar reasons, Germany aided the Irish rebellion during World War I in order to weaken their British enemy. They promoted Ukrainian nationalism during

World War II to undermine the Soviets; the Soviets had encouraged Negro nationalism and separatism, hoping to divide and weaken the United States during the 1920s.[13]

In 1984 Syria intervened militarily in neighboring Lebanon to terminate warfare between heavily armed Palestinian contingents and the Maronite-dominated government of that country. After defeating the Palestinians and forcing them to leave the country, the Syrian army has, to this day, retained a substantial presence in Lebanon as arbiter between its mutually hostile sectarian communities, and as a convenient route for financing and equipping the Shiite Hezbollah movement which harasses their common enemy, Israel.

Examples of the exploitation of ethnic solidarity and of ethnic grievances for strategic advantage by diplomatic pressure, propaganda, financial flows, and military assistance are nearly infinite. It is part of the ancient game of power politics to seek out and take advantage of vulnerabilities among your adversaries. Among these vulnerabilities, the grievances of discontented ethnic communities who might disrupt an adversary's economic performance or military potential are tempting targets.

Intervention to prevent or terminate ethnic conflict

These may be initiated by individual states, by international agencies, or by non-government organizations (NGOs).

Intervention by states[14]

One of the principal foundations of international law is the doctrine of state sovereignty and its corollary that precludes intervention by outsiders in the affairs of sovereign states. Reciprocal respect for this doctrine is intended to insure international peace and stability. Exceptions are acceptable only when a government agrees, by treaty or other expressions of its sovereignty, to allow such intervention. Though this principle has been frequently violated, when stronger powers impose their will on weaker states, as in Syria's occupation of neighboring Lebanon and the US occupation from time to time of several Caribbean countries, it has been and remains normative in international relations and is written into the United Nations' Charter.

The first significant modification of this principle was the series of undertakings intended to protect minorities mainly in eastern Europe after World War I (discussed in chapter 6). These arrangements were to be monitored and enforced by the League of Nations. Bitter opposition by nationalist politicians in the countries affected and the disinclination of the leading members of the League to enforce their provisions led, in the 1930s, to their gradual abandonment.[15]

The most common form of intervention is to provide *good offices* to mediate between contending parties, suspend hostilities, and facilitate negotiations. This may entail "confidence-building" measures designed to overcome distrust between the parties and search for common interests in a peaceful outcome from which both sides would benefit or for compromises that are mutually acceptable. Timing may be critical since contestants may be most amenable to a settlement when they encounter a "hurting stalemate," realizing that neither side is strong enough to impose its will on the other and that the losses and suffering have become unbearable.[16] Other forms of intervention are the provision of humanitarian assistance, foreign aid (technical and economic assistance), non-violent sanctions (military and economic embargoes such as those applied against the apartheid regime, which are intended to punish the party to the conflict that is judged to be the offender), preventive intervention (action by an outsider to prevent a tense situation from exploding into violence), and coercive sanctions (when an outsider applies military power to terminate a conflict or put an end to flagrant violations of human rights.)

Individual states are sometimes in a good position to mediate ethnic conflicts. They are able to act more decisively than international organizations that are obliged to take account of the views of their several member states; they can engage in secret "back channel" diplomacy to lay the groundwork for formal negotiation, a process that is difficult for international agencies; and they can more readily deploy military force to enforce agreements arrived at by moderates on both sides against more militant factions which resist compromise settlements.

President Jimmy Carter initiated the marathon Camp David talks that terminated the long-standing conflict between Israel and Egypt and led to the peace treaty that has survived for a quarter century.[17] The fact that the United States was able to promise large sums of money to both parties once they settled their differences was an important contributor to that happy outcome. The emperor of Ethiopia held talks in his capital, Addis Ababa, in 1972 that led to the suspension for more than a decade of civil war between the Arab-Muslim government of Sudan and its southern peoples, including a power-sharing agreement that conferred regional autonomy on the south. Norway initiated the back channel discussions between officials of the Israeli government and the Palestine Liberation Organization resulting in the Oslo agreement that promised a peaceful settlement of that conflict, only to have it sabotaged by extremist factions on both sides who were unwilling to accept a compromise outcome. Norway has attempted also to mediate and host negotiations intended to terminate the civil war in Sri Lanka and lay the groundwork for a settlement.

The United States in 1995 dispatched a small force to Macedonia, hoping to head off a violent confrontation between its Slavic government and its Albanian minority that could have destabilized the southern Balkans. While such interventions sometimes succeed, there are no guarantees. President Clinton's desperate efforts at the end of his term of office to broker an agreement between Israelis and Palestinians were rebuffed at the last minute by the PLO chairman, Yasser Arafat. At the invitation of the Sri Lankan government, the Indian Army in 1989 sent an expeditionary force to northern Sri Lanka intending to disarm and put an end to the Tamil rebellion, then negotiate and implement a fair settlement. In this attempt at coercive intervention, the vaunted Indian army was unexpectedly so badly mauled by the Tamil Tigers that they were unceremoniously withdrawn from Sri Lanka, their mission unfulfilled. Shortly thereafter, a Tamil woman assassinated the Indian prime minister who had dispatched his army into Sri Lanka.

Intervention by international agencies

Interventions organized and operated by international agencies are perceived as more legitimate than those undertaken by a single state that might be motivated by its own national self-interest. The UN-sponsored economic and military sanctions against the apartheid regime in South Africa symbolizing its pariah status was a major factor in convincing the National Party leadership that their racist system could no longer be sustained. The European Union (EU) made it clear to the Government of Hungary that it could not be eligible for membership unless it put a stop to its destabilizing propaganda concerning Hungarian minorities in neighboring countries. The EU has declined to proceed with Turkey's application for admission, in part because Turkey's treatment of its Kurdish minority falls short of European standards of human rights. The African Union in April 2003 sponsored a 3,500 person peacekeeping mission staffed by South African, Mozambican, and Ethiopian forces to Burundi to enforce the recent truce between Tutsi and Hutu. But because decisions by multi-state organizations to intervene militarily tend to be slow, cumbersome, and often reluctant, they frequently act, even when they act at all, only, as in the case of Bosnia, after great damage has already been done.

The Organization for European Security and Cooperation (OSCE) maintains a High Commissioner on National Minorities whose responsibility is to provide good offices to mediate intra-state conflicts involving national minorities in OSCE member countries and contribute to their resolution. He has been most active in the former Soviet republics and satellites in eastern Europe and central Asia.[18] His interventions are frequently intended to provide early warning of ethnic tensions and head off the outbreak of violence. After a decade of tense negotiations, he succeeded in persuading the Estonian and Latvian governments, despite the deep suspicions they harbor toward the Russian minorities whom they inherited from the Soviet occupation, to liberalize their naturalization procedures and citizenship status. Improved facilities were made available to the Russians for learning the state language. On matters affecting the status and chances of the depressed and excluded Roma minorities in several eastern European countries, the Commissioner has succeeded only in highlighting and clarifying the severity of the problems facing the Roma and their host societies. And in other cases, such as the language rights of the Russian minority in Romanian-speaking Moldova, his proposals were politely received but have yet to be acted on. His energetic interventions have, however, established the principle that, for Europe at least, the protection of minority rights and maintenance of healthy interethnic relations have become legitimate subjects of international concern.

The United Nations Security Council has been called upon to mediate a number of ethnic conflicts, using its good offices to induce the parties to forego or halt violent activity and begin negotiations. Since 1990 there have been no fewer than 41 UN-sponsored peacekeeping operations of which 15 were active in 2002. These involved 44,000 Blue Helmets contributed by 90 states. The Kosovo mission alone required 4,400 police trainers budgeted at $345 million just for the year 2002.[19] When these interventions succeed in suspending hostilities, the UN may be called upon to provide peacekeepers – military contingents seconded by member states to serve as observers and monitors, supervising the truces or armistices to insure that violations by either side do not escalate into renewed violence. In the case of Cyprus, UN Blue Helmets have been in place since 1974 supervising the armistice between Greek and Turkish Cypriots because the parties have been unable to agree on a permanent settlement. UN peacekeeping contingents are stationed in a number of the world's hot spots from Rwanda to Bosnia, Somalia, and East Timor, attempting to maintain precarious truces pending the achievement of permanent agreements. When Namibia gained its independence, a UN force not only supervised the peace agreement, it also managed the election to choose the country's first independent government.

Since UN Blue Helmets are present at the request of both parties to disputes, they are normally not authorized to use force except in self-defense. Situations have arisen, however, where nothing short of superior military power, coercive intervention, would be sufficient to terminate flagrant violations of human rights. In Kosovo where the Serbian military was systematically expelling tens of thousands of Muslim Kosovars from their homes and driving them out of the country (committing the crime of ethnic cleansing), armed forces from the United States and United Kingdom authorized by NATO intervened to defeat and expel the Serbian army, and were followed by a joint military and multinational civilian force to maintain order, resettle returning refugee families, restore the economy, and build the institutions of government.

An earlier example of coercive intervention occurred in Bosnia, where half-hearted attempts by the European Union and the UN to deter the Serbian military by mediation and good offices had proved ineffectual, while thousands had been massacred and driven from their homes. President Clinton finally called a conference in 1995 at Dayton, Ohio. This conference produced a formula that put an end to hostilities and resulted in an international tribunal to try the perpetrators of these atrocities for crimes against humanity. The US and other NATO members took charge of securing order and apprehending war criminals, while a UN-sponsored force, the Peace Implementation Council, became responsible for resettling refugees, organizing a multiethnic government structure, and restoring the economy. In East Timor, which had been ravaged by elements of the Indonesian military even after its independence had been conceded by the Indonesian government, the UN force is responsible not only for maintaining order, but also for organizing and operating a government and managing humanitarian services until the economy has been restored and indigenous personnel have been trained to assume the responsibilities of government.

Intervention by non-government organizations (NGOs)

During the past quarter century there has been a notable decline of confidence in the ability of government to solve society's problems. In the search for alternatives, conservatives have turned to market mechanisms, liberals to civil society. The latter reflects their democratic faith that people can take the initiative to form non-profit, non-government organizations that are responsive to them, address important societal problems, and contribute significantly to their solution. Though most humanitarian relief supplies – food, medicines, and temporary shelter – are provided by governments and international agencies, much of the responsibility for their distribution to civilian victims of ethnic violence, including displaced persons and refugees, is assumed by NGOs often at great risk and peril to their field personnel. Often NGO workers find themselves in danger, accused of favoring one side or the other. There have been numerous instances from war zones in Sudan, Congo, and Bosnia of supplies intended for civilian relief being hijacked by combatants for their own use or for sale in local markets.

Some NGOs oriented to the peaceful resolution of conflicts have attempted to provide their good offices in a number of ethnic conflicts and help the parties in dispute to resolve their differences peacefully. They have attempted to intervene both in local conflicts and in those that involve governments. Though there are many versions of the conflict resolution paradigm, they all emphasize the importance of initiating and sustaining dialogue between representatives of the disputants, moderated by neutral interlocutors who command the confidence of both sides.[20] Participants in these dialogues may be influential non-officials and occasionally officials of the warring parties.

Proponents of the conflict resolution paradigm believe that when the dialogue proves fruitful, it transforms the perspectives of the participants and facilitates mutually satisfactory adjustments and outcomes. The dynamics of dialogue and confidence building are believed to help participants appreciate the sincerity of their opponents, understand the conflict from the other's perspective, realize that their common interest in a peaceful outcome is far more important than rigid adherence to their original goals, agree that reasonable compromises are possible, and commit themselves to their implementation. They believe that NGOs as members of society are more likely than representatives of governments to win the confidence of suspicious parties, because they are not encumbered with national interests in the outcome, and can operate with greater flexibility than functionaries of international organizations.[21]

Because of the optimism, energy, and patience demonstrated by NGOs and the substantial literature they have produced, it is important that students of ethnic conflict be aware
of their philosophy and their efforts. NGOs have scored
many successes as international advocates for womens'
rights, environmental protection, and civil rights for minorities. They have been instrumental in terminating a number of
localized ethnic conflicts. Structured dialogue, the principal
method employed by NGOs, influenced the attitudes of participants in official negotiations, for example the civil war in
Tadjikistan analyzed by Saunders.[22]

The Carter Center founded by former US president Jimmy
Carter is dedicated to working for the peaceful resolution of
conflicts. Under Carter's leadership it has founded an International Network of NGOs concerned with the prevention
and mediation of mostly intra-state (ethnic) conflicts.[23] It
holds periodic consultation sessions to appraise the state of
the art of resolving armed conflicts. Carter has attempted to
mediate, terminate the violence, and bring an end to some of
the most intractable conflicts, including the long civil war in
Sudan, the Eritrean insurrection against Ethiopia, and the
tripartite conflict between Serbs, Croats, and Muslims in
Bosnia. Despite Carter's unique prestige, moral standing, and
dedication, these interventions have seldom proved successful because, like all NGOs, the Carter Center lacked the
muscle and the financial resources needed to nudge reluctant
negotiators to take the final, risky step toward compromise.
The Carter Center has been more successful in monitoring
elections that select post-conflict governments and insuring
that the elections have been free and fair.

There are limits to what NGOs can accomplish. To
help make moderate agreements and compromises stick,
the interlocutors may need to be able to provide coercive
resources to deter hard-liners on both sides and possibly
funds to help the parties implement the settlement and
sweeten the compromises. NGOs are unable to provide
these resources. The Swiss-based Centre Henri Dunant's
patient mediation between the Indonesian government and
the insurgents in Aceh came within striking distance of
success before it was undermined by intransigent militants on
both sides.

Foreign aid and ethnic conflict[24]

The supply of foreign economic assistance from rich to poor countries has stagnated in recent years at about $50 billion, representing only three-tenths of 1 percent of the combined gross national products (GNPs) of the rich (donor) countries (the United States is at the bottom of the donor list, providing only one-tenth of 1 percent of GNP). Nevertheless, foreign aid represents an important contribution to the resources available to governments of less developed countries. Many of them depend on foreign economic assistance to finance a substantial share of their development budgets.

Each of the rich countries conducts its own bilateral foreign aid program, but international agencies such as the World Bank and the UN Development Program as well as some foundations are significant contributors. Since each of them operates according to its own rules and policies, they confront the weak administrative capabilities of recipient countries with the daunting and often unsuccessful task of coordination. Until recently their common assumption has been that the main purpose of the resources they supply is to promote macroeconomic growth in the countries they assist and that the main tests for evaluating individual projects were economic and technical feasibility. "Political" considerations such as the implications of projects for ethnic relations were to be avoided, since they would be viewed as interference with the sovereignty of host countries. (Involvement with their budgets and exchange rates was somehow not regarded as interference.) Economic growth was believed to benefit everyone, to raise all ships, to be the universal solvent for all conflicts.

In addition to promoting market-based economic policies, the scope of foreign aid has recently expanded to cover such "political" goals as good governance, accountability and transparency of public administration, the rule of law, human rights, environmental protection, and the status and opportunities of women. These are advocated both for their intrinsic worth and because they are believed to facilitate economic growth. Donors have hesitated, however, to extend their concerns to the prevention and mitigation of ethnic conflict, fearing that this would involve them too deeply in the political affairs of recipient countries.

It has been found, however, that foreign aid does not affect all ethnic groups equally. Some may benefit, others may be hurt. Though foreign aid administrators may be insensitive to the interethnic effects of their interventions, local politicians and officials are very much aware of them. The government of Sri Lanka induced several major donors to support the Mahaweli scheme, a very large irrigation and land development project in an area that had long been populated by members of the Tamil minority.[25] It then colonized the area exclusively with Sinhalese settlers. In their innocence, donors supported the project because the economic benefit–cost ratios seemed so favorable. To Tamils, however, it appeared to be a naked land grab favoring Sinhalese at the expense of the legitimate rights of Tamils. This was one of the grievances that contributed to the outbreak of the Tamil rebellion, as members of the Tamil community concluded that they could not expect fair dealing from a Sinhalese-dominated government.

The government of Kenya, controlled by an ethnic coalition, was found to be channeling all foreign aid projects, including overseas scholarships, exclusively to members of the government's ethnic coalition, treating foreign aid resources as spoils to be used for patronage to reward their (ethnic) supporters. When the donors discovered this misuse of aid resources, along with evidence of massive corruption, they attempted to impose strict conditions on the use of assistance, releasing funds in segments only after they were satisfied that the terms of conditionality had been honored.[26] One element of conditionality was fair, non-discriminatory treatment of all ethnic communities.

Many similar cases could be cited where the failure of donors to assess the likely ethnic consequences of their assistance resulted in the deterioration of interethnic relations and aggravated ethnic conflict. During the decade of the 1990s, aid donors were pressing Third World governments, in the interest of economic efficiency, to privatize state-owned enterprises. As many governments dragged their feet in implementing this advice, donors failed to recognize that privatization would benefit mainly foreign firms and members of ethnic minorities who were better equipped with financial resources and management experience to acquire and operate these enterprises. Governments are seldom prepared to see important enterprises that have been created by the state pass into the hands of ethnic minorities or foreign corporations.

There are also instances where thoughtful concern for ethnic relations helped prevent ethnic conflict. In Sri Lanka, the aid-financed Gal Oya project to rehabilitate a derelict irrigation system required the cooperation of Sinhalese and Tamil farmers from which they would mutually benefit.[27] While a civil war raged about them, these farmers jointly maintained and operated the restored facilities and protected one another, because they were convinced that the benefits were fairly distributed and that cooperation was essential to their common interest as farmers. Projects that serve the common interest of members of ethnic communities, that create interdependence among them, or where the benefits can be fairly shared are good candidates for preventing conflict.

Foreign aid donors have generally been slow to recognize that the resources they provide may have important, but differential consequences for ethnic communities. They may exacerbate or help to prevent conflict. As aid donors contribute to the rehabilitation and development of post-Taliban Afghanistan it will be interesting to observe how sensitive they are to the interethnic effects on this ethnically plural and violence-prone society of the policies they recommend and the projects they finance.

Conclusion

The contemporary state establishes and enforces the rules that govern the relative status, rights, and opportunities available to members of its component ethnic communities. These include the terms of access to economic resources of all kinds, the degree of respect accorded to languages and religions, and rights to participate in the institutions of government. For this reason, mobilized ethnic communities invest much of their collective energies in attempts to influence the behavior of governments to their benefit, to affect government policies, to gain actual control over the state apparatus, and in some cases to break away and construct their own state.

In our interdependent era, ethnic-based pressures frequently spill over the borders of individual states. Ethnic competitors reach out for external support, while outsiders find reasons to intrude into the ethnic politics of other states. Thus, ethnic conflict has become an important dimension of international relations. International law and practice are gradually recognizing the threat of intra-state (chiefly, ethnic) conflict to human rights and international peace, and the obligation this imposes on governments, NGOs, and international organizations. These outside agencies now act, often hesitantly and ineptly, to forestall, mitigate, and terminate violent ethnic conflicts.

6

Patterns of Pluralism I: Domination

Domination is a pattern of interethnic relations in which one mobilized ethnic community, usually in control of the state apparatus, excludes, limits, or otherwise subordinates members of other ethnic communities. There are two major types of domination: exclusionary and inclusionary. Minority rights are a version of domination that concedes some rights and dignity to subordinated peoples. Middleman minorities represent a special form of ethnic vulnerability.

Exclusionary domination

Exclusionary domination can be formal or non-formal, but in either case the effect is a structure of ethnic stratification with unequal rights, status, and opportunities available to individuals due entirely to their ethnic origins. Intellectuals from the dominant community invent and popularize reasons, biological or cultural, to demonstrate the superiority of their people and the inferiority of the other, which justifies their dominant status. American Indians, during the nineteenth century were demonized as bloodthirsty, heathen savages. Germans under Hitler were glorified as the master race.

Exclusion means inferiority in rights, status, and opportunities, combined with rejection, no possibility of escaping from this ascriptive predicament. The rejection is experienced psychologically as well as tangibly, creating combinations of resignation, self-hatred, and resentment among the victims of discrimination. Resignation and the internalization of a sense of inferiority may help to perpetuate subordination for very long periods of time, as individuals feel that any change or resistance would be hopeless and might result in severe punishment.[1] The long period of passivity among the defeated and humiliated Indian peoples of the Andean highlands can be explained in this way. Yet, out of resentment have arisen movements for liberation and revolutionary change, such as the African National Congress (ANC) in South Africa, Zionism among eastern European Jews, the Irish Republican Army (IRA), and the Pachakutic movement among Ecuadorian Indians.[2]

European colonial societies on all continents were systems of caste stratification, in which any European, no matter how humble, had higher status and enjoyed more rights, privileges, and opportunities than any but a tiny handful of native elites. Except as servants, natives were excluded from European residential areas, social clubs, and schools; senior positions in government, the military, modern economic enterprises, and education were monopolized by Europeans. This social order was enforced by the state security and judicial apparatus. By such methods small contingents of Europeans were able to dominate, control, and exploit large native societies. Japan, a non-European latecomer to the colonial game, employed identical methods in Korea, Formosa, Manchuria, and north China.

A classic example of exclusion and subordination was the operation of the apartheid system in South Africa prior to its collapse in 1990. Non-Whites were excluded by law from participation as voters or office-holders in the political institutions of the state, their cultures were denigrated as savage or childlike, and they were relegated to menial, low-status, low-productivity occupations. Housing and public facilities such as schools, playgrounds, and seating on vehicles of mass transportation were rigidly segregated and unequal. These exclusions were enforced by the police and judicial arms of the state. The weight of separation and institutionalized inferiority was intended to produce a spirit of resigned hopelessness and acceptance among the non-White majority.[3]

During the century preceding the national civil rights legislation in the mid-1960s, Blacks in the southern states of the United States were similarly subjected to "Jim Crow" laws. Provided with separate and unequal facilities, they were excluded by literacy tests and similar devices from political participation, employed only in menial occupations, and frequently intimidated and victimized by mob violence, all despite the language of the fourteenth amendment to the US Constitution which mandated that "no state shall deny to any person within its jurisdiction the equal protection of the laws." The Roma people (Gypsies) in central and eastern Europe have been stigmatized as inferior, a pariah people, rejected as unclean, devious, and unfit for membership in the national society.[4] Persons of non-Yamato ethnic origin are effectively excluded from citizenship and membership in the Japanese nation.

State-induced violence against selected ethnic communities has been one method of enforcing domination. This involves attacks on the persons and property of ethnic minorities by mobs, often inflamed by agents of the state as the police stand by while the mayhem is in progress. Classic examples of state-induced violence were the pogroms in tsarist Russia against Jewish communities during the late nineteenth century. In the year 2002, the Hindu nationalist government of the Indian state of Gujerat incited Hindu mobs to attack Muslims, resulting in 2,000 fatalities and extensive property damage as the police stood aside. Under similar circumstances, Muslim mobs in Indonesia have murdered and pillaged Christian communities while the police failed to intervene. A frequent purpose of such attacks is to divert economic and social grievances from the government and project them on vulnerable minorities who can be softened up by such intimidation for further abuse and extortion. Failure of government to protect vulnerable minorities is an invitation to violence-prone elements among the majority to rob, pillage, and kill, as Muslim extremists in Egypt have felt free to attack the homes and shops of the Coptic Christian minority.

Genocide and ethnic cleansing have been practiced against subject populations since the dawn of recorded history and continue to this day. When the Israelites conquered their promised land, all the local Canaanite tribes were exterminated.[5] The Government of Rwanda sponsored the slaughter of an estimated 800,000 Tutsi by Hutu mobs, the Holocaust against Jews in the 1940s was planned and executed by the German government, and the massacre of Armenians during World War I was sanctioned by the Ottoman authorities. The rulers of Spain in 1492 expelled their Jewish population. In 1755 the British expelled the French-speaking Acadians from Nova Scotia to the Louisiana territory – the origin of the current Cajun people of Louisiana – on the ground that Acadians constituted a security risk, threatening to thwart the British designs on Quebec. During the nineteenth century, the United States government, often in violation of treaties, drove most of the Indian nations from their ancestral homelands and confined the survivors to cramped and impoverished reservations as wards of the state. After World War I, the Turkish government expelled the long-established Greek communities from Anatolia as subversives who had welcomed the Greek invading army prior to its defeat by Turkish forces. After World War II the Government of Czechoslovakia summarily expelled the entire German population of western Bohemia, 2.5 million people, for similar reasons: they had greeted the invading and occupying German forces with enthusiasm.

Genocide and ethnic cleansing are expressions of domination that target entire communities, inflicting unimaginable cruelty on individuals who are held to be collectively guilty of the presumed offenses that occasion such draconian punishment. The response of the Western Powers through NATO in the 1990s to the attempted expulsion of the entire Albanian majority from Kosovo by the Serbian army suggests that a new international norm to prevent or roll back ethnic cleansing may be emerging.[6]

Not all processes of domination by exclusion are the result of laws or government policies. Some are the non-formal consequences of entrenched societal traditions and practices to which the government acquiesces but which it does not enforce. The intimidation, oppression, and humiliation of untouchables (dalits) by high-caste societies in India is forbidden by the state constitution, but persists nonetheless. An excellent example can be found in Brazil, whose opinion leaders boast of the non-racial character of its democracy. There are no laws or official policies authorizing racial strat- ification. Under its present (1988) constitution, racial dis- crimination is a felony, but this policy is not enforced. Yet, its large Afro-Brazilian and mixed race (pardo) population, an estimated 45 percent of the total, is barely visible among its political, professional, business, cultural, educational, or religious elites.[7] Only 5 percent of the members of the National Congress and 3 percent of university students are Afro-Brazilians. Nor do they live in the same neighborhoods as their Euro-Brazilian compatriots. To be born an Afro- Brazilian means that your life chances – opportunities for a good education, family contacts that open doors to favorable marriages and employment opportunities – effectively limit you to low expectations, modest achievements, and discrim- inatory treatment. The favelas, squatter slum settlements sur- rounding Brazil's major cities, are peopled almost entirely by Blacks, while the inhabitants of upper- and middle-class neighborhoods are mostly White. The national myth simply denies that racial differences play any part in Brazilian life. This non-formal process of institutionalized stratification has been challenged in recent years by militant spokespersons for Afro-Brazilians and their sympathizers, but without produc- ing noticeable results.[8] A new era may be dawning, however, since the left of center government which was elected in 2002 has pledged to introduce a system of quotas that would apply to government jobs in all branches of the service, to govern- ment contracts, and to university admissions. Predictably Whites who fear that, despite their superior qualifications, they will be unfairly excluded from government employment, business opportunities, and especially university admissions have begun to protest the use of quotas, arguing that by imposing quotas the government is introducing racial conflict into a previously harmonious situation.[9]

Total or partial subordination or exclusion can be imposed entirely non-formally, by tacit social conventions once known as "gentleman's agreements." Beginning in the 1840s, Americans of Irish Catholic origin experienced discrimination and often physical harassment as undesirables because of their Catholic faith, their alleged sloth and drunkedness, and accusation that they were undermining labor standards by accepting employment at sub-standard wages. Prior to World War II, Irish Catholics were unwelcome in economic enterprises and social institutions dominated by Anglo-Saxon Protestants. It was not until 1960 that an Irish-Catholic American could be elected to the highest office in the land and only after assuring members of the Protestant clergy that he would not be guided in his official responsibilities by instructions from Pope John XXIII in Rome. Similarly, Jews in the United States, were excluded from managerial and professional posts in most major industrial and financial corporations, from law firms, from the faculties of most universities and the medical staffs of most hospitals. These practices were not sanctioned by law, but prevailed nonetheless. Access by Jews to the more prestigious universities and professional schools was regulated by unofficial quotas. They were kept out of social clubs and vacation resorts and denied the opportunity to own property in many residential areas. The trauma of the European Holocaust, Federal non-discrimination laws, and judicial decisions finally succeeded in ending these practices after World War II.

Inclusionary domination: assimilation

Domination can be implemented by the strategy of the velvet glove, by inducement sponsored by public authority. Governments can encourage individual members of minority groups to acculturate to the national mainstream, to become proficient in the national language as prerequisite to higher education, participation in government, professional careers, and economic enterprises. By acculturating to the national mainstream, adopting mainstream lifestyle, and eventual intermarriage, their attachment to their original ethnic community is expected to diminish until succeeding generations identify entirely with the mainstream. Incentives for individuals to acculturate and eventually assimilate are expected to deplete their original ethnic community, while the dominant community is strengthened by the addition of fresh recruits. At any intermediate stage in this transition, individuals may attempt to balance both identities, preferring one at home, the other at work. Gradually, however, the balance is tipped as the mainstream identity eclipses the original which may survive for a generation or two among children of mixed marriages as bits of family nostalgia. The recruits to the mainstream may become the most loyal citizens of the state and the most enthusiastic participants in its culture. No one is to be excluded, all are eligible for inclusion in the ranks of the nation, united and indivisible. The outcome is painless ethnicide, the death of an ethnic community.[10]

Beginning with the French Revolution, the policy of successive French governments, monarchical and republican, conservative and socialist, has been one of aggressive assimilation of minorities. "Nation-building" is often employed to denote this strategy. Homeland peoples – Gascons, Burgundians, Corsicans – as well as immigrants – Spaniards, Poles, Jews – all were to become free, equal, and fraternal Frenchmen, proud participants in one of the world's most prestigious cultures. Under these Jacobin policies of centralization and uniformity, a rigidly standardized national system of compulsory education and military service for young men in the French language, and the active promotion of French culture have historically succeeded in converting persons of diverse backgrounds into Frenchmen. But for the first time in more than two centuries this policy is being challenged by North African Muslim immigrants, many of whom are resisting assimilation and demanding official recognition of and concessions to their separate collective identity and culture.

The Thai government, after earlier efforts to suppress the culture of its large and economically powerful Chinese minority, now practices the policy of consensual inclusion. Persons of Chinese origin are encouraged to adopt Thai names, embrace the Hinayana Buddhist faith, enroll their children in Thai language schools, and intermarry into Thai society. Members of Thailand's revered royal family boast of the Chinese element in their background. This inclusionary policy is succeeding, as education, intermarriage, and occupational mobility attenuate the attachment of Sino-Thai to their ancestral identity and culture. This contrasts with the Malay-Muslim minority in southern Thailand who refuse to assimilate to Thai-Buddhist society. As they cling to their separate identity and culture, the Bangkok government has come reluctantly to recognize and tolerate their distinctiveness as a permanent situation.

The Turkish government strategy toward its large Kurdish minority is one of inclusion through acculturation and assimilation of individuals. This is in pursuit of the vision of Atatürk, founder of the modern Turkish state, that all inhabitants of the state are to be considered members of a unified Turkish nation and that the duty of government is to build that nation. Kurds are not recognized as a separate people and until recently were regarded as "Mountain Turks," members of the Turkish nation with equal rights and duties as individual citizens. Some Kurds who have migrated to Turkey's urban areas in search of employment appear to be acquiescing in this policy, but it is resisted, in some cases violently, in the Kurdish heartland of southeastern Anatolia by the Kurdish national movement that demands official recognition of the distinctive Kurdish language and culture, plus political autonomy for the region. The weight of evidence suggests that the government's efforts, at great cost in lives and property and in Turkey's reputation in Europe, to suppress the insurrection have failed and that government will be compelled eventually to come to terms with their Kurdish minority and recognize this element of diversity in their country.

Efforts to induce members of minorities to yield their original identity and join the national mainstream – in effect, domination by inclusion rather than exclusion – have produced mixed results. Russification, attempted by the tsars and by their Soviet successors, enjoyed some minor successes but failed to eliminate the collective identities of the larger ethnic communities within the Russian and Soviet states. Arabization over the centuries has spread the Arabic language and culture over most of North Africa; many Berbers have been absorbed, but a substantial minority has resisted Arabization and has become increasingly militant in recent years. Over the centuries, Sinicization has incorporated many peoples into the Chinese nation, but faces intense resistance in Tibet and among the Uighurs in China's northwest. Some peoples are sufficiently attached to their original culture and identity that they will decline or forcibly resist efforts to incorporate them into another. They may believe that contrary to the promise of equal incorporation, they would not in fact be accepted on equal terms; they would sacrifice their original identity and culture only to be held at arm's length as second-class citizens. For example, Malayan Chinese who speak Malay and convert to Islam are not eligible for the preferential treatment available to Malays.

Others have proved more amenable to conversion, concluding that the promised benefits exceed the costs of allowing their ancestral identity to lapse. Most of the third and fourth generation of European immigrants to the United States have acculturated and contributed to the English-speaking mainstream and are intermarrying en route to integration, preserving in many cases their original religious affiliation in an increasingly secularized society. When a distinctive ethnic identity is combined with a distinctive religious identity – the cases of Malay-Muslims in southern Thailand and of Hindu immigrants in East Africa – prospects for acceptance of an alternate identity become much more problematical, even when assimilation would convey many practical benefits.

Minority rights

A third method of insuring domination involves neither exclusion nor individual inclusion, but the grant of collective minority rights. This policy is designed to reconcile the minority to their subordinate status by conferring on them valuable individual and collective rights, with no expectation that they will be pressured to assimilate to the majority. Their security and continuity as a separate community is thus confirmed by law, though it may fall short of their aspirations.

We have previously referred to the first international effort under the League of Nations to recognize minority rights. At the end of World War I, the defeated powers, Germany, Austria-Hungary, and Russia, were partly dismembered and in central and eastern Europe a number of nations gained their independence. These included the Baltic states, Estonia, Latvia, and Lithuania, Finland, Poland, Czechoslovakia, and

Yugoslavia. Each of these new states included substantial national minorities, many of whose spokespersons were demanding that the victorious powers, Britain, France, and the United States, vindicate President Woodrow Wilson's promise regarding the "self-determination" of peoples. The victorious powers responded by imposing on several of these new states, as well as on Germany, minority treaties which committed them to guaranteeing members of their national minorities non-discriminatory treatment as citizens plus such cultural rights as primary and secondary education and judicial proceedings in their native languages and the opportunity to maintain their own cultural, recreational, and religious institutions. The provisions of these minority treaties were to be monitored by a section of the new League of Nations Secretariat and enforced, if need be, by the Council of the League, its highest political organ.

These provisions were resisted and resented by the leadership of most of these new states as encroachments on their sovereignty and as discriminatory, since other states were not subject to such requirements. Moreover, they believed they were justified in trying to build integrated nations, rather than perpetuating minorities in their midst. Gradually several of these states, notably Poland and Romania, began to disregard these treaties; the League, including its principal powers, Britain and France, proved unwilling to enforce them; and in 1934 Poland formally denounced these treaties. This proved to be the ignominious end of the first effort to recognize and protect the rights of ethnic minorities by international action.[11]

After World War II, the human rights conventions drawn up under the aegis of the newly established United Nations referred entirely to individuals, not to groups such as ethnic minorities. Gradually, however, the concept of human rights has been interpreted to encompass members of ethnic minorities, enabling the UN on behalf of the international community to intervene on behalf of minorities whose rights had been flagrantly abused. At present such interventions are selective, directed at smaller states, as in the case of Kosovo, but not at more powerful states such as China for its oppression of Tibetans. In Europe, however, the Organization for European Security and Cooperation (OSCE), as noted in chapter 5, sponsors a Commissioner on Minority Affairs who intervenes to prevent or rectify violations of minority rights in member countries. The European Union has signaled its unwillingness to admit new member states which fail to respect the legitimate rights of their ethnic minorities.

Respect for minority rights may be promoted by international action and the relevant rights may be expanded to include some degree of regional autonomy as well as the cultural maintenance that was emphasized by the League of Nations. These constitute restraints on the powers and discretion of governments. There are, in addition, examples of minority rights that have evolved independently of international pressures, such as those guaranteed by Finland to its Swedish minority. These represent concessions by majorities that retain their dominant position, while at the same time insuring the security and dignity of ethnic minorities.

Israel is a Jewish state, but its founding charter conferred citizenship on its Arab-Palestinian minority now numbering 20 percent; Arabic was recognized as an official language, and religious freedom was confirmed for all faiths. Palestinian voters elect members to the Knesset, the national parliament, they have access to the Israeli courts, its universities, its world-class medical and health services, and the network of social services provided by the Israeli government. There is a separate school system in the Arabic language, though it is closely supervised by Israeli authorities. While they enjoy the right to vote and hold office, and their representatives can voice their grievances, they have little influence on government and no Palestinian has ever been invited to serve as a Cabinet member or allowed to exercise executive authority. Though citizens, they are exempt from the military service that is obligatory for young Jewish men and women. In effect, Palestinians are second-class citizens, leading separate but unequal lives. Many Israeli Jews suspect their Palestinian fellow citizens as security risks, prepared, should the occasion arise, to betray their country to its enemies. Israeli Palestinians appear to prefer to remain Israeli citizens, but hope that Israel may be converted into a state for all its people, a bi-national polity in which Palestinians as individuals and as a collectivity might enjoy equal rights with Jewish Israelis. This idea is anathema to the Zionist majority in

Israel, as few would agree to dilute the uniquely Jewish character of Israel. Jews in Israel are clearly dominant, but limited rights are reserved for the Palestinian minority.

Locally born Chinese and Indians are Malaysian citizens. They vote and hold office in all branches of the Malaysian state, including ministerial portfolios. But Malays jealously guard their dominant position in government. No non-Malay can ever serve as prime minister or deputy prime minister or as head of the army or police, and positions in the elite civil service are regulated by a quota of four Malays to every non-Malay. Electoral districts are drawn to insure that Malays will substantially outnumber non-Malays in Parliament. All the symbols of the state are drawn from Malay tradition, the head of state is a Malay sultan, Islam is the state religion, Malay is recognized and promoted as the sole official language of government and of secondary and higher education. Though non-Malays resent their unequal treatment, they recognize that they enjoy significant minority rights including participation in, and a voice in, government, primary schools for their children in their ancestral languages, religious toleration, and economic opportunities that enable them to maintain a higher average standard of living than their Malay compatriots. They also realize that the Malay-controlled security services would crack down vigorously on any challenge to the current regime. Malay domination is not based on exclusion of minorities, nor is there any expectation that non-Malays would wish to assimilate into Malay-Muslim society or would be readily accepted. The formula is domination combined with significant minority rights.

Official language minorities in Canada, English-speakers in Quebec, Francophones in English-majority provinces, are guaranteed by the national constitution the right to elementary and secondary education in their minority official language where numbers warrant. This is similar to concessions to minorities elsewhere, such as the right of Muslims in India to have disputes over domestic relations and inheritance adjudicated under Islamic canon law (sharia). Canada's policy of multiculturalism subsidizes at government expense the cultural institutions of ethnic minorities in order to help them perpetuate and further develop their cultural heritages and thus invigorate what Canadians believe to be their ethnic mosaic.

(Canada, according to former Prime Minister Trudeau, has two official languages, but no official culture.) During the four centuries of Ottoman rule in the Balkans and the Middle East, Christian and Jewish minorities were excluded from civil and military positions in government and were required to pay a special tax. They were, however, as "people of the book," afforded a large measure of self-government and economic freedom under their respective religious authorities, applying religious law, as long as they did not challenge the authority of their Ottoman Muslim overlords.

Minority rights are concessions by a dominant majority to subordinate communities that institutionalize the dominant-subordinate relationship, yet guarantee the minority significant rights intended to give them a valuable stake in the status quo.

Middleman minorities

Middleman minorities are members of ethnic groups with some commercial skills and experience, who migrate to peasant societies in search of economic opportunity. There they occupy niches as traders, moneylenders, and processors and marketers of agricultural commodities between peasants who are inexperienced in such occupations and the ruling elite of warriors, administrators, and priests who disdain commercial pursuits. Beginning often as peddlers, petty traders, and shopkeepers, their more successful operatives may evolve into wealthy industrialists, bankers, and international merchants. Middleman communities tend to maintain their culture and separate collective identity and not to mix socially with the indigenous society.[12] While they seldom integrate socially with the native people, they retain important transnational links with ethnic kinfolk. Transnational firms operated by overseas Chinese have been and remain the largest and most dynamic examples of capitalist enterprise in Southeast Asia.[13]

Because of these differences and because they appear to be more prosperous than the local peasantry who frequently become their debtors, they are likely to become the collective targets of envy, suspicion, and hatred. Economically potent but politically weak, conspicuous yet vulnerable, they attract the attention of the rootless, nationalist intelligentsia and of aspiring politicians who seek to build constituency support by charging these "foreigners" in their midst with sharp dealing, economic exploitation, disrespect for the native culture, and even conspiracies to subvert the national government. To protect themselves, the more enterprising members of middleman minorities cultivate influential personalities among the ruling elites by gift-giving, ill-disguised bribery, serving as their economic agents, and by offering them shares as silent partners in profitable business ventures, often in exchange for valuable licenses or economic concessions provided by the state. In Malaysia such arrangements came to be known as "Ali-Baba" contracts; Ali being the Malay front man who protects the enterprise and shares in the profits, but has no role in its financing or management; Baba is the Chinese businessman who provides the funds, entrepreneurship, and management. In this way middleman minorities seek to buy security for themselves and their community and scope for their economic energies, but at the price of further alienating themselves from the majority.

Middleman minorities were prominent among Greeks (Phanariots), Armenians, and Jews throughout the Ottoman Empire and in Russia and eastern Europe during the seventeenth, eighteenth, and nineteenth centuries, among Overseas Chinese throughout Southeast Asia, Indians in eastern and southern Africa, Lebanese and Syrians in West Africa. These unpopular minorities do well as long as there are few indigenous competitors and the elites of society continue to protect them. But when that protection for any reason is withdrawn, popular resentment against their relative wealth and outsider status expose them to pillaging, oppression, and mass violence. During the last quarter of the nineteenth century, the Russian tsars, cultivating the support of the clergy of the Russian Orthodox Church and of rabble-rousers among the emergent populist intelligentsia, launched pogroms against the Jewish minority. Idi Amin, the Ugandan dictator during the 1960s, summarily expelled the entire Asian community and divided their confiscated property among his supporters – with disastrous consequences for Uganda's economy. (A later government invited the Asians to return and restored some of their property.)

When the long-serving Suharto dictatorship in Indonesia ended in 1998, the Chinese minority was stripped of its protection and became immediately vulnerable. They were blamed for the subsequent collapse of the economy and the consequent hardships suffered by rank and file Indonesians. The dictator and his family had maintained conspicuous and lucrative ties with leading Chinese tycoons; in return, the increasingly unpopular regime had provided protection for Indonesian Chinese and their economic operations. When the dictator and his regime were ousted, Chinese leaders were forced to scramble for new strategies to protect themselves and their community. Meanwhile, mobs, angered by economic hardships and inflamed by local politicians and lower-level military personnel, began to attack, pillage, and burn Chinese shops and neighborhoods, though these local merchants had nothing to do with the Suharto regime. Chinese became scapegoats for the economic distress of native Indonesians; many Chinese lost their lives, many more their property and life savings as the police and the army stood by.

To deflect responsibility from their own failings and to cultivate support among the ethnic majority, politicians and governments often resort to scapegoating. Ethnic minorities, most notably middleman minorities, are convenient, available, and defenseless targets. They are charged with responsibility for any and all of society's ills, from high prices for consumers to low prices for farm products, from outbreaks of pestilence to corruption in high places and affronts to the true faith. Middleman minorities are especially vulnerable: suspected and resented as untrustworthy outsiders; envied for their relative prosperity, which is popularly believed to be the ill-gotten fruit of sharp practices and economic exploitation; and often identified as the willing accomplices of corrupt, discredited rulers.

Conclusion

The most common form of domination is exclusionary and the reasons are obvious. It conveys important advantages on even the most humble member of the dominant community.

In addition to preferential access to most of the good things in life – jobs, housing, business opportunities – its members enjoy the satisfaction of belonging to the group that is in charge, that writes and enforces the rules that others must live by, while their language must be learned and used by others who wish to get ahead in the world. Their intellectuals have no difficulty celebrating the special virtues of their people, which fully justifies their domination over others. No surprise, then, that the beneficiaries of domination are so reluctant to give it up when the time comes.

Minority rights and inclusionary domination (induced assimilation) are more subtle and less draconian methods of maintaining control. In both cases the subordinates have something to gain: security and the legally recognized right to maintain their culture (minority rights) and the opportunity to join the mainstream (inclusionary domination). In the latter case, individuals decide whether the benefits they will derive from joining the mainstream are worth the price of forsaking their inherited culture and the society that nurtured them, a sometimes painful choice. The logical consequence of a successful policy of induced assimilation is the withering and slow disappearance of a minority culture.

7
Patterns of Pluralism II: Power-sharing

Domination as analyzed in chapter 6 is not the only, nor is it the inevitable, pattern of pluralism. As it has proven possible for ethnic communities to coexist peacefully in the same locality, they can coexist as well within the same state through processes of shared rule. The main premises of power-sharing are that: (1) ethnic communities are permanent and legitimate components of society; (2) they should enjoy security and a large measure of self-determination; and (3) they are entitled to equitable participation in the affairs of the central government which is their common and joint responsibility and to share equitably in its benefits.

For some ethnic communities, power-sharing within a pluralistic system is an alternative to full independence, either because they value membership in a larger security and economic community, or because the anticipated costs of achieving independence are deemed not to be worth the price, or because independent statehood is simply not feasible. One of the principal expressions of factionalism within ethnic communities focuses on this very question: would our people be better served by complete independence or by remaining within the current multiethnic state? A faction of the Basques in Spain, ETA, has employed terrorist tactics in its struggle for independence, but has failed to persuade a majority of its compatriots, who continue to acquiesce in the current pattern of regional autonomy (power-sharing) within the Spanish state and to oppose terrorist methods by voting consistently for the Basque National Party (PNV) which governs the Basque autonomous region.

There are two principal patterns of power-sharing: federalism and consociationalism.[1]

Federalism

Federalism is a territorial arrangement that applies to homeland peoples who seek a significant measure of autonomy and self-government within their territorial homeland, along with a fair share of participation and influence in the affairs of the central government. Not all the many examples of federal systems in today's world are relevant to our interest in ethnic conflict. Some systems that are federal in form are not federal in substance. In form, the late Soviet Union was a voluntary federation of ethnic-based republics which, under the Stalin Constitution of 1936, even had the right to secede; in actuality it was a unitary and centralized state because its ruling organs, the Communist Party, the KGB (secret police), and GOSPLAN (economic planning agency) operated as highly centralized institutions of government. The Ethiopian constitution of 1994 proclaimed self-determination as the inherent right of all the nation's many ethnic communities; this policy was to be implemented by the establishment of 9 states for the largest ethnic communities. Yet, the domination of the central government by the Tigrean military, which imposed its will on these state governments, has nullified the constitutional promise of self-determination.[2] Federalism in Nigeria is more illusory than real because the central government controls oil royalties, the principal (80 percent) source of public revenues. This reduces the 36 states to the role of petitioners for access to the central government's largesse. Genuine autonomy and effective federalism are impossible unless regional units, like the states in the US and the provinces in Canada, have independent or guaranteed sources of revenue.

Other federal systems, some of them long-lasting and effective, are not intended for the management of ethnic conflict, but rather for the recognition of historical differences and enduring regional loyalties. These may be combined with elements of political engineering – to divide governmental authority among several units in order to diffuse political power and prevent excessive concentration in a single unit of government, as well as to provide more opportunities for competition and meaningful political participation. The United States, Germany, and Brazil are examples of this pattern of non-ethnic federalism.

India, Canada, and Switzerland, are examples of stable federal states with mobilized homeland peoples that would, in all likelihood not have held together were it not for the autonomy and self-government provided by their federal structures. The founders of modern, independent India visualized a secular state with a centralized government and planned economy in which India's numerous communal (religious, caste, and ethnic) identities would be subsumed under an overarching national identity. These inherited identities would lose their political significance and individuals would enjoy equal rights and immunities as citizens of a united democratic and socialist Indian commonwealth. This vision was rudely shattered during the first decade of independence when the persistence of India's many-faceted pluralism became politicized in the form of demands for linguistic states, to which India's leaders were compelled to acquiesce, language being a surrogate in India for collective ethnic identity. India has since been divided into 28 states with a substantial measure of self-government. Each state is dominated by its largest ethnic community, conducts its business and educates its children in the majority ethnic language within the state. Interstate relations and transactions with the central government are conducted in Hindi or English. This policy has complicated the processes of government, but, except in Kashmir, it has successfully accommodated aspirations for self-government among its principal ethnic communities and eliminated any significant demands for separation. The Hindu-Muslim cleavage cannot, however, be managed by territorial federalism, since the Muslim minority, estimated at 120 million, is present in many of India's states.

In 1840 Lord Elgin, Canada's governor-general, observed that Canada was a case of "two nations warring within the bosom of a single state." Canada's survival as a single polity would be highly problematical were it not for the autonomy and degree of self-rule provided by its federal institutions for the Francophone majority in Quebec. Canada's vast size, regional economic differences, and historical loyalties are other reasons for its federal structure of government, but French-Canadian nationalism centered in Quebec distinguishes it from the rest of Canada where English-speakers are a substantial majority. This calls for a structure of government that allows a large measure of self-rule for Quebec, sufficient to provide security for its distinctive society and enable its French-speaking culture not only to survive, but to reproduce itself and to flourish. Federal systems are not without tensions between the central government and the regions, and even within the regions themselves. Canada has evolved a complex language regime that recognizes English and French as the two official languages of the Government of Canada and all its institutions and agencies, while the individual provinces are free to adopt their own language policies that apply to matters under the jurisdiction of the provincial governments. Quebec, for example, has declared French to be its sole official language and has attempted to make French the principal medium for work in private enterprise as well as government, and for the conduct of everyday affairs. Each province, however, is required by Canada's constitution to make elementary and secondary education available in the minority official language, wherever there is sufficient demand.

Quebec society has been divided nearly equally between sovereignists who favor independence for Quebec and federalists who prefer to maintain the present membership in the Canadian federation. Since 1976 when the sovereignist Parti Québécois (PQ) was first elected as the government of Quebec, it has alternated in office with the federalist Liberal Party of Quebec (PLQ). PQ governments have twice sponsored referenda that would permit them to negotiate terms of separation from Canada and failed both times. The second time, 1995, they lost by a margin of less than 1 percent. The majority of French-speakers actually voted for separation, while the English-speaking minority and their allies among recent non-French-speaking immigrants voted overwhelmingly against it. The future of Quebec is in the hands of its voters and to date they have not opted for independence.

Meanwhile the Ottawa government has implemented a policy of "balanced participation" in its civil service, attempting at all levels to insure that French-speakers are represented in numbers equivalent to their proportion in the national population. They are guaranteed three of nine positions on the Supreme Court of Canada. The national capital region, Ottawa and its environs, maintains a bilingual environment. And since 1968 every Canadian prime minister with one brief exception has been from Quebec, all but one a native French-speaker and vigorous federalist. Thus, Canadian federalism provides substantial autonomy and self-rule for its principal homeland-based ethnic minority, plus significant participation in the institutions of the central government.

The Ottawa government in recent years has also attempted to recognize, subsidize, and provide autonomy for its many Indian and Inuit communities. It has carved out a separate Inuit-majority province, Nunavut, from the Northwest Territories. Since 1971 it has operated a program of multi-culturalism under which it subsidizes the cultural institutions of its several ethnic communities to enable them to preserve and develop their inherited cultures.

Ethnic federalism in Russia is an evolving work in progress. There are 21 autonomous republics, 19 with formal treaties regulating relations between Moscow and the individual republics. Some of these arrangements appear to violate the Russian constitution. Except for Chechnya, there is little separatist sentiment due to the accommodative posture of the Moscow government, the absence of strong ethnic solidarity in most of the republics, and the legitimacy imparted by the treaties. In only 5 of the republics does the titular ethnic group constitute the majority. Chechnya is clearly the exception. There the Chechens, a Muslim people, are a large majority with a history of violent resistance to external centralized rule. The apparently endless cycle of insurrection and repression in Chechnya is a tragic exception to the otherwise successful management of ethnic federalism by the current Russian government.[3]

We should also note that some systems of government have important federal-like features, but are not fully federal. In 1997 Scotland, after a lapse of 290 years, was successful in achieving an elected Scottish Parliament and Scottish Executive with taxing powers and control over a large number of subjects important to the daily lives of the Scottish people. Individual Scots continue to occupy important posts in the British government, especially when the Labour Party is in office. Yet, Scotland's substantial autonomy is a matter of powers devolved by the London government, powers that could be revoked just as they were granted by what remains, constitutionally, the highly centralized British state. Similar powers have, in the past, been devolved to Northern Ireland, but subsequently withdrawn. In a genuinely federal system, powers of government are distributed by its constitution between the center and its regions and these cannot be changed except by complex amendment procedures. So, what Scotland enjoys is a federal-like grant of powers from the central government in London. Scottish opinion is divided between the majority who appear to be satisfied with the present degree of autonomy, and a vigorous minority in the Scottish National Party who argue that the interests of the Scottish nation would best be served by complete independence from Britain, combined with membership in the European Union.

The benefits of federal arrangements are quite straightforward. They provide political space for homeland people to manage their own affairs and develop their own culture, yet participate in a much larger economic unit and enjoy the protection of a larger security community.[4] The post-Saddam settlement in Iraq will almost certainly include a federal or federal-like structure to protect the minority homeland peoples, Kurds and Turkomans in the north and Sunni in central Iraq, from the Shiite majority in the south.

At the same time federal systems are not trouble-free. Regional units may appreciate their autonomy, but believe they are being short-changed or discriminated against by the central government that is dominated by another ethnic group. For many years Slovenes and Croats complained that the Yugoslav federation, dominated by Serbia, was short-changing them in its allocation of resources and concluded that they would be better off as independent states. Slovaks came to the same conclusion in Czechoslovakia. There is also the central government's chronic fear of the "slippery slope," with federal autonomy likely to be only a way station to subsequent demands for independence. This was the position of the Franco dictatorship in Spain, which refused to countenance any political or cultural autonomy for Basques and Catalans – the very pattern of regional autonomy that was conceded to these two peoples by the successor democratic regime. The Ankara government fears that any concession of regional autonomy to its Kurdish minority would be only the prelude to future demands for secession.

Another troublesome problem is what provisions should be made for minorities *within* the territorial homeland claimed by an ethnic community. Many of these minorities believe their interests are overlooked or deliberately thwarted by the dominant group in federalized units. The Indian peoples, Cree and Mohawk, in Quebec have no interest in the French language and culture and believe their interests would be better served by the central government in Ottawa than by the provincial government of Quebec; thus, they are unalterably opposed to independence for Quebec. Christian minorities in the Muslim-dominated states of northern Nigeria oppose the introduction of Islamic criminal law, and for their opposition they have been victimized by mob violence. The Nepali minority in northwestern Bengal has no interest in Bengali, the majority language in the state of West Bengal. They demand the right to educate their children in their own language. Matters of this sort can be negotiated and compromised, usually by awarding autonomy to these minorities within minorities, but all too often the dominant ethnic community in what they regard as their homeland is reluctant to recognize the rights of minorities in their midst. Most of the Québécois who assert, in the name of self-determination, their right to secede from Canada are not prepared to grant the Cree nation, which occupies a large swath of territory in the north of the province, the equivalent right to secede from Quebec.

Consociationalism

Consociation, as a process of power-sharing, applies mostly in situations where ethnic communities are so intermixed in their settlement patterns that federal arrangements are impossible. Consociation means that two or more ethnic communities come together and agree, through their leadership, to mutually recognize the rights and interests of one another and to share in operating their common government according to an agreed set of rules and understandings. The underlying premise is that a consensual political system is possible among peoples who do not share a common culture or speak a common language.

The leading student and advocate of consociational politics has been Professor Arend Lijphart.[5] While consociational regimes must be anchored in a set of cooperative dispositions and mutual respect among the leaders of the component communities, there are four basic principles, according to Lijphart, that underlie any successful consociational system. These are: (1) the government executive must be based on a *grand coalition* or cartel in which the leaders of all the component ethnic communities are represented and participate, and in which they can promote their group interests, while bargaining out their differences in order to achieve consensual decisions. The bargaining should occur in camera, so that differences should not be allowed to stir up the mass of their constituents and make the necessary compromises more difficult to reach and to implement. (2) Minorities must retain the *right to veto* decisions which, in the judgment of their leaders, threatens one of their vital interests. This provision, which may retard the pace of decision-making and result in occasional deadlocks, provides iron-clad assurance to minorities that their basic rights and interests can be effectively protected. (3) *Proportionality* in all aspects of government insures that each community will be represented in all the organs of the state according to their share in the total population, that positions in the civil and military agencies will be similarly allocated, and so will the resources, facilities, and services provided by the state. Proportionality implies the assurance of fair and equitable treatment for all ethnic groups. (4) *Internal autonomy* for all communities, reserving for their own institutions control of matters that are of particular concern to their maintenance, such as education of their children in their ancestral language and the operation and control of their separate religious and cultural institutions. Consociational autonomy is not territorial, it is instead institutional, with government agreeing not to interfere in this aspect of self-management.

Lijphart also identifies some conditions that are not essential, but which facilitate the operation of consociational systems, including publics that are inclined to defer to their leadership, a relatively small territory, and prior experience of cooperation and good will among the leadership.

Consociational theory proved to be highly attractive to students of democratic government, since it asserted that democratic government is possible even in culturally divided societies.[6] Lijphart and his followers identified several such cases, including Belgium, Malaysia, and Lebanon, as well as others that were not fully consociational but included several power-sharing features. Nevertheless, consociational theory drew a substantial body of criticism. Some held that it froze ethnic categories into rigid molds, denying individuals the right to alter their ethnic affiliation or transform their identities in the direction of a non-ethnic society. Others argued that in postulating deferential publics, it was anti-democratic because of its emphasis on the necessity of leadership control; thus, it is entirely unsuited to the democratizing trends of the late twentieth century. It tended to overlook instances where arrangements agreed to by the leadership were rejected by the majority of their constituents, and many cases where the rank and file proved to be more moderate in their judgments than their leaders. Still others contended that consociationalism is implemented by constraints on leadership such as mutual vetoes, rather than by offering incentives for leaders to behave moderately toward other ethnic communities.

Perhaps the most damaging critique of consociationalism has been based on the strong possibility of outbidding. Consociational bargaining in a grand coalition requires leaders to compromise the claims or demands of their followers in order to reach agreements with their colleagues representing their ethnic partners. Such compromises inevitably provoke ambitious politicians in any ethnic community who are not part of the prevailing power structure to attempt to build their own constituencies by championing the more militant demands of their fellow ethnics, while insisting that the current moderate leaders have "sold out" the legitimate interests of their people. Moderates on both sides then face the unwelcome choice of backing away from their compromises or losing the support of important segments of their community. As moderates retreat from their compromises and move toward more extreme positions in order to protect their political flanks, compromises which are necessary for the functioning of consociational systems become harder and harder to achieve. Thus, the process of outbidding is likely to doom consociational experiments to failure and further to demonstrate that this form of power-sharing is impossible in democratic political systems.[7] A number of recent experiences demonstrate the iron logic of the outbidding process, including the collapse of the power-sharing Sunningdale compromise in Northern Ireland in 1973 negotiated by moderates among Catholics and Protestants under the auspices of the governments of Great Britain and the Republic of Ireland. In the face of violent, intractable opposition by the Irish Republican Army on the Catholic side and militant Protestant unionists on the other, this effort had to be abandoned.

Though full-blown consociational regimes have been few in number and some have not long survived, consociational elements are present whenever power-sharing solutions are proposed for the management of ethnic conflict and where members of ethnic communities are inextricably mixed. The 1995 Dayton accords for ending the bloody conflict in Bosnia envisioned a power-sharing executive in which the three communities – Serbs, Croats, and Muslims – would be equitably represented. A similar arrangement, the Good Friday agreement, was agreed to for Northern Ireland in 1998 as the outcome of mediation by former US Senator George Mitchell and was actually implemented. (It was later subjected to intense strain by the unwillingness of the IRA to surrender its weapons.) International mediators continue to search for power-sharing arrangements that might finally settle the long standoff in Cyprus between Greek and Turkish Cypriots and reunify the country which, for three decades, has been split into two sectors and governed by an armistice supervised by a UN peacekeeping force. Consociational schemes have been proposed for managing the conflict between Hutu and Tutsi in Rwanda and Burundi. In post-apartheid South Africa, however, consociational democracy, advocated for that country by Lijphart and supported by the Afrikaner and Zulu leaderships, was rejected by the African National Congress and its allies as a reversion to tribalism and a source of division and conflict within African society. They insisted instead on a non-racial majoritarian democracy.

Federalism and consociationalism in combination

Federal and federal-like arrangements can be effective when ethnic communities are territorially concentrated in their homelands and complete separation is either undesirable or unfeasible. Yet, this leaves aside the question of their representation in the central government which is likely to retain considerable powers, such as foreign affairs, national defense, macroeconomic policy, and resource allocations that are important to ethnic communities. This is the case in Belgium, once a unitary state dominated by French-speaking Walloons which, since World War II, has undergone a complex process of regionalization under which many of the powers and functions of government have been devolved to its Walloon region in the south and its Flemish region in the north, plus the French-majority capital enclave of Brussels. But in order to maintain parity between Flemings and Walloons in the central government, it is now required that half the ministers be French-speakers and half Flemish-speakers, while the prime minister may be either. Positions in the civil service must be equitably distributed between the two communities, maintaining the principle of parity even though Flemings now outnumber Walloons. In Canada, following the principle of rough proportionality, three of the nine Supreme Court justices must be French-speakers, the Ottawa civil service strives for balanced participation, French-speakers must be present in any national cabinet, and serious candidates for the office of prime minister must be competent to function in both official languages.

At the time of writing (2002–3), negotiations are in progress, under Norwegian auspices, to settle the long and bloody civil war between Tamils and Sinhalese in Sri Lanka.

Any successful outcome must include federal-like features, where Tamil-majority areas will be granted considerable autonomy and self-rule, functioning in the Tamil language. (Which areas are to be included in this Tamil region are at the moment in dispute, as well as the rights of non-Tamils within the Tamil majority areas.) It is likely that the Tamil negotiators will demand some guaranteed representation in the central government not only to provide jobs for their constituents, but also to insure that in the executive and judicial agencies of the state Tamil interests will be represented. They may also demand that the Tamil language be granted official status both in the Tamil region and in the central government. These consociational elements will be difficult pills for Sinhalese nationalists to swallow and it may be that negotiations will be stalled even more on these consociational demands than on the question of regional boundaries.

Similarly any settlement of the protracted and sanguinary civil war in Sudan between the Arab-Muslim north and the Christian-pagan south would involve both territorial autonomy for the south and a significant share of participation and division of oil revenues in the central government, a consociational provision that the Arab-Muslim regime in the north might not be willing to accept. The Indian federal system, which provides regional autonomy for its major ethnic communities, has avoided demands for consociational participation in the center, because the All-India services are already broadly representative. There was, however, a significant demand to reduce the notable overrepresentation of a few ethnic groups in the Indian military services, a residue of the British colonial policy of staffing the military with members of a few designated "martial races" whose absolute loyalty the British raj believed they could count on. These included Sikhs, Rajputs, Pathans, and Gurkhas. At the time of Independence, Sikhs who comprised a mere 2 percent of the population constituted 25 percent of the officer corps. It became clear that in a democratic state no institution of government, especially one as powerful and prestigious as the national army, could continue to be so unrepresentative of India's diverse population. The government solved this problem by declaring all of India's ethnic communities to be martial races with distinguished military traditions. A policy of broader recruitment has been implemented to insure that the military at all ranks is broadly representative of the national society. This policy became especially urgent after Prime Minister Indira Gandhi was assassinated by her Sikh bodyguard.

Transitions

Ethnic relations are a dynamic phenomenon. They evolve with changes in the relative numerical and economic strength, with the mobilization and cohesiveness of the ethnic communities, with the behavior of government, and with external forces that affect their relationships. From its establishment in 1830, French-speaking Walloons dominated the Belgian state.[8] In education, economic development, and cultural self-confidence they were far superior to the mostly peasant, poor, undereducated, Dutch-speaking Flemings. "French in the parlor, Flemish in the kitchen" was a popular slogan that epitomized this relationship. Members of the Flemish bourgeoisie learned French, but few Walloons bothered to learn Flemish. Gradually, however, Flemings were able to improve their educational levels, and after World War II to attract substantial foreign investment in new industries to their region, capitalizing on the excellent port and transport facilities anchored in the harbor of Antwerp which became a gateway to the emerging European Economic Community, forerunner of the European Union. Their population increased, while that of their Walloon compatriots stagnated; their industrial base expanded while the older nineteenth-century industry in Wallonia became obsolescent. As their educational levels rose along with their standards of living, their self-confidence grew and their political organizations became more effective to the point that they were no longer willing to accept a subordinate status within the Belgian state. They vigorously promoted their demand that in the Flemish majority areas of the country the Flemish language and Flemish culture must prevail. As an example, the renowned French-speaking Pontifical University of Louvain located in a Flemish-speaking area was transformed into the Flemish-speaking University of Leuven, while a new French-speaking institution, Louvain-la-Neuve was established in Wallonia. The French-speaking national capital, Brussels, is an enclave within the Flemish-speaking region. Flemish politicians have been insisting that its suburbs, inhabited mostly by French-speakers who work in Brussels, conduct their public services, including schooling, entirely in Flemish. In the central government in Brussels, equality prevails between the two communities in the distribution of cabinet posts and civil service positions. Any institutional reform requires a double majority of both French-speakers and Flemish-speakers. Yet, most of the functions of government have been devolved from the central government to the unilingual regional authorities, so that Belgium, in the language of its 1993 constitution, has been formally transformed into a "federal monarchy."[9]

From political and cultural domination by French-speakers in a centralized unitary state, the relationship of the ethnic communities has been transformed into a pattern of formal equality; but since Flemings now outnumber Walloons and enjoy a stronger economic base, the balance has tipped in their favor. While ethnic competition in this small country has been intense, it has followed democratic procedures and remained non-violent.

Northern Ireland, whose leader once boasted of "a Protestant state for a Protestant people," has been moving with fits and starts toward a new pattern of power-sharing between Protestants and Catholics. The Catholic share of the population has increased and Catholics have mobilized to demand equality of treatment, including a fringe faction (the Irish Republican Army) that for more than three decades has brought terrorist tactics to this region and evoked a terrorist response from militant Protestants who have difficulty accepting the diminution of their privileged position. The Castilian domination in Spain that suppressed all expressions of ethnic diversity during the long Franco dictatorship has yielded to a general pattern of regional autonomy, especially in Catalonia and the Basque country, but also in Galicia and Andalusia under the successor democratic state. The settlement that is being negotiated in Sri Lanka would transform that state from one of Sinhalese domination to a power-sharing relationship under which the Tamil minority would be in effective control over their region.

The residents of the Caribbean islands of Trinidad and Tobago enjoy a high standard of living due to royalties from their petroleum deposits. Its two main ethnic communities, about equal in number, 40 percent each, are Afro-Trinidadians or Creoles, descendants of former slaves, and Indo-Trinidadians, descendants of indentured laborers from the subcontinent. For three decades following independence from Britain in 1962, Afro-Trinidadians dominated the country's politics, arguing that they comprised the nation and that others are late arrivals who should strive to acculturate to the Creole way of life.[10] Control of government meant that they tilted government services toward their Afro-Trinidadian constituents. Their political vehicle was the People's National Movement (PNM). Indo-Trinidadians have been campaigning to redefine the content of Trinidadian nationality to include Indian-derived culture as a legitimate and equal component of the national identity.

In 1992, however, the unthinkable occurred as the Indo-Trinidadian United National Congress (UNC) won a narrow majority in the Parliament. For the first time Indo-Trinidadians formed the government, a transformation in the structure of Trinidadian politics. Politics in Trinidad is now a contest between two equal ethnic parties, the winner depending on its ability to get its supporters to the polls and to gain the backing of persons from the smaller minority communities, Chinese, White, and mixed race. Though the situation is amenable to consociational power-sharing, so that both ethnic groups would participate in decision-making roles in government, the political leadership has retained their winner-take-all legacy of the British parliamentary system. During their term of office, only one of the country's major ethnic communities is in power, the other comprises the official opposition and is excluded from decision-making roles in government.

The cases that I have cited all involve transitions from ethnic domination to some form of power-sharing through federalized or consociational methods. But there are other patterns as well. From its independence in 1957 until 1969 Malaysia's government operated as a consociational-type system in which non-Malay participants in government exercised real power, including the ability to block or attenuate measures that negatively affected their constituents. When in

1967 Malay militants demanded that the constitutional status of Malay as the national language be enforced, a tense and potentially explosive confrontation was defused when the Malay leadership yielded to demands from their non-Malay partners to attenuate the enforcement of this provision, allowing non-Malays more time to learn the Malay language, and "liberal" use of English in parliamentary debates. After the riots of May 1969, Malays assumed firm control of government, brushing aside objections from their erstwhile non-Malay partners and began to implement economic, educational, and cultural policies that their non-Malay associates could not agree to, but were forced to accept. Malays were calling the shots and non-Malays who opted to participate as junior partners in government retained a voice, but no longer a veto, over measures that their constituents regarded as discriminatory. This was a transition from power-sharing to Malay domination.

With the sudden collapse of the Soviet Union in 1989 and the reemergence of the Baltic republics, Estonia, Latvia, and Lithuania, as independent states, Russians in these countries became endangered minorities. Under Soviet rule, they had been secure, belonging to the dominant community, speaking the more prestigious language, participating in the more prestigious culture, holding the more remunerative jobs, entitled to the best amenities. With little warning, they awakened one day as foreigners, unable to speak the new national language, shorn of political support, suspected of disloyalty to the new governments, holding their jobs, housing, and other amenities at the sufferance of a hostile indigenous majority. They were trapped in these countries, since there were no jobs or housing in Russia that they could return to. From membership in the dominant community, they had been transformed into a powerless and vulnerable minority. The language and other civil rights that were eventually conceded to them they owed to the good offices of the Commissioner on Minority Affairs of the European Organization for Security and Cooperation (OSCE) and to the European Union, which these three states are eager to join and which requires decent treatment of minorities as a condition for admission.

These are examples of the volatility of interethnic relationships. Even as apparently rigid as race relations appeared to be in apartheid South Africa, suddenly and unexpectedly they were reversed with the abandonment of the apartheid state and the emergence of a democratic, non-racial polity in South Africa. Africans and other non-Whites were empowered politically and legally, a major transformation, though economic assets and professional and managerial positions remained mostly in the hands of the better-educated and better-endowed White minority.

Some proposed transitions, though favored by majorities among the concerned ethnic communities, encounter resistance from determined minority factions who are prepared to resort to violence to prevent the negotiated compromises from being implemented. When this occurs, those who negotiated the new arrangements must be willing to use force against the ultras in their own community, a very painful choice which is likely to cost them domestic support, or witness the destruction of their negotiated agreement and a reversion to armed conflict.

In December 1921, after five years of brutal warfare, of ambushes and reprisals, the leadership of the Irish insurrection and the British government arrived at an agreement that provided for effective Irish independence, an Irish Free State, the long-sought goal of Irish nationalism. There were two conditions, however: that the Free State remain a dominion of the United Kingdom, its office-holders swearing allegiance to the British crown, and that the six northern counties with their Protestant majorities were to be detached from the Free State and remain part of the United Kingdom. The ultras in the Irish Republican Army refused to accept these conditions. The Provisional Government under its legendary leader, Michael Collins, decided, nonetheless, to proceed with the agreement as a historic achievement that would bring peace to Ireland and as the best deal that was possible under the circumstances. The result was a bloody civil war between the majority and minority Irish factions that was eventually won by the Provisional Government, which then proceeded to implement the Free State agreement. The Provisional Government had to be willing to resort to force against a faction of their own people, including many of their former comrades-in-arms, in order to implement the agreement. Similarly, if Israel and Palestine are to achieve a negotiated compromise and *modus vivendi*, both the Palestine Authority and the Government of Israel must be prepared to use force against their own extremists, the Islamic Hamas and the religious and secular advocates of a Greater Israel, who are willing to resort to violence, including terrorist methods, to thwart any compromise settlement and whose incompatible goals make any agreement impossible. The lesson here is that some beneficial changes which enjoy majority support may have to be enforced coercively against internal opposition by uncompromising minority factions.

Non-formal power-sharing

Federalism and consociationalism are formalized structures of government that institutionalize the norms and processes of power-sharing, imparting robustness and staying power to what otherwise might be fragile undertakings. Some observers have argued that, in addition, there are non-formal practices that serve the same purpose. They point to recent examples of governments that take care to insure that key positions are awarded to members of all significant ethnic communities, so that none will feel left out, while facilities and services provided by the state are equitably distributed. Sensitivity to ethnic interests and concerns by political leaders, they argue, serves the same purpose as more formal systems of power-sharing, citing such African examples as Tanzania, the Ivory Coast, and Kenya.[11]

A difficulty with this approach is its dependence on the sensitivity, skill, and judgment of individual political leaders. Leadership failure may fatally undermine these informal relationships and understandings, with no institutional back-up to buffer them. This was the sad experience of the Ivory Coast, one of the cases cited in support of this proposition. Felix Houphouet-Boigny, during his long tenure as president, had been reasonably successful in distributing positions and facilities in ways that appeared to satisfy his several ethnic constituencies. His successors had no such luck. In 2002 an insurrection broke out among Muslim ethnic communities in the underdeveloped northern provinces, leading to a full-scale civil war in what had been touted as one of the most suc-

cessful African examples of economic and political development. In the absence of institutional support, these informal
power-sharing arrangements proved too fragile to survive a
serious challenge.

Conclusion

The main theme of this chapter is that relations between
ethnic communities within the same political space need not
be characterized by domination and subordination, with the
imminence of violence that is inherent in coerced inequality.
Nor need they result in separation. Power-sharing through
federal or consociational institutions affords more equitable
and consensual alternatives. They provide the framework and
the processes that enable peoples with different cultures to
coexist peacefully under the same political authority. Conflict
is not eliminated, as contending parties and their factions
remain free to promote their interests vigorously through
channels provided by federal or consociational systems.
Politics in consociational Belgium during the past thirty years
have seldom been free of harsh controversy over ethnic interests, and India has witnessed ethnic-based violence, including
the assassination of two prime ministers, that its federal institutions were unable to avert. The relevant question is whether
the alternatives – separation or domination – would have
yielded greater security, stability, and satisfaction to members
of these ethnic communities. The management of power-
sharing institutions that require brokering, negotiation, and
conciliation of legitimate competing demands calls for higher
levels of political skill than the regulation of relations
between stronger and weaker. The brutal, iron-fisted Franco
dictatorship in Spain required far fewer political skills than
its democratic successor, which has initiated and managed
federal-like power-sharing arrangements with its Catalan,
Basque, and other regional minorities. Even when such skills
are not readily available, federal or consociational institutions that compel political give-and-take may compensate for
their absence.

8
Patterns of Pluralism III: Integration

Ethnic pluralism and liberal individualism

Integration is the application of the principles of liberal individualism to ethnic relations. In liberal thought there is no place for ethnic or cultural diversity. Liberalism is premised on the belief that individuals, not groups, are the appropriate unit of value in public affairs, that all individuals regardless of ethnic origin, racial features, or religious beliefs should be equal before the law, that any form of preference or discrimination based on ethnicity, race, or religion is illegitimate, and that there can be no official recognition of ethnic identities or ethnic differences. All citizens by birth or naturalization are endowed with equal rights and responsibilities as individuals in the indivisible nation. The discomfort of many western social scientists with ethnicity as a social and political phenomenon, as discussed in chapter 2, can be traced to their commitment to liberal individualism as the sole legitimate basis for democratic societies. They fear that ethnic solidarity places the group above the individual and compromises individual freedom. A colleague once reported to me that he liked my earlier book on ethnic politics, but "detested" the subject.[1]

A fine line separates policies of assimilation, described in chapter 6 as a form of domination, and integration. In both cases the intended outcome is a common culture and national society. Assimilation, however, implies that newcomers as well as indigenous minorities are to be absorbed by the host society without leaving any mark on that society. Integration, by contrast, is closer to the melting pot metaphor, implying that each wave of new arrivals makes its unique contribution to the ever-evolving whole. Elements of ethnic cultures survive, but these are shared by others, while all participate in an increasingly common culture and mixed society.

The French version of assimilation is premised on an established French culture whose content is fixed by public authority, including the prestigious French Academy. This standardized culture is inculcated by a highly centralized and uniform system of compulsory public education, mass media that adhere to the established rules, and until recently universal compulsory military service. This becomes the norm, the mainstream to which both indigenous minorities (Breton, Basque, Burgundian) and later arrivals are expected to adapt and conform through education, participation, and eventual intermarriage, but not to contribute. This mainstream culture provides opportunities for newcomers and their offsprings to participate in the institutions of French society and achieve social mobility, so that individuals of Spanish, Polish, and Jewish backgrounds may become authoritative critics of the French literary classics, French patriots, members of the Parliament and of the French Academy, and speak with pride of "our ancestors, the Gauls." The goal of this nation-building strategy is to transform native minorities and immigrants into Frenchmen. As it absorbs newcomers, France positively frowns on and resists expressions of ethnic diversity, as in the controversy over headscarves for Muslim schoolgirls, and efforts to discourage the use of "franglais" (English words such as "weekend" and "e-mail").

The United States, as an integrationist system, is prepared to tolerate greater cultural and social diversity and to absorb elements of exotic cultures as well as individuals – one only has to think of the popularity of ethnic foods such as tacos, bagels, sushi, and pizza. In integrated states, according to liberal thought, one ethnic group cannot dominate others, nor is ethnic power-sharing possible, since it is only individuals that count. Yet, there is a charter people who were there first and who continue to claim pride of place, at least informally. Their culture, especially their language – Portuguese in Brazil, English in the United States – becomes the norm for communication, the mainstream which later arrivals are expected to learn and to use. It is taught in public schools, propagated by the mass media, and employed at work and in the marketplace.

While there can be no formal or official recognition of ethnic differences, ethnic-based organizations are permitted to function on a voluntary basis. Individuals may contribute or not contribute, and participate or not participate in ethnic cultural, educational, recreational, mutual assistance, or defense organizations entirely as a matter of personal choice. Ethnic associations exist primarily to maintain the inherited culture, to facilitate adjustment to the new environment, and to provide fellowship through such institutions as schools, churches, publications, sporting groups, youth and women's associations, and fraternal lodges. Since they deploy no coercive resources, they must rely on the incentives and informal sanctions they can muster to retain the interest of their members. With each passing generation this becomes more problematical, as the pressures of mainstream culture, mainstream education, occupational and residential mobility, and intermarriage attenuate the bonds that link individuals to their ethnic heritage.[2] The once proud and powerful German-American community, the largest ethnic group in the United States, with its vigorous and extensive network of cultural, recreational, and sports organizations and publications was virtually destroyed during World War I when all things German were stigmatized as unpatriotic. *Deutschtum-in-Amerika* never recovered, as German-Americans were quickly absorbed into the mainstream. The New York-based Yiddish language *Daily Forward* which flourished before World War II with a daily circulation exceeding 200,000, which owned its own building and operated its own radio station, struggles today to survive as a weekly, half in English, half in Yiddish, with barely a tenth of its former readership. More than half of ethnic Japanese in the United States now marry outside their ethnic community. The offsprings of these mixed marriages are likely to identify with neither of their parents' backgrounds, but to function entirely within the framework of the mainstream. Persons of German, Italian,

Puerto Rican, and Jewish extraction join their Irish friends and neighbors participating in the annual St Patrick's Day festivities in New York.

In addition to mutual assistance and the maintenance of culture and community, ethnic associations may perform a political function, serving as public relations vehicles or interest groups on behalf of their ethnic community. Thus, the Italian Sons and Daughters of America strives to overcome the identification of Italian-Americans with organized crime, and the Arab-American Anti-Defamation League works to counteract discrimination against their constituents and the association of Middle Easterners with subversive activities. They may also raise funds to support the political campaigns of their compatriots, collect contributions for charitable purposes in their country of origin, and attempt to influence the nation's foreign policy on behalf of the old country. Tamils in Britain and Canada raise funds to support the Tamil insurrection in Sri Lanka, Chinese in Hawaii financed the Chinese republican rebellion in 1911, and German-Americans strove to prevent the United States from entering World War I on the side of the Allies. Disputes over such political issues often are the occasion for factionalism within ethnic communities, as the Chinese diaspora in Southeast Asia was split for many years over support for the Kuomintang regime on Taiwan or the communist government on the mainland.

The more prestigious the receiving culture, the more powerful its government and economy, the more incentives it provides for outsiders to identify with it and join the mainstream. The cultural prestige, economic strength, and military power of the United States provide such incentives to individuals from a variety of backgrounds. Chinese immigrants in the United States, and especially their children, willingly integrate culturally and many pass socially into its mainstream. By contrast, Chinese, who consider themselves products of one of the world's high cultures, find limited incentives to abandon their birthright and integrate into Indonesian society which, in their eyes, lacks cultural prestige, economic strength, and political power. The propensity to integrate is, in part, a prudential calculation, in part – as the behavior of Muslim immigrants in France demonstrates – a matter of principle and pride.

Two dimensions of integration

There are two dimensions of integration, the cultural and the social. Cultural integration involves the adoption, for purposes of everyday communication, of the mainstream language and of mainstream dress, cuisine, popular entertainment, and lifestyles. Social integration entails living in mixed neighborhoods, participating in mainstream institutions such as churches and social clubs, and eventual intermarriage. Cultural integration normally precedes the social by as much as several generations and individuals may spend their lifetime culturally but not socially integrated.

The French pattern of cultural and social assimilation, in which the substance of the mainstream remains rigid and unchanging and minorities are expected to do all the adjusting and disappear into mainstream society has been attempted by others. Such policies as Arabization, Russification, and Sinicization have been implemented with the goal of absorbing minorities without any changes in the mainstream culture or social structure of the dominant ethnic group. All adjusting is to be done by the minorities. The Thai government's policy has been to absorb all minorities, indigenous and immigrant, into the culture of central Thailand, a recent exception being its toleration of Malay-Muslim culture in its southern provinces bordering Malaysia.

The American pattern of creating a nation from successive waves of immigrants has reflected the more decentralized and pluralistic structure of American society and government. Voluntary ethnic associations have been tolerated as a useful stage of immigrant adjustment to their adopted country, confident that Americanization will occur in the natural course of events. The success of this policy has been confirmed by the mobilization of energies and support for American participation in both world wars and by the spontaneous expressions of national sentiment following the terrorist attacks of September 2001. America's nationalism is not based on an ethnic model. It can best be described as civic nationalism, based on love of country and commitment to a common set of political ideals, governmental institutions, and aspiration to a common way of life.

Societies committed to integration regard diversity as individual traits, rather than as attributes of communal solidarity. Barriers to social intercourse are lowered and taboos against intermarriage are eroded. Though some offsprings of mixed marriages choose to identify with and participate in the community of one of their parents, the majority pass into the national mainstream, leaving their parents' communities behind. After a few generations, and in the absence of reenforcement through immigration, ethnic communities become depleted, their institutions can no longer be supported, and the community struggles to survive through the dedication of a core of loyalists, reduced increasingly to nostalgia and the recounting of history. Some members of the mainstream become curious about their roots, but this involves little change in their current mainstream lifestyle. Such has been the experience of Dutch, Scottish, Swedish, French, and Czech communities in the United States and others are following in their wake.

Where ethnic communities are coterminous with a distinctive religious inheritance, as among Greeks, Armenians, Jews, and Sikhs, communal solidarity is strengthened and the process of integration is retarded, but not blocked. The same is true when fellow ethnics in their erstwhile homeland are threatened, as with Irish nationalists in Northern Ireland, Jews in Israel, and Tamils in Sri Lanka. The fact that the majority of young Jews in the United States now marry outside the faith demonstrates the powerful incentives and attractiveness of integrative behavior in that environment. The higher the levels of education and of social and occupational mobility, the more individuals are prone to leave their ethnic community behind. The remnants of several groups manage to survive as viable entities – for example the Amish, Hasidic Jews, Navajos, and other Indian nations – successfully resisting the appeal of the mainstream. Continuing immigration replenishes the ranks of Puerto Rican, Mexican, and Dominican communities, even as large numbers of their second and third generation intermarry and pass into the mainstream. The principal exception is African-Americans, whose social integration in large numbers is blocked by persistent prejudice.

The American mainstream culture is continuously evolving and expanding, incorporating elements from recent immigrant communities.[3] Jewish humor (Jack Benny, Woody Allen, Seinfeld), Italian cuisine (espresso, pizza, pasta), German education (kindergarten, research universities), and African-American music (spirituals, jazz, rap) have been incorporated into mainstream culture. There are powerful pressures on persons of all backgrounds to conform to the prevailing version of mainstream culture. As the children of immigrants become culturally integrated, they prepare the way for their social integration, to be accepted as neighbors, friends, and marriage partners. Throughout this process of culture change and social absorption, some older elements of the mainstream culture have remained quite stable and changed very slowly. These themes include the English language, the work ethic, individualism, patriotism, religious identification, ambivalence about government, and the propensity to organize for common causes; these would be readily recognized by nineteenth-century Americans.

Thus, the American concept of the mainstream differs from the French assimilationist goal of abandoning previous identities in favor of conforming to a standard Paris-based French model of the good citizen. The emergent American culture is believed to be enriched by contributions from its diverse citizenry so that the American version of the English language incorporates elements derived from its ethnic mix (chutzpah, gourmet, numero uno), and its panoply of heroes expands on the Anglo-Saxon Protestant roots of its Founding Fathers to include Martin Luther King, Pulaski, Columbus, and Eisenhower. The rich array of ethnic associations that thrive in the United States comprise important elements of the civil society. With generational succession these associations become less and less viable as membership declines, participation assumes a lesser role in the daily routines of their members, and social and geographic mobility deplete ethnic neighborhoods. The author who challenged the ideology of an American mainstream by celebrating the "unmeltable ethnics" in the 1970s has been proved simply wrong.[4]

Brazil has welcomed immigrants to help develop and populate that vast territory and to achieve its manifest destiny as a great power. Germans, Italians, Jews, and Japanese have been integrated into this Portuguese-speaking culture and together they comprise a larger share of the national population than persons of Portuguese origin. Yet, despite the carefully nurtured myth that racial stratification has been banished, the descendants of slavery which was abolished as recently as 1888 continue, as described in chapter 6, to occupy subordinate positions in all dimensions of Brazilian society. Brazil's official integrationist ideology holds for immigrants from Europe and Asia, but not for its large Afro-Brazilian and mixed-race minorities, who are integrated officially but remain outside the pale.

During its long struggle for racial equality, the South African National Congress (ANC) adhered rigorously to its goal of a non-racial, egalitarian, democratic state and society. It resisted the call for militant Black separatism from its Pan-Africanist opposition ("one settler, one bullet") and for emphasis on ethnic autonomy and separatism from Zulu and other tribal spokespersons, a position fostered by the tribal homelands and "separate development" policies of the former Afrikaner leadership. Now that they hold office, the ANC leadership is confronted with the challenge of realizing in practice their goal of non-racial democracy. Politically the integrationist goal has been largely achieved as the ANC has won elections and rules in the national capital and 8 of the 10 provincial governments. But, socially, South Africa remains a highly pluralistic society. The constitution of 1994 recognizes 11 languages as official languages, their adherents entitled, where practicable, to education and other public services in their own medium. These include 2 European languages, English and Afrikaans, and 9 African languages, of which Xhosa, Tswana, Zulu, and Sotho each claim more than 5 million speakers. Economically, the gap between Whites and Blacks remains very large in the ownership of assets, professional and managerial positions, living standards, educational achievement, and similar indices of socio-economic attainment. De facto segregation remains the reality in public schools, because of the persistence of separate residential neighborhoods. As long as class differences re-enforce ethnic differences, in South Africa as elsewhere, social segregation will persist and these differences will inevitably be reflected in political behavior. Until these economic and social gaps have been substantially reduced, the ANC's goal of non-racial integration will remain elusive, despite the dramatic progress that has been realized at the political level.[5]

As a rule, immigration flows, legally and illegally, to countries that enjoy economic prosperity and provide job opportunities for people from countries that lack such opportunities. Even countries such as Japan, which as a matter of public policy discourage immigration, nevertheless tolerate, *sub rosa*, large numbers of immigrants because of the exigent need of employers for cheap labor to perform the dirty, heavy, dangerous, low-wage, unskilled tasks that local people disdain. Notwithstanding the extended, if illegal, presence of many thousands of foreign workers, Japan has evaded the question of their status, hoping apparently that the problem will go away. Third and fourth generation members of the Korean minority, Japan's largest, continue to be treated as resident foreigners, denied the opportunity to naturalize or to integrate into Japanese society. The oil-rich Persian Gulf states deal with their need for large numbers of foreign workers, some performing highly skilled tasks, by hiring them on a contract basis, stipulating that they will be required to return home when their contracts have expired. Permanent residence and citizenship are out of the question. When Iraq invaded Kuwait in 1991 and the PLO announced its support for Iraq, the Kuwaiti government summarily expelled its 10,000 resident Palestinians, many of whom had lived in Kuwait for decades and held responsible professional and technical positions.

In those countries where naturalization is possible and persons locally born can qualify for citizenship, the pluralism resulting from immigration is attenuated and gradually disappears in three or four generations as the progeny of immigrants are absorbed into the national mainstream. An example is the heavily industrialized Pittsburgh region which attracted large numbers of European immigrants from many ethnic backgrounds during the late nineteenth and early twentieth centuries. "The ethnic enclaves that are Pittsburgh's colorful quilt of European nationalities still exist, but their intensity fades with every decade . . . The number of ethnic churches and clubs has dwindled. Between the national censuses of 1990 and 2000 the percentage of local residents counting themselves among the European immigrant groups that settled in the Pittsburgh region declined for nearly all nationalities . . . ," including the largest, Germans, Irish, Italians, and Poles. In the words of a local Polish-speaking priest, "when you have intermarriage and people moving out to the suburbs, everything changes. . . ." In his parish, persons of Polish ancestry declined by one-third between 1990 and 2000.[6] All have acculturated to the American mainstream and speak English in their homes.

Where the flow of immigrants continues, as with Mexicans and Caribbean peoples into the United States, their diasporas are renewed with fresh recruits. Many of the newcomers remain poorly integrated into mainstream society and, as economic migrants, look forward to eventually returning home. The diaspora's links with the old country are reinforced by these new arrivals, their separate institutions are sustained, and the pluralism continues, even though many offsprings of earlier arrivals, especially those who have achieved higher education and social mobility, loosen their links with the diaspora as they are absorbed into the mainstream.

The implications of the rapid and virtually uncontrolled flow of immigrants into the United States during the past quarter century, much of it illegal, has been the subject of intense controversy. As 40 percent of the total is from neighboring Mexico, opponents of the current trend fear that unless the flow of illegals is curbed, the effect will be an "alien nation" within the United States, complete with its own cultural and social institutions, continuously renewed by fresh arrivals, creating a large, unintegrated, permanent minority.[7] Those who do not share this fear argue that members of the current wave of Latin American immigrants, like their predecessors from Europe, will continue to acculturate and integrate into the English-speaking mainstream. Unlimited immigration is supported politically by a coalition of employers seeking sources of low-wage, non-union labor; by civil libertarians convinced that freedom of movement is a human right; and by the increasingly influential Hispanic voting bloc that is poised to punish at the polls any political party advocating restrictions on immigration.

Persistent barriers to integration

The process of integration is not always as smooth and certain as the previous paragraphs might have suggested. The two principal obstacles are resistance from the receiving society and resistance within the body of immigrants.

An important source of resistance in receiving societies stems from racial differences, especially from the rejection of Africans and other peoples of color in many White societies.[8] Despite rapid acculturation and some intermarriage, the barriers erected by White racism continue to impede integration, especially in Europe and North America and, to a lesser extent, in Latin America as well. The majority of Blacks, it appears, would be content to be treated as individuals, free to integrate into the mainstream. This was the expectation of many students of social pluralism; they expected that following the elimination of official discrimination in the United States, African-Americans would follow the pattern of European immigrants, achieve economic and social mobility, intermarry, and be gradually integrated into the mainstream. This, however, has failed to occur either in North America or Europe. In some sectors of the economy, such as professional athletics, the military, the entertainment industry, and higher education, a significant measure of integration has been achieved; elsewhere and especially in social relationships and residential patterns, rejection and segregation persist.

As a result, White hostility and rejection have produced a separatist reaction among many African-Americans, expressed in such movements as Black is Beautiful and rejection by a substantial minority of inherited Christian beliefs and associations by embracing the Muslim faith – for example, the Nation of Islam. African-Americans who are citizens by birth and English-speaking are slower to integrate – or be allowed to integrate – socially than immigrants from Asia and Latin America who have arrived recently with no English at all. A substantial majority of Whites, especially in the South, now support the Republican Party, reversing in many cases the political identity of generations of their forebears, because that party is considered less sympathetic to the claims of the African-American minority than the Democrats, who now attract the great majority of Black voters. Despite legislation and judicial decisions banning racial discrimination in voting, housing, education, employment, and public facilities, and despite the emergence of a substantial Black middle class, informal racism persists as a popular sentiment, impeding the process of integration.

The source of resistance to integration may originate also within immigrant communities. Many Muslim immigrants from North Africa do not aspire to become Frenchmen, since this, they fear, would force them to compromise their religious faith and their culture. They have come to France, they say, for economic reasons, not to join the French polity or embrace its infidel culture. Unlike Jewish immigrants who were happy to be accepted as Frenchmen, they have not (yet?) succeeded in innovating a form of Islamic culture that is compatible with contemporary secular European civilization. In Germany these two patterns of resistance have converged. After World War II, Germany admitted as citizens thousands of ethnic German refugees and displaced persons, many of whose families had lived in eastern Europe for centuries. Most Germans, however, are reluctant to accept Turkish Muslims as German compatriots, to dilute the ethnic purity of the German nation, convinced that Turkish Muslims, even those who have been born and educated in Germany, can never be assimilated into German society; they are too different. Meanwhile, many Muslim Turks unto the third generation of fluent German-speakers are disinclined to integrate, to become German citizens, even though laws and procedures governing naturalization have been relaxed and simplified in their favor. They can continue to earn a decent living in Germany without adopting an infidel culture, without becoming Germans. As a result, Germany is confronted with a large bloc of permanent foreigners who decline to join the nation. Similar anti-immigrant sentiments, targeted mainly toward Muslims, have become an important issue in public affairs throughout Europe. The outcomes of recent national elections in Austria, France, Denmark, and the Netherlands have been affected in large measure by hostility to immigrants.

Indigenous minority groups may also reject the opportunity to integrate, even though individuals among them follow that course. Having been decimated, dispossessed, and in many cases, driven from their homes, the remnants of North American Indian nations are now segregated in reservations (reserves in Canada). Invited to integrate as individuals – as many among them already have – and though most communicate readily in English, they have instead preferred to maintain their distinctive communities and cultures, even though life for most of them as assimilated individuals might be easier were they to abandon their tribal identities and join the mainstream.[9] Similarly, a number of African nomadic peoples, such as Masai in Kenya, have resisted the efforts of African governments, to abandon their economically inefficient nomadic way of life and become settled agriculturalists with the prospect of benefiting from government services such as education and health, earning higher incomes, and integrating into the national community. Such efforts to entice nomads into the mainstream have usually failed as African governments provide insufficient incentives for nomadic peoples to sacrifice their familiar ways of life.

There may be many way stations on the slow road to ultimate integration. Some individuals are more inclined than others to abandon their ethnic ties and pass into the mainstream. Pride in and respect for their inherited culture, family ties, friendships and business associations, or the sense that their community is being unjustly treated may induce some individuals to maintain links with their community and renew their affiliation, even when full integration into the mainstream is an option.

In English-speaking Canada the integration of individuals from many ethnic backgrounds is proceeding apace, a trend similar to that in the United States. Canada has been host to a large Ukrainian diaspora centered in Manitoba. Spokespersons for the Canadian Jewish Congress requested that an elderly man of Ukrainian origin be deported, as he was charged as a prison guard with the murder of several Jewish inmates of a Nazi death camp during World War II. The organized Ukrainian community responded vigorously in defense of one of its own and for several years there were strained relations between the two ethnic groups.[10] Though both Ukrainians and Jews had integrated culturally into Canada's English-speaking mainstream, and social integration is underway, a sufficient number maintain ties to their community and their separate institutions and are prepared to rally to its defense when the occasion arises. Several generations may pass before these ethnic institutions atrophy for lack of membership and membership interest. If the diaspora is renewed by fresh arrivals, the community may be able to support itself and its institutions for many years, perhaps indefinitely, even as some members opt to pass into the mainstream.

The fact that a state is committed by its constitution and its ethos to an integrated society, and that individuals are steadily passing out of their ethnic communities into the mainstream, does not spare them the trauma of ethnic conflict. Even as they integrate culturally, some individuals are likely to remain attached to their community, to support its institutions, and to promote and defend what they believe to be its interests when these are challenged by other ethnic groups or by governments. Countries that experience continuing immigration are especially likely to witness the persistence of ethnic communities. The result may be conflict, pursued mostly by political means, but some may lead to collective violence. The aforementioned dispute between Jewish- and Ukrainian-Canadians is an example of ethnic conflict in an integrating system. In South Africa, conflict between Zulu and Xhosa over access to land has led to thousands of deaths in the province of Kwazulu-Natal. In the Miami area, Americans of African and of Cuban backgrounds have clashed violently over charges that the former, despite their native origin, are being squeezed out of employment opportunities because they do not speak or understand Spanish in what they believe to be an English-speaking country. Nativists, many recently recruited from immigrant ethnic communities into the mainstream, champion the exclusive use of English in public affairs, and dispute with Mexican- and Puerto Rican-Americans over such issues as bilingual education and Spanish-language ballots and public notices.

Even as the mainstream continues to attract recruits from ethnic communities, some choose to cling to their ethnic roots. Others, including African-Americans in the United

States, are culturally integrated, but social integration for them has proved to be difficult if not impossible. For such reasons as these, complete integration is a long-term process and in the interim ethnic conflict remains a live possibility.

The open society: liberator or executioner?

The open society welcomes individuals of all backgrounds to accept and contribute to the national culture and join the mainstream with equal rights and obligations for all individuals. As the Abbé Emmanuel-Joseph Sieyès is reputed to have announced to France's recently emancipated Jews following the French Revolution, "to Jews as individuals, everything; to Jews as a people, nothing." Join the mainstream as equal citizens; you may for a time encounter social prejudice and economic discrimination, but these will not be sanctioned by the state and will gradually disappear, along with ethnic pluralism in an increasingly homogeneous and indivisible society. Maintain your social and cultural institutions if you wish to preserve and develop your culture, but expect no help or support from the state and no power, except as they agree, to regulate the behavior of individual members of your community. This is the promise of integration, a cosmopolitan society of equals in which the individual is liberated from the crippling constraints of ethnic conformity and free to participate in the cultural and social mainstream, while society is liberated from the parochialism and conflicts that are likely consequences of ethnic pluralism.

The counter-argument begins with the premise that every culture is unique and inherently valuable, the distinctive expression of many generations of irreplaceable human experience, and that the responsibility of the state is to help preserve and develop cultures, not to participate in destroying them. Cultural diversity is to the human species what biodiversity is to the natural world, a source of strength and richness for the entire species. From the individual's perspective, the enjoyment of one's culture is a precious human right that should be fostered by governments and protected by the international community. The international community has gradually come to realize that the individual human rights proclaimed in the 1948 UN Convention need to be expanded to incorporate the rights of peoples as well.

A common language may be helpful, but not essential, for facilitating economic transactions and the business of government, but this should not preclude the flourishing of multiple cultures, their art, music, literature, sacred beliefs, modes of dress, and distinctive cuisines, and, where desired, self-governing autonomy. Homogenization of cultures and integrationist societies rob peoples of their birthrights and reduce the content of the resultant culture to its lowest common denominator, much like the fare provided by contemporary Hollywood films and commercial TV. The popularity of ethnic foods in North America is a popular reaction against the bland and colorless offerings of the pervasive fast food industry. Thus, the indictment runs, integration amounts to a vicious and needless process of ethnicide, destroying much that is precious, unique and irreplaceable in the human inheritance.

Among the current attacks on informational and economic globalization is the fear that it brings in its wake a common culture derived from the popular culture of the most powerful states. Imagine, they say, a globalized nightmare in which indigenous cultures had been swept away by McDonald's cuisine, Disney entertainment, Nintendo games, CNN News, Beatles tunes, Levi's fashions, and high-pressure advertising on the annual super-bowl classic. Is integration a liberating experience that eliminates an important source of social tension and violent conflict, releases the individual from the narrow constraints of traditional cultures, opens opportunities to participate in a more cosmopolitan society, and fulfills the ages-old aspiration for a common humanity? Or is it the homogenizing executioner of inherently valuable cultures that embody irreplaceable human experience and deserve to be cultivated and developed?

Conclusion

While power-sharing presupposes the indefinite continuation of ethnic pluralism, integrationist strategies foresee its gradual reduction and eventual disappearance as individual members of minorities voluntarily accept the invitation to join, participate in, and contribute to the mainstream. Cultural integration becomes a way station to eventual social integration and full incorporation into the mainstream. Meanwhile the mainstream evolves and is enriched by adopting elements of the cultures that are contributed by its new recruits.

While this process is underway, ethnic conflicts may occur, involving still active members of communities that are in the process of integration, as well as others who resist integration and those whose integration is resisted by elements of the mainstream. While the process may be slow, extending over several generations, the ultimate goal of integrationist strategies is the elimination of ethnic diversity and social pluralism, which is the precondition for ethnic strife and the achievement of cultural and social cohesion in an indivisible nation.

9
The Management of Ethnic Conflict

An overriding goal of public policy is to prevent ethnic pluralism from lapsing into violence, to maintain peaceful if not necessarily friendly coexistence among ethnic communities, and to establish procedures for dealing with demands and grievances through legitimate, non-violent channels. Seldom can ethnic-based differences be definitively settled or resolved as long as the parties are present under the same political roof. As they remain on the scene, fresh occasions for grievances and disputes are likely to arise. The best that can be expected is that successive differences can be managed or regulated in ways sufficiently acceptable to the parties and to their major factions and that peace can be maintained and the intensity of ethnic differences reduced. The ability of governments to keep the peace depends both on their skill in regulating disputes that affect mobilized ethnic communities; and on the efficacy of their security apparatus, their ability to prevent or control violence by factions that are dissatisfied with the government's decisions.

In this chapter we focus on the policies and practices of governments that are intended to regulate interethnic relations within their borders. We organize this discussion around the general patterns that we have followed in this book: domination, power-sharing, and integration.

Conflict management in domination systems

We divide domination systems into two categories, authoritarian and democratic.

Authoritarian systems tend to rely on the liberal use of official force – police, judiciary, and military – to maintain the peace. They are likely to proscribe the mobilization of ethnic associations that might prove troublesome to the regime by branding them as subversive and suppressing them, imprisoning their leaders, and intimidating their members. Thus, the Alawite minority government in Syria turned its troops loose on a center of Sunni resistance in February 1982 in the city of Hamma, slaughtering between 10,000 and 25,000 mostly unarmed civilians, then bulldozing every structure so that the entire dissident community was simply wiped out. The lesson had been learned, for during the next two decades there were no further demonstrations of opposition to the Alawite dictatorship. Saddam Hussein's government used poison gas to suppress an uprising among Kurds in northern Iraq. The Indonesian military has used strong-arm tactics to suppress ethnic opposition in East Timor, Aceh, and West Irian. A gang of Fijian thugs in that ethnically divided country, with significant support from the Fijian-dominated military, intervened in May 2000 to overthrow the Indian-led government that had won a recent election. They believed this government, led by descendants of former indentured Indian laborers, threatened Fijian control of the state to which many Fijians believe they are entitled as the indigenous people of that country. After a lengthy stalemate new elections were held that resulted in a new Fijian-led government.[1]

Authoritarian systems may attempt to preempt ethnic opposition by sponsoring and patronizing organizations that operate in the name of an ethnic community, but are supervised and controlled by the regime. This method was used by the Soviets to promote activities among their ethnic minorities that they considered innocuous and offered no challenge to the regime, "national in form, socialist in content." The system of ethnic-based republics, closely supervised by the highly centralized and Russian-controlled Communist Party and KGB (secret police) offered symbolic political power and

cultural respect to the non-Russian peoples, featuring ethno-
graphy and folk dancing, but no real opportunities to mobilize
politically or to vent their grievances. Ethnic identity was
considered a transitional phenomenon under socialism; eventually, in the transition to communism, national sentiments
were expected to disappear and to be succeeded by a common
socialist culture and Soviet collective identity, all speaking
the Russian language. Meanwhile, national sentiments were
to be tolerated but, neutered politically under indigenous
leaders who joined the Communist Party, were subjected to
its discipline and acceptable to the Soviet leadership. Similarly,
the apartheid regime in South Africa promoted a policy of
"separate development" in their tribal homelands (13 percent
of the most barren land for 75 percent of the population)
under indigenous governments selected and financed by
the apartheid authorities and closely supervised by its police.
The homelands were intended to create the illusion among
Africans of autonomous power. Meanwhile, they would have
the effect of keeping the African majority divided by tribal
affiliation, impecunious, and dependent on the apartheid government for their security and financial support.

The Chinese government operates an academy in Beijing
to train indigenous members of minority populations to serve
as Communist Party cadres and junior administrators in their
regions. They function as intermediaries between the PRC
state apparatus and minority peoples, such as Tibetans and
Uighurs. They administer Chinese laws and government policies under the watchful eyes of PRC civil and military officials; their tenure in office depends on faithful service to the
Chinese state. Thus, the will of foreign rulers is to be executed by persons who resemble and speak in the accents of
the indigenous minority peoples.

More subtle authoritarian states have maintained control
of ethnic minorities by the grant of minority rights which are
intended to reconcile minorities with their subordinate status,
thus reducing the costs of control without compromising
their dominant position. An instructive example was the
millet system operated by the Ottoman Empire, which
granted internal self-management to its Christian and Jewish
minorities, allowing them to be governed by their own legal
systems administered by their own religious leaders. Thus, the

Muslim Ottoman state maintained undisputed political and military control of its infidel minorities, while insuring their security, economic opportunity, and survival.[2]

The bottom line is that authoritarian regimes are prepared to use coercive means to maintain their domination over dissident and potentially dissident ethnic minorities by preventing their political mobilization and by vigorously repressing opposition when it does emerge. Symbolic concessions may be provided to minorities to produce the illusion of autonomy and self-determination; a thin layer of indigenous elites may be persuaded that the existing regime is genuinely beneficial for their people, the best that can be expected under the circumstances, as well as profitable for them personally. Allowing them to maintain a legal existence enables the regime to monitor their activities more closely. But, the velvet glove promptly gives way to the mailed fist when the power of the controlling regime is challenged. Very little latitude is available to the potential opposition. They may function within permitted cultural and religious organizations, playing a cat-and-mouse game with the authorities who debate whether and when to close them down. Potential opponents are forced to go underground, to organize mass resistance, and to seek external support – weapons, funds, and protected sanctuaries beyond the reach of the regime. Thus, when the African National Congress (ANC) was banned by the apartheid government in 1960 and driven underground, it maintained a legal presence, the United Democratic Front (UDF), that managed to operate within the letter of the law. The ANC moved its headquarters to safe sanctuaries in sympathetic neighboring states from which it conducted its diplomatic, propaganda, fund-raising, and military training activities.

The maintenance of ethnic dominance is not limited to authoritarian states. It also happens in states that qualify as *political democracies* in that they hold free and regular elections, while free speech, a free press, and freedom of organization permit the unimpeded expression and circulation of political views. The classic example was Northern Ireland. In that majoritarian, winner-take-all system, the Protestant majority elected an all-Protestant government from which the Catholic minority was totally excluded. Their elected representatives in Parliament were always outvoted. As a result, the government governed in the interest of its all-Protestant constituency and could safely ignore the grievances of the Catholic minority. A similar situation prevailed in Sri Lanka. Though the Sinhalese divided their vote between two competing Sinhalese parties, the Tamil minority was excluded from government and their grievances were ignored. In both these instances elements of the minority responded to their exclusion by launching armed insurrections with conspicuous components of terrorism directed at civilian populations.

The alternative, more subtle tactic of domination practiced by democratic governments is to ignore the grievances of minorities, keep them off the political agenda, and then brand the opposition, once it mobilizes, either as cranks or as subversives. For many years, Turkish governments simply refused to acknowledge that there was a Kurdish problem. The Kurdish minority, 20 percent of the population, were officially designated as "Mountain Turks" with the same rights and privileges as other Turkish citizens. Expressions of opposition to this assimilationist strategy were ascribed to banditry, then to terrorism, and finally, after lengthy, costly, and often brutal military campaigns of repression, there was grudging recognition of limited cultural autonomy, but rigorous refusal to concede political autonomy for the Kurdish majority region or to depart from the Kemalist ideology of Turkey as a unitary state and nation. The French Jacobin state long denied, even in international forums, that it harbored any minorities, let alone minorities with unsatisfied demands. The first break came in the 1970s when Breton activists succeeded in calling attention to their demands for inclusion of Breton language instruction in the curricula of the region's public schools and for Breton language programs on radio and television. This was followed by outbreaks of terrorist violence in Corsica which finally induced the government in Paris in January 2000, after extended debate, to offer an unprecedented degree of autonomy to the Corsican National Assembly. These devolved powers include instruction in the Corsican language in elementary schools as well as control over cultural affairs, environment, infrastructure, agriculture, and economic development. These measures split the French Socialist Party government of the day, as two ministers resigned to protest what they charged were ill-advised concessions to terrorism and a dangerous fragmentation of the indivisible French nation.

Israeli government behavior toward its Palestinian minority, as outlined in chapter 6, has been one of consistent marginalization. As citizens, Palestinians vote and elect members of the Knesset, Israel's parliament, and most of them are proficient in Hebrew. Yet, their representatives have never been included in any of Israel's many coalition governments, nor have they any role in Israel's state apparatus. Elementary and secondary education is available in Arabic, an official language in Israel, but curricula are closely supervised by Israeli officials. There is virtually no social contact between Jewish and Palestinian Israelis. Palestinian citizens are second class in most respects and the amenities provided by Israel's government to Palestinian communities are notably inferior to those available to Jews. Most Palestinians do not accept the legitimacy of the Zionist state and would prefer that Israel be transformed into a bi-national, consociational state (a state for all its citizens) in which Palestinian and Jewish values and symbols would have equal status, in effect a power-sharing system. Among Israel's Jews, their Palestinian fellow citizens are widely suspected as potential security risks and the police would unhesitatingly respond to any overt act deemed to threaten Israel's security. Until a peace settlement has been reached with Palestinians in the West Bank and Gaza, and until Israel has been accepted as a legitimate entity by Arab governments, this situation is unlikely to change; Palestinians in Israel, notwithstanding their status as citizens, will continue to be suspect, and experience individual and collective discrimination in this democratic state. Though its institutions are democratic, Israel's Palestinian citizens are a dominated minority.

Conflict management in power-sharing systems

Power-sharing is an inherently accommodative set of attitudes, processes, and institutions, in which the art of governance becomes a matter of bargaining, conciliating, and compromising the aspirations and grievances of its ethnic communities, and a search for common interests that benefit all the communities and distribute benefits and costs more or less equitably. The fact that the rules of the game call for moderation and respect for the expressed interests of the other party does not prevent spokespersons for each of them and factions within them from presenting and arguing their case vigorously, even aggressively. It does mean that the tacit understandings and the machinery of government in federal and consociational systems should be conducive to consensual settlements, so that neither party emerges from confrontations as complete winners or complete losers.

In terms of autonomy, complete separation cannot be dismissed as an option, distasteful as this normally is to state elites who refuse to believe that they were entrusted with high office in order to preside over the dismemberment of their state.[3] Yet, when tensions between the parties prove unmanageable, separation may prove to be the preferable alternative, transforming destabilizing domestic conflict into international relations governed by international law. The separation of Ireland from the United Kingdom in 1922, of Bangladesh from Pakistan in 1971, of Slovakia from Czech-dominated Czechoslovakia in 1992, of Slovenia, Macedonia, and Croatia from Serb-dominated Yugoslavia has virtually eliminated conflicts between these nations where previous relations within the same state had been characterized by chronic, often acrimonious conflict. Yet, separation is no guarantee of conflict reduction. After two decades of armed struggle, in 1991 a new government in Ethiopia finally agreed to the separation of Eritrea, which became an independent state. Shortly thereafter, in 1998, war broke out between these two states over a strip of disputed territory. As a component republic in Yugoslavia, Bosnia had prospered, while its ethnic communities, Serbs, Croats, and Muslims, had managed to coexist peacefully. As independence was thrust upon Bosnia, nationalist extremists in neighboring Serbia and Croatia began to stir up separatist sentiments and to supply armed fighters and weapons to their more militant co-ethnics in Bosnia, promising to partition the territory and reunite their ethnic kinfolk with their neighboring homelands. Government in Bosnia-Herzegovina broke down, civil war ensued, hundreds of thousands of refugees were driven from their homes, accompanied by enormous property damage, human atrocities, and war crimes, leading finally to international intervention to stop the slaughter and impose some form of civilized order. Bosnia had been much better off as a republic within multiethnic Yugoslavia than as an independent entity.

There are two methods of managing ethnic conflict within *federalized* systems. The first is to increase the scope of autonomy for the regionalized units. Since the Quiet Revolution of the 1960s, the Government of Canada has gradually yielded to Quebec control over such subjects as immigration, manpower development, urban affairs, labor relations, and higher education. Canada has also increased the range of autonomy, including control over valuable natural resources, to its aboriginal peoples, Indian nations and Inuit. Belgium has devolved nearly all the functions of government, except foreign affairs, national defense, and macro-economic management to its Flemish and Walloon regional authorities.

Current negotiations about ending the civil wars in Sri Lanka and Sudan focus on the territory to be included in the regional units (the disputed border between north and south in Sudan straddles rich petroleum deposits), the status and rights of minorities within these regions, and the functions of government to be devolved to the regional authorities. The latter must sometimes settle for second best, since central governments may draw a line at the maximum autonomy they are prepared to concede. The government of India resolutely resists any suggestion of separation and independence for regional units, but has been quite flexible in authorizing new states within India to satisfy the aspirations of ethnic minorities. Kurds in Iraq, Iran, and Turkey aspire to a united, independent Kurdistan, but this would be vigorously resisted by all three governments and would not gain significant international backing. As a result, they must, for the time being at least, limit their demands to regional autonomy within their three host states. None of these states has as yet yielded even to this demand.[4]

Drawing on India's experience, Professor Kohli argues that in democratic states with well-functioning institutions that provide both effectiveness and legitimacy and whose elites are prepared to practice accommodative politics, regionally based movements for ethnic self-determination are likely to follow the pattern of an inverted U curve. Democracy stimulates ethnic mobilization and demands for self-determination, but accommodative responses from the center that permit significant autonomy for the ethnic community are likely to result in demobilization and a new political equilibrium in a power-sharing federal relationship.[5] Where the center's behavior is unaccommodating, as in Kosovo and Sudan, the result is likely to be cycles of insurrection, repression, and violence.

The status of minorities within federalized regions can be a source of contention, as the dominant regional group, motivated by intense nationalist sentiments, may be disinclined to recognize or concede to minorities in its midst the same right to self-determination that they demand for themselves. In the current negotiations over terms of autonomy for a Tamil region in north and northeast Sri Lanka, Tamil negotiators have demonstrated little patience with the concerns of local Muslim and Sinhalese minorities. Though the rights of Quebec's large but diminishing English-speaking minority have been and remain the subject of controversy and suspicion, the provincial government of Quebec provides them with publicly financed education in the English language from kindergarten through university and government services including hospital care in English, while local governments in English-majority districts may be conducted in English. The English-speaking community has, however, vigorously contested the provincial legislation that requires all commercial signs, even on English owned business serving primarily English-speaking customers, to be primarily in French.

Aside from territorial autonomy, the principal demand of federalized ethnic regions is greater influence in the central government as a means of protecting their interests, and particularly for strengthening their claims on the financial resources of the central government. We have already noted that Canada has committed itself to increasing Francophone participation in its military and civil services and on the Supreme Court; membership in Belgian cabinets must be equally distributed among Walloons and Flemings. The several state governments in India compete vigorously to tease out increased financial support from the central government in the form of development projects and transfer payments. Before the dissolution of Yugoslavia, the richer republics, Slovenia and Croatia, complained that the foreign exchange they earned and the taxes they paid to the central government were being dissipated and squandered on the backward and lazy peoples of Macedonia and Montenegro. Economically for them, Yugoslavia was a losing proposition, they received from the federation much less than they paid in as foreign exchange and taxes; economically, they would be better off as independent entities than as cash cows for the Serb-controlled central government and the backward regions. The Yugoslav government replied that taxing the richer regions to help develop the economies of the more backward regions was a reasonable policy from which all would eventually benefit. Though regional competition for resources from the center is an inherent reality of federal systems, it becomes especially acute when the component units represent different ethnic communities.

As an alternative to ethnic federalism, a prescription for attenuating ethnic militancy is to split ethnic regions into several states or provinces. Each such unit would then struggle to achieve its own distinctive advantage and maximize its share of central government funds and services, thus diminishing the ethnic factor in its political behavior. Unlike the original large ethnic regions, no single state would be able to threaten the stability of the central government. This form of political engineering was implemented by Nigeria's military rulers following its devastating civil war (1966–9). The three large ethnic regional authorities have been replaced by 36 states, each with its separate political institutions and interests. The effect has been to diminish the intensity of ethnic solidarity and hostility between Yoruba, Ibo, and Hausa-Fulani. It has not, however, put an end to ethnic violence in Nigeria. There have been lethal clashes between Muslims and Christians in several of the northern states and between smaller ethnic communities, for example Ijaw and Itsekiri competing for employment opportunities in the offshore oil industry in the Niger River delta.

In planning for post-Saddam Iraq, one option is a federal state that splits the three ethnic regions (Kurds in the north, Sunni in the center, Shia in the south) into a dozen or so provinces following the Nigerian precedent.[6] Would this reduce the intensity of ethnic solidarities and thus make the future Iraq more governable? How vigorously would the leadership of these three mobilized communities resist this policy, designed as it is to weaken their political clout? Could it even be implemented? If so, what are the prospects that it could achieve its purpose? Or would the cure be worse than the disease?

Consociational systems are explicitly designed to manage conflicts where the distribution of ethnic populations does not allow for federal arrangements. Conflicts are to be regulated by agreements struck by the leaders of coalition governments who are then responsible for "selling" these compromises to their respective ethnic constituents. In chapter 7 we cited a number of examples of successful consociational management, recognizing, however, that it is a fragile arrangement requiring highly skilled political leadership and an abundance of good will. Consequently, consociational systems are vulnerable, after a period of time, to breakdowns.

Allowing each community to manage its own institutions in its own language insures their security and the continuity of their culture, while the volume of business that falls to the central government is thereby limited. In this way the system is able to tolerate the delays and sometimes deadlocks to which consociational systems are vulnerable when agreement eludes the coalition's leadership. Proportionality is an element of consociational relations intended to insure each participating ethnic community, particularly the smaller parties, fair shares of representation and of the resources available from the state. While this may minimize conflict, it cannot eliminate it. We have mentioned before that disputes may arise over charges of discrimination against better-qualified individuals and over what constitute accurate numbers on which the proportions are to be based. Veto power, which is advocated by Lijphart and others to protect the vital interests of minorities is, however, of dubious value as a method of conflict management. As a temporary measure it may cause the majority to rethink its position and enable further negotiation. But, thwarting the majority in a consociational system is more likely to provoke than to prevent or diminish conflict.

The process of outbidding by extremist factions in both camps is what threatens most consociational systems, as the ultras on both sides become tacit allies in undermining the compromises negotiated by their more moderate leaders. In consociational systems it is essential that moderate leaders maintain their influence within their respective communities, so that the necessary trade-offs can be bargained out and implemented. Inability to do so marks the end of consensual power sharing. The inability of Northern Ireland moderates, who accepted the 1998 Good Friday consociational settlement, to control their extremist factions has jeopardized the implementation of that agreement.

Another version of power-sharing has been called by its proponents "institutional engineering," focusing on the institution of elections. This theory argues that election systems in ethnically divided societies should be so structured that candidates and their parties have strong incentives to appeal for support to voters outside their own ethnic community. This means that successful candidates must take into account the interests and views of ethnic communities other than their own. In negotiating for such support, they must engage in dialog with representatives of other communities. This is likely to favor candidates who take moderate, accommodative positions on matters of interest to other communities, who highlight matters of common interest, and who de-emphasize matters of potential conflict. This process has been labeled "centripetalism," forcing candidates who hope to win office to eschew the militant expression of narrow ethnic demands and move toward the moderate center. Voting arrangements that allow the second preferences of defeated candidates to be transferred to voters' second choices may be elements of centripetal systems. It is believed to foster the formation of moderate inclusive coalitions and even of ethnically inclusive parties.[7]

The weakness of this very attractive theory for partisans of democratic politics is the very limited number of cases where this approach has been tried and can be empirically evaluated. It applies only to situations where ethnic populations are mixed, are not territorially separated. Reilly could identify only a handful of cases where this form of institutional engineering had been attempted. These include Sri Lanka, Fiji, and Northern Ireland, hardly examples of successful conflict management. His two successful examples were Estonia and Papua New Guinea, especially the latter. There, when centripetal election rules applied, the result was accommodative campaigning. After the rules changed to majoritarian voting, the result was more extreme expressions of narrow ethnic interests, accompanied by enhanced electoral violence. Despite the limited empirical evidence, however, this approach may be a future option, especially in large, mixed ethnic cities.

While Afro-Trinidadian and Indo-Trinidadian political parties continue to compete for political office, they have to date relied on winner-take-all elections to rotate in office, rather than on consociational power-sharing between the two ethnic communities that are nearly equal in numbers. Can this unstable and unpredictable rotation in office continue to satisfy the defeated party that is excluded from government at least until the next election? All depends on the self-restraint of the winning party in not pressing their temporary advantage too far.

In chapter 7 we discussed non-formal methods of power-sharing. In Afghanistan an effort was underway in late 2003 to draft a constitution for the post-Taliban state. Representatives of the minority ethnic communities – Tadjiks, Uzbeks, and Hazara – were concerned that the largest group, Pushtuns and their allies, who had long dominated Afghan affairs, would seek to maintain their hegemony by controlling the powerful presidency that they were advocating. The minorities insisted that more powers be vested in the Parliament to check the authority of the executive. In Parliament the minorities believed they would have sufficient representation to balance the president, a rough, informal pattern of ethnic power-sharing. At the time of writing, this issue, which is central to the structure of the future Afghan state, had not been resolved.

Conflict management in integrative systems

Integrative systems are committed to the gradual supplanting of ethnic loyalties and solidarities by membership and participation of individuals in a common national mainstream, which incorporates the contributions of its diverse ethnic components. But, though integration is the policy and the goal, the continuing reality of ethnic differences during the transition period keeps cropping up. And though ethnic conflicts are regarded as temporary and distracting, they must of necessity be dealt with.

The first impulse of governments is that of non-recognition, the attempt to ignore ethnic-based grievances and demands and keep them off the public agenda. Though they glorified the Indian contribution (*indigenismo*) to its dominant mestizo (mixed race) culture, Mexican governments for decades refused to acknowledge the grievances or the special needs of their Indian minorities. It was not until the Chiapas rebellion in the 1980s, which became front-page news and drew international attention to Mexico's neglected and impoverished Indian peoples, that the government was forced to begin addressing their special needs. Frequently, it is only after confronting violent protest that governments are compelled to face up to discontents in their ethnic communities. The British government failed to respond to complaints by non-White immigrants of widespread discriminatory treatment at the hands of police and other government agencies until riots in London and other major cities made the issue impossible to avoid.

When it becomes evident that the avoidance of minority grievances and demands will not silence them, governments then attempt symbolic recognition and mollification. These do not commit the government to policy changes or to altering in any significant way the prevailing distribution of power and resources. The classic method of symbolic recognition in the United States is to arrange for the appointment or election of a respected member of the minority community to a dignified position, such as a judgeship, hoping that this token of recognition and respect will appease his or her community and perhaps induce its members to reward the party responsible for this friendly gesture with support at the polls. The designation of Martin Luther King's birthday as a national holiday was intended to demonstrate to African-Americans that their heroes are national heroes and that they are respected members of the American nation. It did not, however, address the social and economic problems confronting large numbers of African-Americans.

In the English-speaking provinces of Canada, persons of non-British stock are rapidly integrating into the Anglophone branch of the Canadian nation. In their passage to full integration, official multiculturalism was intended to recognize symbolically that each of these diaspora communities has achieved an honored position in Canadian society, even though, unlike French-speakers, their language has not been awarded official status. Multiculturalism, however, has not retarded their gradual integration as individuals into the English-speaking mainstream and is not likely to do so in the future. When an individual of Black Caribbean background is inducted into the British House of Lords, this is meant to be a gesture of good will by the British establishment toward that minority. The same can be said for the constitutional designation of nine African languages as official languages of South Africa. Since English will be the language of government, business, and higher education, parents who want their children to succeed in life will see that they are English-educated, while the African languages will, notwithstanding their official status, in practice be relegated to vernaculars.

Symbolic recognition may be all that some communities demand in their passage toward integration. The large Italian-American community is integrating rapidly into the American mainstream. Having secured official designation of Columbus Day as a national holiday in recognition of an Italian's pioneering role in American history, no further collective demands were felt to be necessary. All that was asked is that Italian-Americans as individuals should expect non-discriminatory treatment and equal opportunity in education, employment, and government. With higher education, occupational mobility, and economic success, Italian-Americans have been moving away from ethnic neighborhoods, inter-marrying, and participating in the mainstream. When, in November 2002, Nancy Pelosi was chosen to lead the Democratic Party in the US House of Representatives, she was hailed as the first woman to have achieved that honor. Her Italian origins and Catholic faith were never mentioned.

But the transition is not always so smooth. Some representatives of the fast-growing flow of Latin-American immigrants to the United States have argued that immigrant communities have a right to preserve and maintain their cultures, a right that governments should abet and for which they should provide public services, including education in the Spanish language. Prompted by the Federal courts, Federal state, and local governments have attempted to accommodate this demand, including bilingual schooling, with the expectation that bilingual public notices, ballots, and health services would be temporary measures that would ease the inevitable transition to complete Americanization. Some more militant Hispanic intellectuals have, however, insisted that the purpose of bilingual services should not be to ease the transition to English, but to preserve Hispanic culture; respect for diversity, they argue, is a human right that governments are obligated to foster. This has led to the "English-only" backlash, its advocates fearing that government support for bilingual education penalizes Hispanic children, while threatening to balkanize the United States. The United States, they argue, is an English-speaking country, the English language being a major link that unites this polyglot nation. Therefore, on arrival immigrants should be expected to conform to this language regime. This has led to a long-running, often emotion-laden debate over the merits and effectiveness of bilingual education, and to referenda in several states on the exclusive use of English in government and education.[8] Thus, a well-meaning attempt to accommodate a large ethnic minority has generated considerable conflict, spurred by many who fear that this concession to Hispanics threatens the integrative mission of American society. The slow rate of naturalization among Latin-American immigrants is a further source of concern to opponents of bilingual services.

Those who would encourage the transformation of domination or power-sharing systems into integrative societies based on liberal individualism advocate a number of strategies for bringing this about. Prominent among them is to break down ethnically segregated institutions by opening them to persons of all ethnic backgrounds. This applies to institutions such as public schools, so that children of all origins might become acquainted with one another and share a common formative experience. The same applies to employment both in government agencies and in private enterprises and to membership and activist roles in political parties. Cross-cutting memberships in professional organizations, athletic and recreational societies, and labor unions should be fostered, so that persons of different ethnic origins may develop friendships and learn to share common interests within these non-ethnic associations, instead of limiting personal relationships to individuals of the same ethnic background. Over time, it is hoped that these multiple memberships in organizations and participation in activities that cross ethnic lines will diminish the importance of ethnic identities and ethnic associations in favor of the non-ethnic, national mainstream. In societies where there are strong incentives to join the mainstream, such as the United States and Australia, this process has been largely successful with most ethnic minorities, but less so with African-Americans. In other situations, where the incentives are less obvious, such as Bosnia and Lebanon, these initiatives have not been robust enough to counteract pressures to retreat to the shelter of ethnic associations when tensions develop between ethnic communities.

Affirmative action reflects recognition by the United States government that African-Americans remain seriously under-represented in higher education, skilled employment, and the professional and managerial ranks of government and industry. Elimination of discriminatory practices, though necessary, would not suffice to close these gaps, because the legacies of institutionalized racism have compromised their ability to compete. They need a helping hand in the form of preferential access until such time as these handicaps have been overcome. This attempt at accommodation by government has produced a backlash among many, who regard affirmative action as reverse discrimination (quotas), denying deserving Whites educational and employment opportunities for which they would otherwise be qualified and violating the principle of equal opportunity based on competitive merit.[9]

Some of the beneficiaries of affirmative action are from middle-class African-American backgrounds, those who least need preferential treatment, often at the expense of lower-middle-class and working-class Whites. The extension of affirmative action to other groups believed to have been underrepresented because of previous discrimination (Hispanics, women, Asian-Americans, Native Americans) has diluted its effectiveness for African-Americans, without mollifying the sense of injustice felt by many White males. It has helped to create and consolidate a substantial African-American middle class which has been integrated culturally into the American mainstream, though for most of them social integration has not been realized. It has failed to reach large numbers of the African-American underclass that remains trapped in poverty and hopelessness in the nation's large urban centers.

A nation of fully integrated individuals remains central to the American belief system. But, temporarily at least, diversity persists and is recognized by government. This brief discussion has barely explored the complexities attendant on affirmative action and bilingual education in a society based on liberal individualism and committed to cultural and social integration.[10] Official preferences designed to overcome the effects of past discrimination have generated resentment and conflicts wherever they are implemented, whether for Malays in Malaysia or dalits (untouchables) in India. A recent proposal by the newly elected president of Brazil to institute a system of preferential quotas for university entry to benefit members of the depressed Afro-Brazilian population has aroused intense opposition from Whites who fear that they would be unjustly penalized by that policy. Such conflicts are particularly bitter in integrative systems such as the United States because they are considered by many to be inherently illegitimate, violating the principle of non-discriminatory individualism on which the polity is premised.

Societies committed to integration are not spared the tensions of ethnic hostility or the trauma of ethnic violence, even as more and more individuals are absorbed into the mainstream. Lethal warfare between Mexican and Black youth gangs in south Los Angeles over control of turf and drug traffic has strained the resources of local law enforcement agencies and mobilized the efforts of religious leaders, civic organizations, and officials of state and local government attempting to mediate the conflict and prevent its recurrence. Such efforts at mediation and conflict resolution by locally based third parties often rely on methods of structured dialogue and confidence-building similar to those that are employed by NGOs and other transnational outsiders intervening in ethnic disputes, as discussed in chapter 5.

Often, these well-intentioned efforts can only scratch the surface of deep-seated social pathologies such as undereducation, broken homes, drug addiction, and absence of employment opportunities. Most conflicts involving ethnic communities are, however, managed through non-violent processes, such as elections and contentious propaganda campaigns. Mexican-Americans in California punished the Republican Party at the polls in 1998 for the Republican governor's anti-immigrant initiatives. The controversy between organizations speaking for Jewish-Americans and Arab-Americans for influence over US policy in the Middle East has been waged entirely by propaganda and the application of political pressure.

Efforts of governments to de-emphasize ethnic identities by creating and fostering overarching national identities have met with limited success, especially in the short run. Notable recent failures were the efforts of the Titoist regime in Yugoslavia to build an overarching Yugoslav identity and of the Soviets to develop a new model Soviet socialist citizen. A similar effort is under way in Singapore, a tiny but very prosperous island state with a 75 percent Chinese population (15 percent Malay, 10 percent Indian and other), surrounded by Malaysia and Indonesia with Malay-Muslim majorities, suspicious of any sovereign Chinese presence in their area. As a matter of national security, Singapore's authoritarian elites promote the concept of a Singaporean identity and rigorously repress any expression of ethnic politics. Government, education, and business are conducted in the neutral English language. Though pride in ethnic cultures is cultivated, it is closely supervised to prevent any encroachment on politics or public affairs.[11]

Allocation formulas

This discussion raises the question of criteria by which scarce and valuable resources should be allocated among competing individuals and ethnic communities. In most *domination* systems, the allocative methods, if not stated in formal law, in practice favor members of the dominant community and either exclude or disadvantage others. This applies to eligibility for public office, language policy, educational opportunities, employment in the more lucrative and prestigious occupations, access to capital, credit, land, and other economic resources, and membership in prestigious clubs and similar social institutions. This was the practice in apartheid South Africa and was also evident in Iraq (for Sunni Arabs), Sri Lanka (for Sinhalese), and Russia (for ethnic Russians). In some cases the dominant group in control of government allows members of minorities access to important economic opportunities as long as they share their profits with officials of the dominant community. This is the common experience of middleman minorities, Chinese in Indonesia, Asians in East Africa, Jews and Greeks in seventeenth- and eighteenth-century eastern Europe. In Malaysia the dominant Malays insure control of government, provide exclusive official status for the Malay language and the Islamic faith, maintain preferential access for Malays to government employment, ownership of agricultural land, higher education, capital, credit, government contracts, and ownership shares in privatized enterprises. Non-Malays protest these discriminatory practices, but have found sufficient slack in the system to continue to educate their children and to benefit from an expanding economy.

In *power-sharing* systems, especially in consociational polities, the allocation rules are designed to share access in rough proportion to population numbers. While disputes over population numbers may introduce a contentious element into these arrangements, proportionality is intended to provide a roughly fair inter-group formula for regulating access to government employment, public contracts, and higher education. In consociational Lebanon, under the National Pact of 1943, government jobs were allocated according to a strict formula

of six Christians to five Muslims. While proportionality prevails in government-related activities, economic life may be
governed, as it is in prosperous Belgium, by market rules of
competition.

In federal systems rough proportionality may be realized
as each regional unit attempts to skew economic opportunities in favor of its ethnic constituents (local residents are preferred for university admissions and local companies are
preferred for government contracts). Thus, the government
of Quebec created several large government corporations and
staffed them with French-speakers, many of them products
of the recently expanded network of French-speaking universities. They also created government agencies to provide
capital and credit to enable French-owned and -operated
businesses to expand and gave them preferential access to
government contracts. The purpose was not to damage
English-owned and -operated enterprises, but to increase the
proportion of underrepresented French-speakers, their constituents, in ownership and managerial roles in the Quebec
economy. Numerical proportionality may be pursued in
central governments, as the Government of Canada strives
for "balanced participation" of Anglophones and Francophones in its civil and military services and guarantees three
French-speaking members for its nine judge Supreme Court.

In *integrationist* systems, where all individuals are to be
treated equally, access is formally regulated by meritocratic
rules of individual competition or by market processes, which
are believed to provide a level playing field for all entrants
and to reward superior qualifications and efficient performance. It is presumed to be color-blind and indifferent to
ethnic origin, thus to combine social justice with efficient
performance. The difficulty has been that these rules of the
game often reward those who enter the competition with
superior preparation – better education, wealthier and better-
connected family backgrounds. The effect is to penalize or
effectively exclude persons who by birth lack these initial
advantages and to favor those who are born into these privileges, contributing thereby to the intergenerational succession of elites.

In the United States where meritocratic rules of allocation
have formally prevailed, informally a regime of preferences

was for many years applied in favor of White Anglo-Saxon Protestants (WASPs). This discriminated against non-Whites and non-Protestants in access to the more prestigious universities, professional schools, managerial positions in the major financial, commercial, and industrial firms, and in social clubs, resorts, and residential neighborhoods.[12] After World War II, prompted in part by Federal legislation and judicial decisions, in part by reaction to the horrors of the European Holocaust, these practices were gradually relaxed and persons of Jewish, Italian, Polish, and Asian origins gained more equitable access to these competitive opportunities. But, despite the political successes of the civil rights revolution, African-Americans continue to be underrepresented in higher education, professional and managerial employment, the skilled trades, and ownership of corporate assets. To overcome these disparities, affirmative action measures were introduced in the early 1970s as a temporary departure from the meritocratic regime, with consequences that were discussed earlier in this chapter.

Affirmative action, in effect preferences, was instituted as a temporary substitute for meritocratic rules to enable young African-Americans to compensate for the effects of institutionalized racism. The new rule substituted fairness of outcomes for equality of opportunity, setting aside, for an undetermined but temporary period, meritocratic rules in favor of proportionality, to govern access of African-Americans to many of the competitive educational and occupational opportunities in the American economy. We cannot here review the history and controversies produced by this social experiment. The point to emphasize is that meritocratic and open market competition between individuals, which are hallmarks of liberal individualism in integrative systems, may have consequences that penalize members of some ethnic communities; and that this may create the need, for a time at least, to substitute some other rule of access, proportionality perhaps, to meet the need for interethnic fairness.

One inherent difficulty with affirmative action preferences is that, once established temporarily, they tend in fact to become permanent, as spokespersons for ethnic communities that have benefited find reasons that require their continuation. Malaysia's New Economic Policy, which provided important economic preferences for Malays, was launched in 1970 and intended to last for twenty years. At the end of that period, non-Malays pleaded for its termination, but pressures from Malay interests claiming that its purposes had not been sufficiently fulfilled persuaded the government to extend it in modified form under a different name, this time for an undetermined period of time.

Conclusion

The powers of the modern state are challenged both from above and from below. From above, economic globalization and regional associations are eroding the control of governments over economic policies and information flows, while sub-national mobilization, especially by ethnic communities, threatens their powers from below. Yet, people continue to look to their governments to protect their security, provide necessary public services, and regulate conflicts; in failed states where government ceases to function, there is no law and men with guns rule as the people suffer.

The role of outsiders, including states, international organizations, and NGOs in regulating, as well as generating, ethnic conflict, has been treated in chapter 5. Yet, the principal burden of managing ethnic conflicts, as reviewed in this chapter, remains with the state apparatus. Governments normally attempt to maintain peace and order, but their methods vary with the structure and basic rationale for statehood including the patterns they have selected for managing conflicts. Since ethnic politics are always contentious, violence prompted by aggrieved elements is an ever-present possibility, regardless of the posture of government. The maintenance of peace depends both on the political skills of government officials and on the capacity and willingness of the security forces, especially the police, to enforce order when it is threatened.

10
What of the Future?

Three scenarios

One can identify three competing scenarios for the future.

The first scenario regards ethnic pluralism as a likely, if not inevitable, source of conflict. While ethnic communities may coexist for extended periods of time in mutual respect, they tend to maintain their boundaries so that the "other" remains the "other." Events occur that produce differences of perception or interest which are magnified by ethnic entrepreneurs, causing these communities to mobilize and to move apart. The consequence is conflict, similar to the movement of one people into the territory claimed by another. These conflicts may spin out of control, resulting in destructive violence, but when managed by wise policy and firm security measures, may lead to peaceful outcomes. This scenario recognizes the enduring, adaptive character of collective ethnic identities and the possibility of conflict when they exist in the same political space. It is shared, despite their many differences, by most who practice the domination and the power-sharing patterns.

The second scenario predicts the reduction and eventual elimination of ethnic differences by policies of integration or by induced or coerced assimilation. Its advocates would welcome the disappearance of politicized ethnic identities and solidarities and the needless conflict they have spawned during the past two centuries. Many of them have been nurtured in the western liberal tradition that looks forward to the day when ethnic differences will happily disappear and all persons will participate on equal terms and be evaluated by their individual character and performance, independently of their ethnic origins.

A third, less prominent, scenario is gaining followers, especially in elite circles in North American universities, armed services, and industries. Ethnic diversity is celebrated as a virtue in itself, enriching the lives of all members of society. All cultures are held to be intrinsically valuable, worth preserving, and should be helped to develop, while the death of any culture represents a net loss to the quality and vitality of human civilization. There need be no conflicts between cultures or between their individual members if all are treated with equal respect. This multicultural scenario visualizes the permanence of cultural pluralism, but recognizes no need for conflicts between its members, as long as society's authorities create and maintain an environment that treats all cultures with respect and all individuals equally.

A hy-brid of the third scenario that nevertheless reaches the same end point as the second holds that while ethnic diversity should be regarded as a national blessing rather than a burden, a subsequent and perhaps final stage is emerging and should be welcomed. This final stage may be called "mongrelization," the mixing of cultures and of blood. This its supporters advocate for the United States and other advanced societies. They believe the United States is becoming the model of the mongrelized society that is pointing the way for others to follow: a twenty-first-century version of the melting pot?[1]

Readers who have followed the course of my argument up to this point will recognize that I believe the first scenario to be the most likely for most countries for the future. While ethnic mixing continues to occur, even under unfavorable circumstances – between Tamils and Sinhalese in Sri Lanka, Hausa and Ibo in Nigeria, Serbs and Muslims in Bosnia, Hutu and Tutsi in Rwanda, Tibetans and Han in China, French and North Africans – such unions occur on the margins of their societies. Some states populated by recent and continuing immigration, such as the United States, Brazil, and Australia, may incorporate some features of the second (integrationist) scenario, yet even they are not spared the problems of ethnic tensions during the long transition to an integrated society. More significant for most countries are the continuing salience and politicizing of collective identities, the conflicts they engender, and the challenges they pose to persons of good will within and outside these societies to innovate and implement peaceful coexistence and equitable relations between them. This, I judge, to be the most common scenario for the foreseeable future.

Each of these scenarios entails a normative set of propositions, reflecting the value their proponents attach to ethnic distinctiveness. In this concluding chapter we shall not attempt to resolve these disputes over values, but focus instead on prospects for the outbreak and management of ethnic conflicts and the means available to divert such conflicts into channels that allow for peaceful regulation.

From modernization to globalization

An influential group of scholars in the generation following World War II promoted the concept of "modernization," which they believed to be a universal stage in social evolution.[2] At different rates, societies move from tradition to a new stage characterized by industrialization, urbanization, secularization, and participation in modern science and technology. In their passage to modernization, traditional ascriptive identities such as ethnicity become increasingly irrelevant to the common needs of a more "rational" society, and are destined gradually to wither away. Modern identities, by contrast, are based on state citizenship, occupational roles, class, and ideological choices. Like their successors, the globalizers, they were confounded by the persistence of ethnic identities and ethnic mobilization in societies such as the United States, France, and the United Kingdom, which they considered to have been pioneers in modernization.

As we concluded in chapter 1, economic and informational globalization with its promise of a borderless world and a universal culture will neither eliminate ethnic differences nor mitigate ethnic conflicts. Instead, free trade and the global mobility of capital may create fresh grievances as foreign imports threaten to destroy local livelihoods, and foreign investments appear to benefit members of some ethnic communities and to inflict pain and hardships on others. Power and prestige seem to flow to the sources of globalization, while members of societies on the periphery that have fallen behind often feel diminished and resentful. The emergence of Islamist revivalism and radical politics can be explained in this way.[3] Ethnic communities that had long been unmobilized may be stirred into action by the impact of globalization, like the Indian peoples of Ecuador's highlands whose way of life was threatened by the encroachment of foreign firms on the resource frontier in their homeland.[4] They have organized into a political bloc, the Indigenous Nationalities Federation, and their support was critical to the success of a friendly candidate for president in the 2002 election. Some previously dormant peoples are challenged by the incursion of globalization into their world and stubbornly refuse to sacrifice their collective identity and melt into the national mainstream, despite the incentives presented to them. Large numbers of Berbers in Algeria refuse to be Arabized, Tatars in Russia decline to be Russified, Amish farmers, Indian nations, and Hasidic Jews in the United States reject integration, preferring to maintain their separate collective identities and distinctive way of life.

Chronic roots of conflict

It is difficult to visualize a scenario of the future in which all peoples who claim homeland status can be endowed with political sovereignty. The reasons are quite straightforward: (1) either the territory they inhabit is controlled by a powerful state whose leaders will not allow it to be dismembered; or (2) residence patterns are so intermixed that it is impossible to carve out a viable state for an ethnic minority without engaging in unacceptable, coercive transfers of population. The first situation is illustrated by the several Indian tribes (or nations) in the United States whose government will not agree that chunks of its territory should be detached to create independent polities for its indigenous nations. Nor would the Indian state or the Russian federation agree to the secession of any of its territorially concentrated national minorities. They are destined to coexist, though the terms of coexistence may become subjects of contention and negotiation by methods that do not exclude violence.

The second situation is illustrated by Bosnia. There, despite the post-conflict legacy of mutual fear, hatred, and distrust between Serbs, Croats, and Muslims – who not long ago coexisted in relative harmony – settlement patterns preclude the division of the territory into three viable political and economic entities, without even more coerced transfers of populations. There is no feasible alternative to maintaining Bosnia as a single system through some form of power-sharing arrangement that has yet to be worked out.[5] The same holds for Lebanon, Trinidad, South Africa, and Northern Ireland, where homogenization is not desired by any party, territorial partition is simply unfeasible, and peoples must therefore find ways to coexist and manage the differences that arise between them. Many indigenous homeland peoples are destined to remain unassimilated within pluralistic political systems.

Nor is transnational migration likely to diminish. It has already exceeded all previously recorded levels, generated by the radical differences in labor market conditions between richer economies that need and can absorb large numbers of workers and poorer economies where job opportunities have failed to keep pace with new entrants into the labor force. Instant communication by telephone and the internet, and cheap, reliable, safe transportation facilitate transnational migration. As migrants and their children form diaspora communities in host countries, as these communities continue to be renewed by fresh arrivals, as there is much traveling back and forth between host and home countries as well as telephone traffic and financial remittances, these communities are unlikely to disappear. As detailed in chapter 5, conflicts inevitably arise between "natives" (often the products of earlier migrations) and the newer arrivals to the point that in contemporary central and western Europe they have become a prominent divisive item on the political agenda of every

country. As far as we can imagine the future, these population movements will continue to produce ethnic pluralism.
Already they have altered the demographic proportions of
central and western Europe and North America where a
diminishing proportion of the population is White and a
growing proportion people of color. In the United States,
despite rapid acculturation to the mainstream, in 2000 as
many as 20 percent of households conversed at home in languages other than English.[6] Grievances and threats resulting
from tensions between natives and new arrivals will result in
conflicts that cannot be kept off the political agendas of these
countries.

   Some integration and ethnic mixing will occur as individual migrants and their offsprings decide to acculturate to the
national mainstream, accept local citizenship where this is
permitted or encouraged, leave the diaspora community,
blend into the mainstream, and eventually intermarry. This is
happening among Hispanics, the largest contemporary source
of immigration in the United States; 25 percent of persons of
Hispanic origin now marry non-Hispanics.[7] Others, however,
decline to integrate. Some, like many Turks in Germany,
dream of one day returning to their fatherland; others,
insulted by the unwillingness of native Germans to accept
them as equals, react by rejecting German society even
though they have no intention of ever leaving Germany.
North African Muslims in France, 5 million strong, fear that
acculturation is a slippery slope that would force them to sacrifice their proud Islamic heritage, a price they are unwilling
to pay. Others, like many Afro-Caribbeans in Britain, feel
that they are effectively barred from first-class acceptance
into the mainstream because of their color, complaining that
they continue to be harassed by the police and suffer discrimination in housing and employment. They prefer the
status of resident foreigners to second-class citizenship. All of
which implies that racially visible immigrants of exotic cultural backgrounds will continue to harbor grievances and
encounter hostility that will extend their diaspora status well
into the future. In their daily lives they may suppress these
grievances in order to get along and avoid potentially damaging and disagreeable conflict. But they will maintain their
separate communities. Spokespersons for these minorities

will find ways to express grievances and make demands, and representatives of the mainstream community and of the state will find it necessary to respond. Ethnic conflict will recur, mostly through civic channels, some, however, through violence. In domination and power-sharing systems, ethnic differences are built into the society, so that conflicts are certain to arise.

This is not to argue that ethnicity is the sole line of political cleavage or even the most important in many societies. Class, occupation, ideology, region, family, and even personal ambitions may form the critical cleavages in some societies. These may combine with ethnicity, as in ranked situations where ethnicity reinforces class stratification (where those at the bottom of the socio-economic ladder happen also to be composed of a single ethnic community).

Terrorism

Terrorism has been on many people's minds following the atrocities of September 11, 2001. It can be defined as violent, even lethal, assaults more often on civilian than military targets through clandestine means by non-uniformed assailants. Their motives range from publicizing grievances, radicalizing and raising the morale of the community they claim to represent, to intimidating and punishing their purported enemy. It is a form of guerilla warfare mounted by groups that lack access to the heavy weapons and repressive apparatus of government. Many terrorist organizations spring from aggrieved ethnic communities, such as Hamas from Palestinians, Tigers from Sri Lankan Tamils, ETA from Spanish Basques. Others, however, have no ethnic connections at all, including narco-terrorists in Colombia, anarchists and romantic revolutionaries like the American Weathermen and the European Bader-Meinhoff gang of the 1970s. For the foreseeable future, the threat of terrorist tactics will remain a reality among groups that claim to act in the name of ethnic communities that have been thwarted or believe themselves to have been collectively affronted. The perpetrators of September 11 claimed to be avenging Islam for humiliations

inflicted by the United States in the interest of infidel Cru-
saders (Christians) and Jews.

Lessons learned

Where ethnic-based grievances and demands are sources of
political cleavage and conflict, the parties are likely to clash
over such issues as those outlined in chapter 4, namely: (1)
the dignity and respect displayed by government and by
outsiders to an ethnic community and its members; (2) its
political status and rights, either for self-determination and
autonomy, or for enhanced participation and voice in public
affairs; (3) the status accorded to its culture, especially to its
language, religion, and historical traditions; and (4) terms
and conditions of access to scarce and valued resources and
opportunities, including higher education, employment, land,
capital, credit, and business licenses.

An ethnic community whose members are satisfied on all
these counts is unlikely to feel the need for mobilization
except, perhaps, to defend the positions it has achieved
against challenges from others. Those that are aggrieved on
all scores will have powerful incentives to mobilize and struggle, unless they are blocked both materially and psychologically by the state or by the power of a superordinate ethnic
community. For example, the Indians of the Andean highlands in Ecuador, Peru, and Bolivia were so decisively beaten,
humiliated, and psychologically disarmed in previous centuries by Spaniards and their local successors that only in
recent years have they developed the collective will, with the
encouragement of foreign NGOs, to challenge the status quo
and begin to demand their rights. Factionalism is a common
reality in the internal politics of ethnic communities. One
source of factionalism within ethnic communities reflects dif-
fering interpretations of the strategy that would best serve its
collective needs and interests.

The twenty-first century is certain to witness episodes of
ethnic-based conflict as ethnic communities struggle for
degrees of self-determination that the rulers of their state consider unacceptable – note the unrelenting struggle between

Abkhazians and South Ossetians against the Georgian state; of Tibetans against the Chinese state; of Aceh against the Indonesian state; and between Tamils and Sinhalese in Sri Lanka – some through civic channels, some through violence. And as transnational migration continues unabated, the seeds of ethnic conflict are sown, even in such countries as Denmark and Japan that recently believed they were homogeneous. The question that arises is not whether ethnic conflict is to be expected, but how it is to be managed. Will governments and the leaders of ethnic communities and international agencies, the principal actors in these confrontations, display the wit and the will to manage the conflicts that will inevitably occur through peaceful debate, negotiation, give-and-take, and accommodation, as they have in Canada, Malaysia, and post-apartheid South Africa, or will there be still more Palestines, Chechnyas, Sri Lankas, and Rwandas? The reality of ethnic pluralism and the conflicts they breed cannot be wished away or written off as the poisonous effects of elite manipulation or as the misperception of reality among the contestants. These are genuine clashes of group interests as perceived by their principal contestants. The challenge, as we illustrated in chapter 9, is to guide them in the direction of accommodation and compromise, so that the lives of innocents can be spared and the horrors of terror and warfare averted, so that ordinary men and women can at least coexist with members of other communities in the same political space, and look forward to fulfilling their lives in security and peace.

Enough has been learned during the past three decades about the dynamics of ethnic conflict to provide cautious guidance for their management, recognizing that the specifics of every conflict situation call for the exercise of guarded judgment in prescribing courses of action.[8] The circumstances in Fiji and Trinidad, in Malaysia and Uganda, in Catalonia and Quebec, may appear on the surface to be quite similar, yet variable factors in each case require the exercise of informed judgment and willingness to learn and adjust with experience. We know that domination systems, whether authoritarian or democratic, tend to preempt or suppress conflict by the use of force, physical and psychological, hoping to forestall the mobilization of ethnic dissidence, nip it in the bud, or overwhelm it should it turn violent. Power-sharing systems maintain themselves by a combination of autonomy, territorial or cultural; and equitable participation, fair shares in decision-making and in the benefits and costs of governance. Integration systems aim normatively at the consensual transformation of distinct ethnic identities into a common national identity based on individual equality of rights and status. In the interim they attempt to direct ethnic-based grievances away from violent confrontation and into institutional channels where they can be regulated by give-and-take that involves government as well as the ethnic parties to disputes. Outsiders may attempt to intervene in pursuit of their own goals; as conflicts spin out of control, individual states, NGOs, and international organizations may attempt to mediate or to impose settlements. It may at times be necessary for majority factions that have concluded com-promise settlements of disputes to use force to suppress vio-lence initiated by minority factions within their own ranks that remain unreconciled to the compromises.

The new century may witness the consolidation of a prin-ciple that has been struggling to gain international acceptance: that the international community, through its organizations, is authorized, even required to take action to prevent or to ter-minate flagrant violations of human rights, including abuses of ethnic communities. The international norm that appears to be emerging is that state sovereignty which recognizes the exclusive power of governments over the populations within their borders implies a commensurate responsibility to respect the human rights of individuals and of ethnic minorities. When these rights are flagrantly abused, the international commun-ity is authorized to intervene by coercive means, if necessary, as in Bosnia, Kosovo, and East Timor to vindicate human rights and prevent further bloodshed and suffering. However, to deter capricious or self-interested interventions, the power to intervene coercively should be legitimated only when autho-rized by an international organization.

Methods of intervention range from mediation to military force and international judicial tribunals to punish crimes against humanity, such as those perpetrated by the former Serbian president, Slobodan Milosevic. The OSCE in Europe has pioneered in establishing norms and procedures for such action (as described in chapter 5); and the United Nations, notwithstanding its cumbersome processes of decision, has confronted and succeeded in acting in several such situations. State sovereignty no longer guarantees immunity from international scrutiny and ultimate intervention when the rights of ethnic communities are judged to have been severely violated. There are a number of obstacles, conceptual and operational, to the implementation of this principle, including the difficulty of proceeding against more powerful state violators such as China in Tibet and Russia in Chechnya. Yet, is seems unlikely that this new norm will be allowed to lapse. It is strongly supported by public sentiment and active NGOs, especially in Europe and North America. As it gains acceptance, the prospect of international scrutiny and intervention may succeed in deterring governments and protecting ethnic minorities from at least the more flagrant abuses of their rights.

We now understand that:

- Ethnic pluralism is not a sufficient condition for ethnic conflict. Ethnic communities have coexisted in peace within the same political space for extended periods of time.
- Many individuals are deeply attached to their ethnic community; others are more indifferent, able should the opportunity arise to improve their prospects by passing into another community or into a national mainstream. Most ethnic communities survive and evolve over long periods of time, while others pass out of history. Their members are absorbed or assimilated by others or are integrated as individuals into a national mainstream. Fresh circumstances may occasion the emergence and mobilization of new collective identities with their separate cultures and distinctive interests.
- Mobilization and conflict may ensue (1) when the dignity or honor of an ethnic community is challenged by government or another ethnic community; (2) when its vital interests are believed to be threatened; or (3) when fresh circumstances provide opportunities for ethnic communities to achieve goals that were previously considered to be out of reach.

- Conflicts between ethnic communities cannot be dismissed as irrational affairs or as misperceptions of reality; they involve differences over real values or interests. Yet, ethnic contestants are capable of inventing or believing rumors about the intentions of their adversaries, of demonizing them, and of committing horrendous atrocities, prolonging the conflict and inhibiting the search for an equitable settlement.
- Some ethnic grievances are suppressed by the superior power of governments or of dominant ethnic communities. Suppression, however, only intensifies the grievances that may eventually erupt into protest and violence. Others are channeled into political processes where they can be negotiated, accommodated, and compromised, greatly reducing the risk of violence.
- The main task facing social scientists, and officials of governments and international organizations is to improve the instruments of conflict management by NGOs, governments, and international organizations that can produce timely action to forestall or limit the incidence and costs of interethnic violence.
- The parties to ethnic conflict espouse contrary views of what would constitute a fair settlement of their dispute. Though mutual distrust, as well as rigid conceptions of their group interest plus extremist factions in their midst, may impede the search for settlement, the resources of diplomacy with assistance from civil society and internationally sanctioned coercive intervention, will play an increasingly active role in nudging the parties to compromise settlements and helping to implement their terms. Like warfare in general, ethnic warfare can be limited and contained, if not completely prevented.

Academics will continue to argue, as outlined in chapter 2, over the essence of collective ethnic identity and solidarity – whether it is historically rooted or socially constructed. Meanwhile, communities that define themselves as ethnic (or religious, or racial) and are so defined by others are pragmatic realities, pursuing their collective interests in ways that may threaten the interests and ambitions of other ethnic communities or of governments, often with catastrophic costs in lives and suffering. The need to regulate such conflicts in an increasingly interdependent world is evident.

Though much remains to be learned, enough is now known about the origins, dynamics, and outcomes of ethnic conflicts to provide observers and participants with useful guidance for conceptualizing and acting in constructive and humane directions. The purpose of this short volume has been to summarize that state of knowledge at the outset of this century.

Suggested Readings

The subject of ethnic conflict has generated a very extensive literature, most of it during the last quarter of the twentieth century. Some of these studies focus on individual countries, others treat the subject in comparative or theoretical terms. Most of the books that deal with ethnic conflict include lengthy bibliographies, a good example being John F. Stack and Lui Hebron (eds), *The Ethnic Entanglement: Conflict and Intervention in World Politics*, Westport, CT: Praeger, 1999. Since these bibliographies are readily accessible, I will not add another. Instead it would be more useful to suggest a small number of influential books for readers who wish to begin exploring the subject in greater depth.

- Ted Robert Gurr, *Minorities at Risk: a Global View of Ethnopolitical Conflicts*, Washington, DC: US Institute of Peace, 1993. This is a path-breaking data-based presentation and analysis of the scope and incidence of ethnic conflict, identifying the particular communities, the duration and magnitude of their disputes, and recent trends in ethnic mobilization. The first four chapters contain useful comparative information.
- Donald L. Horowitz, *Ethnic Groups in Conflict*, Berkeley: University of California Press, 1986. Though lengthy and somewhat dated, this remains one of the most informative, insightful and comprehensive available treat-

ments of the causes, processes, and consequences of ethnic conflict, plus a number of proposals for its management, mainly from an integrationist perspective.

- Timothy Sisk, *Power-sharing and International Mediation in Ethnic Conflicts*, Washington, DC: US Institute of Peace, 1996. This short book outlines and evaluates the several processes of power-sharing which, as discussed in chapter 7, is one of the more promising strategies for the peaceful management of ethnic conflict. The standard presentation of the consociational approach is Arend Lijphart, *Democracy in Plural Societies*, New Haven: Yale University Press, 1977.
- David Lake and Donald Rothchild (eds), *The International Spread of Ethnic Conflicts*, Princeton University Press, 1998. Stephen Ryan, *Ethnic Conflict and International Relations*, Brookfield, VT: Dartmouth Publishing Company, 1990. From different perspectives, these two books provide good cross-sectional treatment of the impact of ethnic conflict on world politics and of external intervention in domestic ethnic disputes.
- R. A. Schermerhorn, *Comparative Ethnic Relations: a Framework for Theory and Research*, New York: Random House, 1970. A classic in political sociology, this book presents a rigorous analysis and interpretation of the sequences of interaction between dominant and subordinate communities and the conditions that foster or prevent the integration of ethnic minorities into the mainstream of their societies.
- Anthony Smith, *Nationalism: Theory, Ideology, History*, Cambridge, UK: Polity, 2001. Nationalism has been the most influential political ideology of the nineteenth and twentieth centuries. It has yielded entire libraries of scholarship and controversy. Nationalism based on ethnic communities (ethnonationalism) has been and remains a powerful mobilizing force. This book is a skillful summary and interpretation of this extensive literature.
- Stephen Cornell and Douglas Hartman, *Ethnicity and Race: Making Identities in a Changing World*, Thousand Oaks, CA: Pine Forge Press, 1998. As constructionism has captured the allegiance of so many social scientists, readers may find it instructive to consult this well-

informed and nuanced elaboration of the constructionist position on how collective identities are formed and maintained.

- Daniel Chirot and Martin E. P. Seligman (eds), *Ethnopolitical Warfare: Causes, Consequences, and Possible Solutions*, Washington, DC: American Psychological Association, 2001. Readers interested in exploring the psychological insights into ethnic conflict will find these essays instructive, especially the chapters by Chirot (chapter 1), Hewstone and Cairns (chapter 20), and McConley (chapter 21).

This is one scholar's selection from a much larger set of excellent studies, many of which have been cited in the notes to the chapters of this book. Serious students and researchers investigating ethnic politics and ethnic conflict should become acquainted with *Nationality and Ethnicity Terminologies: an Encyclopedic Dictionary and Research Guide* compiled by Thomas Spira and published in 1999 by the Academic International Press. This two volume work defines the key concepts from all the social sciences that are encountered in the literature on this subject.

Glossary

diaspora Communities of migrants who settle in a host country, construct their own institutions, and attempt to maintain their own culture apart from native society. They tend to submit to local political authorities and interact economically with local society, but are slow to integrate culturally or socially.

ethnicity 1 A self-conscious community or collective identity based on perceived common descent, fictive kinship, historical experience, and culture, especially a common language.

ethnicity 2 As a working definition, any community or collective identity based on culture, race, or religion that can be mobilized to act politically in pursuit of its collective interests.

irredenta A state that seeks the acquisition of part of the territory of another state that is inhabited by their ethnic kinfolk. Also, a minority community who seek the transfer of their territory across an international border so that they may be united with their ethnic kinfolk.

multiculturalism The policy and practice of celebrating cultural diversity and entitling the culture of every ethnic community to equal respect and treatment by educational and governmental authorities.

nation   A political community or people that aspires to self-determination in the form of autonomy in a federal system or sovereign independence. A nation may be based either on common ethnic origin (ethnonation) or on residence within the jurisdiction of a state and loyalty to its institutions (civic nation).

nationalism   An ideology that glorifies the nation and elevates it to the supreme object of loyalty for its citizens. In extreme form it exalts one's nation as superior to others, including the right to dominate and rule over them.

race   A community based on self-perceived or externally assigned common physical features, especially skin color.

racism   An ideology that imparts moral, intellectual, and physical superiority to a particular racial community and relegates one or more others to inferior and subordinate status.

religion   A community based on a common belief system about the nature and destiny of humankind, combined with functionaries and practices that institutionalize it for the faithful (sometimes referred to as confessions or sects).

Notes

Chapter 1   Incidence and Scope of Ethnic Conflict

1   Two or more ethnic communities may, however, encounter one another in a political space that is outside the effective control of any government.

2   Ashutosh Varshney, *Ethnic Conflict and Civil Life: Hindus and Muslims in India*, New Haven: Yale University Press, 2002.

3   Ted Robert Gurr, "Peoples Against States: Ethnopolitical Conflict and the Changing World System," *International Studies Quarterly*, 38/3, September 1994, pp. 347–77.

4   Ted Robert Gurr, *Minorities at Risk: a Global View of Ethnopolitical Conflicts*, Washington, DC: United States Institute of Peace, 1993, p. ix. The Minorities at Risk project maintains an extensive database that is available to students and researchers at *www.minoritiesatrisk.com*.

5   James D. Fearon and David Laitin, "Ethnicity, Insurgency, and Civil War," *American Political Science Review*, 99/1, February 2003, pp. 75–90.

6   Contrast the treatment of ethnic solidarity by two prominent scholars: Walker Connor, *Ethnonationalism: the Quest for Understanding*, Princeton University Press, 1994; and Benedict O'G. Anderson, *Imagined Communities: Reflections on the Origins and Spread of Nationalism*, London: Verso Press, 1991. Connor emphasizes the historical roots of ethnonationalism, while Anderson argues that they are intellectually constructed, thus more transient and contingent.

7 Robert Melson, *Marxists in the Nigerian Labor Movement: a Case Study in the Failure of Ideology*, Cambridge, MA: MIT PhD thesis, 1967.

8 Kenneth McRoberts, *Quebec: Social Change and Political Crisis*, Toronto: McClelland and Stewart, 1988.

9 Though citizenship has been conferred on the 250,000 ethnic Japanese returnees (*nikkeijin*), they are not fully accepted as Japanese. Joshua A. Roth, *Brokered Homeland: Japanese-Brazilian Migrants in Japan*, Ithaca, NY: Cornell University Press, 2002.

10 One such effort, expanding on the insights of the German sociologist Max Weber, is the brief monograph by Ashley J. Tellis, Thomas S. Szayna, and James A. Winnefeld, *Anticipating Ethnic Conflict*, Santa Monica, CA: Rand Corporation, 1997.

11 For influential examples of this literature on inter-group relations, see Milton Gordon, *Assimilation in American Life*, New York: Oxford University Press, 1964, and Robin M. Williams Jr, *Strangers Next Door: Ethnic Relations in American Communities*, New York: Prentice Hall, 1964.

12 Typical of this literature was the treatise by Cyril E. Black, *The Dynamics of Modernization: a Study in Comparative History*, New York: Harper and Row, 1966.

13 Varshney, *Ethnic Conflict*.

14 Matthew Evangelista, "The Chechen Wars: will Russia go the way of the Soviet Union?", Washington DC: Brookings Institute Press, 2002.

15 Actually, the "Malaysian Malaysia" slogan is now illegal. Most non-Malays, nevertheless, continue to adhere to the principles it represents.

16 Nagorny Karabakh is a majority Armenian enclave entirely within Azerbaijan. The Armenian army has created and continues to occupy a 40 mile corridor within Azerbaijan, linking Armenia and Nagorny Karabakh. The Armenian diaspora in France and California has financed the construction of a modern highway within this corridor. Though members of these two peoples had long coexisted amicably in both countries, the resultant conflict has created an estimated 25,000 casualties and as many as 750,000 refugees, Azeris expelled from Armenia and Nagorny Karabakh and Armenians forced to flee from Azerbaijan. These refugees subsist in misery and penury on both sides of the border. Though both countries continue to suffer economically from this conflict, all efforts to conciliate this dispute have been thwarted by militants on both sides. See Thomas de Waal, *Black Garden: Armenia and Azerbaijan Through Peace and War*, New York: New York University Press, 2003.

17 This apparent dilemma is explored by Benjamin Barber in his astute and entertaining volume, *Jihad vs. McWorld*, New York: Times Books, 1995.

18 Stephane Paquin, "Globalization, European Integration, and the Rise of Neo-nationalism in Scotland," *Nationalism and Ethnic Politics*, 8/1, Spring 2002, pp. 55–80.

19 Joel Kotkin, *Tribes: How Race, Religion, and Identity Determine Success in the New Global Economy*, New York: Random House, 1993.

20 Yahya Sadowski, *The Myth of Global Chaos*, Washington: The Brookings Institution Press, 1995.

Chapter 2 Ethnic Sentiments and Solidarities

1 For technical definitions, check the glossary, pp. 211–12.

2 As stated by Rodolfo Stavenhagen, "We may define an ethnic conflict as a protracted social and political confrontation between contenders who define themselves and each other in ethnic terms: that is, when criteria such as national origin, religion, race, language and other markers are used to distinguish the opposing parties" (*Ethnic Conflicts and the Nation State*, London and New York: St. Martin's Press, Inc., 1996, p. 284).

3 Walker Connor, *Ethnonationalism*. Also Clifford Geertz, *The Interpretation of Cultures*, London: Fontana, 1973; and Harold Isaacs, *Idols of the Tribe: Group Identity and Political Change*, New York: Harper and Row, 1975.

4 Johann Gottfried Herder is recognized as the founder of this school. See his *Philosophical Writings*, ed. Michael N. Foster, Cambridge, UK: Cambridge University Press, 2002.

5 Pierre Van Den Berghe, *Man in Society: a Biosocial View*, New York: Elsevier, 1978. See also David Carment and Frank Harvey, *Using Force to Prevent Ethnic Violence*, Westport, CT: Praeger, 2001, which elaborates a bio-social interpretation of ethnic solidarity.

6 For an extended treatment of circumstantialism and a systematic comparison of primordialism and circumstantialism, see Stephen Cornell and Douglas Hartman, *Ethnicity and Race: Making Identities in a Changing World*, Thousand Oaks, CA: Pine Forge Press, 1998, pp. 64–8. Also Stephen Steinberg, *The Ethnic Myth: Race, Ethnicity, and Class in America*, New York: Atheneum, 1981.

7 Eric Hobsbawm and Terence Ranger, eds, *The Invention of Tradition*, Cambridge, UK: Cambridge University Press, 1983. For a Marxist perspective see Emmanuel Wallerstein, *The Cap-*

italist World Economy, Cambridge, UK: Cambridge University Press, 1979.

8   For a review of the Bosnian conflict and its aftermath, see Sumantra Bose, *Bosnia after Dayton: Nationalist Partition and International Intervention*, London: Hurst and Company, 2002.

9   Ashutosh Varshney, "Nationalism, Ethnic Conflict, and Rationality," in American Political Science Association, *Perspectives on Politics*, 1/1, March 2002, pp. 85–99, presents a technical refutation of the rational choice position on this subject.

10   An influential version of social constructionism is Benedict Anderson's treatise, *Imagined Communities*. See also Tarja Vayrynen, "Socially Constructed Ethnic Identities," in Haken Wiberg and Christian P. Scherrer, eds, *Ethnicity and Intrastate Conflict*, Aldershot, UK: Ashgate Publishing Ltd, 1999, pp. 125–44. For a constructionist perspective on the relationship between ethnicity and race, see Cornell and Hartman, *Ethnicity and Race*.

11   See Pauline Marie Rosenau, *Post-Modernism and the Social Sciences*, Princeton, N.J.: University Press, 1992.

12   Lydia Polgreen, "For Mixed Race South Africans, Equity is Elusive," *New York Times*, July 27, 2003, p. A3.

13   Myron Weiner, ed., *Modernization: the Dynamics of Growth*, New York: Basic Books, 1966; and David Apter, *The Politics of Modernization*, Chicago, Illinois: University of Chicago Press, 1967.

14   In the 2002 legislative elections, ethnonationalists were victorious among Bosnian Serbs, Croats, and Muslims. Those who advocated a united Bosnia were defeated in all three communities.

15   Rogers Brubaker, *Nationalism Reframed: Nationhood and the National Question in the New Europe*, Cambridge, UK: Cambridge University Press, 1996, p. 7.

16   Anthony Smith's short classic, *Nationalism: Theory, Ideology, History*, Cambridge, UK: Polity, 2001, is a useful brief introduction to the subject. It contains an excellent bibliography.

Chapter 3   Origins of Ethnic Pluralism

1   Rosemarie Rogers and Emily Copeland, *Forced Migration: Policy Issues in the Post-Cold War World*, Medford, MA: Fletcher School of Law and Diplomacy, 1993. This monograph contains reliable data from the early 1990s and an excellent summary of the status of coerced migrants.

Chapter 4   For What Do They Contend?

1   Donald L. Horowitz, *The Deadly Ethnic Riot*, Berkeley: University of California Press, 2001.
2   James C. Scott, *Weapons of the Weak: Everyday Forms of Peasant Resistance*, New Haven: Yale University Press, 1985.
3   This is a common assumption among foreign aid donors. See, for example, George Psacheropoulas and Henry Anthony Pattinos, *Indigenous People and Poverty in Latin America*, Washington, DC: World Bank, 1994. For an evaluation of the economic determinist thesis, see Milton J. Esman, "Economic Performance and Ethnic Conflict," in Joseph V. Montville, ed., *Conflict and Peacemaking in Multiethnic Societies*, Lexington, MA: D. C. Heath and Co., 1990, pp. 479–90.
4   Milton J. Esman, "Ethnic Politics and Economic Power," *Comparative Politics*, 19/4, July 1987, pp. 395–418.
5   Brian Weinstein, ed., *Language Policy and Political Development*, Norwood, NJ: Ablex, Publishing Corp., 1990. Also David Laitin, *Language Repertories and State Construction in Africa*, Cambridge, UK: Cambridge University Press, 1992.
6   David Kertzer and Dominique Arel, eds, *Census and Identity: the Politics of Race, Ethnicity, and Language in National Censuses*, Cambridge, UK: Cambridge University Press, 2002.
7   Rotimi Suberu, "The Politics of Population Counts," *Federalism and Ethnic Conflict in Nigeria*, Washington, DC: United States Institute of Peace Press, 2001, chap. 6, pp. 141–70.
8   For an excellent review of the literature on the psychological dimensions of ethnic conflict, see Miles Hewstone and Ed Cairns, "Social Psychology and Inter-group Conflict," in Daniel Chirot and Martin Seligman, eds, *Ethnic Political Warfare: Causes, Consequences, and Possible Solutions*, Washington, DC: American Psychological Association, 2001, chap. 20, pp. 319–42. Also Vamik Volkan, "Psychological Aspects of Ethnic Conflict," in Montville, *Conflict and Peacemaking*, pp. 81–92.
9   Much of that decline resulted from the ravages of diseases introduced by the Europeans. The numbers have gradually recovered, reaching 2.7 million in 2001 (*Statistical Abstract of the United States*, Washington, DC: US Census Bureau, 2002, p. 16).
10   John W. Burton, *Conflict Resolution and Prevention*, New York: St. Martin's Press, Inc., 1990; also Miles Hewstone, "Contact and Categorization: Social Psychological Interventions to Change Inter-group Relations," in C. N. Macrae,

C. Stangor, and M. Hewstone, eds, *Stereotypes and Stereotyping*, New York: Guilford Press, 1996.

11 Mary Anderson, *The Experiences of NGOs in Conflict Prevention: Problems and Prospects*, Cambridge, MA: The Local Capacities for Peace Project, 1995.

Chapter 5 The Contemporary State and Outsider Intervention

1 For useful case studies on this theme, see Paul Brass, ed., *Ethnic Groups and the State*, Totowa, NJ: Barnes and Noble Books, 1985. Also Milton J. Esman and Itamar Rabinovich, eds, *Ethnicity, Pluralism, and the State in the Middle-East*, Ithaca, NY: Cornell University Press, 1988.

2 OECD data reported in the *Economist*, Special Section on "Globalization and its Critics," September 29, 2001, p. 14.

3 Ashutosh Varshney, *Ethnic Conflict*.

4 Royal Commission on Bilingualism and Biculturalism, *Report and Annexes*, Ottawa: The Queen's Printer, 1967–9. Its recommendations regarding official languages are summarized in book 1, pp. 147–9.

5 These provisions in Bill 22 of 1972 became more rigorous in 1977 when the newly elected separatist Parti Québécois government enacted Bill 101, the Charter of the French Language.

6 Michael Dziedzic, Laura Rozen, and Phil Williams, "Lawless Rule Versus Rule of Law in the Balkans," Special Report 97, Washington, DC: United States Institute of Peace, December 2002.

7 Karen Ballentine, "Beyond Greed and Grievance: Reconsidering the Economic Dynamics of Armed Conflict," in Ballentine and Jake Sherman, *The Political Economy of Armed Conflict* (a project of the International Peace Academy), Boulder, CO: Lynne Rienner Publishers, 2003.

8 Naomi Chazan, (ed.), *Irredentism and International Politics*, Boulder, CO: Lynne Rienner Publishers, 1991.

9 Nevertheless, in 2003 an insurgency emerged in Narathiwat province. It attacked and murdered government personnel, burned schools, and committed other terrorist offenses in pursuit of its separatist objective.

10 Gabriel Sheffer, ed., *Modern Diasporas in International Politics*, New York: St. Martin's Press, Inc., 1986.

11 Reported in the *New York Times*, April 4, 2002, p. A13.

12 Reported by Thomas L. Friedman in the *New York Times*, August 6, 2002, p. A17.

13 To illustrate the cynical nature of strategic intervention: when the Soviets began to seek allies in the 1930s against the threat of German fascism, they abandoned their campaign for Negro militancy and instead celebrated American patriotism.

14 This and subsequent sections summarize the findings in Milton J. Esman and Shibley Telhami, eds, *International Organization and Ethnic Conflict*, Ithaca, NY: Cornell University Press, 1995.

15 The story of these post-World War I minorities treaties has been told by Inis Claude, *National Minorities: an International Problem*, Cambridge, MA: Harvard University Press, 1955.

16 William Zartman, "Conflict and Resolution: Context, Cost, and Change," *Annals of the American Academy*, 158, 1991, pp. 11–22.

17 Shibley Telhami, *Power and Leadership in International Bargaining: the Path to the Camp David Accords*, New York: Columbia University Press, 1990.

18 Walter A. Kemp, ed., *Quiet Diplomacy in Action: the OSCE High Commissioner on National Minorities*, The Hague: Kluwer Law International, 2001.

19 Data from *UN Peace Operations, Year in Review*, New York: United Nations, 2002. See also United Nations, *The Blue Helmets: a Review of United Nations Peace-keeping*, 3rd edn, New York: United Nations, 1996.

20 Harold H. Saunders is a distinguished former US diplomat who has devoted his retirement to the peaceful resolution of intrastate, mainly ethnic, conflicts. His book *Public Peace Processes: Sustaining Dialogue to Transform Racial and Ethnic Conflicts*, New York: St. Martin's Press, Inc., 1999, is an authoritative description of the conflict resolution paradigm with a manual for organizers and moderators.

21 While some NGOs are religiously sponsored, it does not follow that religious functionaries necessarily contribute to moderating conflict. Militant rabbis and fanatical imams speaking from their pulpits have helped to inflame the conflict between Israelis and Palestinians, as have Sinhalese Buddhist clergy and Tamil priests in Sri Lanka.

22 Saunders *Public Peace Processes*, pp. 147–60.

23 For specifics, see *Resolving Intra-national Conflicts: a Strengthened Role for Intergovernmental Organizations. A Consultation of the International Negotiation Network, Feb. 17–19, 1993*, Atlanta, GA: The Carter Center of Emory University, 1993. See also Rod Troester, *Jimmy Carter as Peacemaker: a Post-presidential Biography*, Westport, CT: Praeger, 1996, esp. chap. 5, pp. 51–74.

24 The material in this section summarizes the volume edited by Milton J. Esman and Ronald J. Herring, eds, *Carrots, Sticks, and Ethnic Conflict: Rethinking Development Assistance*, Ann Arbor: University of Michigan Press, 2001. See also Robert J. Muskat, *Investing in Peace: How Development Aid Can Prevent or Promote Conflict*, Armonk, NY: M. E. Sharpe, 2002.

25 Ronald J. Herring, "Making Ethnic Conflict: the Civil War in Sri Lanka," in Esman and Herring, *Carrots, Sticks, and Ethnic Conflict*, pp. 140–74.

26 John M. Cohen, "Foreign Aid and Ethnic Interests in Kenya," in Esman and Herring, *Carrots, Sticks, and Ethnic Conflict*, pp. 90–112.

27 Norman T. Uphoff, "Ethnic Cooperation in Sri Lanka: Through the Keyhole of a US Aid Project," in Esman and Herring, *Carrots, Sticks, and Ethnic Conflict*, pp. 113–39.

Chapter 6   Patterns of Pluralism I: Domination

1 Readers who recall the musical *Fiddler on the Roof* observed how Jews in tsarist Russia adjusted to their powerless situation. Prior to the civil rights movement some African-Americans attempted to lighten their skin and straighten their hair. "Black is Beautiful" was an effort to counteract this sense of racial inferiority. In the 2003 Hollywood film *The Human Stain*, Anthony Hopkins, who plays the leading character, is a talented, light-skinned African-American who rejects his background, fearing that it would block his career as an academic. He assumes a White Jewish identity, refusing to reveal his origins, even to his wife. When accused of directing racist remarks at African-American students, he chooses to lose his professorship at a prestigious university, rather than sacrifice his false identity. When he dies he is interred in a Jewish ceremony.

2 Pachakutic was the greatest of the pre-Conquest Inca rulers.

3 Afrikaner intellectuals propounded a theory of "separate development" for their African subjects. All Africans were assigned to a tribe and their permanent residence was considered to be a self-governing tribal homeland – 13 percent of inferior land for 75 percent of the population. Outside these Bantustans, Blacks were required to carry special pass books, permitting them to live and work temporarily in White cities and farms,

while their families remained in the tribal homelands or in "townships," large native slums on the outskirts of the cities. Other non-Whites, Indians, and mixed race peoples (Coloreds), were assigned segregated residential areas outside the major cities. That social order was enforced by the state security services.

4 For a well-documented survey and analysis of the contemporary status of the Roma in an integrating Europe, see Dana Ringold, Mitchell A. Orenstein, and Erika Wilkins, *Roma in an Expanding Europe: Breaking the Poverty Cycle*, Washington: The World Bank, 2003 (Conference Edition). Also Zoltan Barany, *The East European Gypsies: Regime Change, Marginality, and Ethnopolitics*, Cambridge, UK: Cambridge University Press, 2002.

5 Joshua 10–11.

6 On ethnic cleansing, see Norman M. Naimark, *Fires of Hatred: Ethnic Cleansing in the Twentieth Century*, Cambridge, MA: Harvard University Press, 2002; and Stuart J. Kaufman, *Modern Hatreds: the Symbolic Politics of Ethnic War*, Ithaca, NY: Cornell University Press, 2002.

7 Similar patterns of non-formal racial stratification and exclusion are evident in other Latin-American countries including Venezuela and Colombia. Mestizos look down upon and discriminate against Indians, lighter skinned mestizos discriminate against darker skinned mestizos, and Whites discriminate against all persons of color.

8 Rebecca Reichmann, "Brazil's Denial of Race," Washington, DC: NACAL Report on the Americas, 28/6, May–June 1985, pp. 35–6.

9 Larry Rohter, "Racial Quotas in Brazil Touch Off Fierce Debate," *New York Times*, April 5, 2003, p. A5.

10 Dominant groups historically have employed coercive measures, not to exclude weaker communities but to compel them to join the mainstream. The rapid spread of Islam by fire and sword in the seventh and eighth centuries is a historical instance of coerced inclusion.

11 Inis Claude, *National Minorities*.

12 Edna Bonacich, "A Theory of Middleman Minorities," *American Sociological Review*, 38, October 1973, pp. 583–94.

13 Milton J. Esman, "Overseas Chinese in Southeast Asia," in Gabriel Sheffer, ed., *Modern Diasporas*, pp. 130–63. For more extended treatment see Victor Purcell, *The Chinese in Southeast Asia*, London: Oxford University Press, 1965.

Chapter 7   Patterns of Pluralism II: Power-sharing

1   Timothy D. Sisk, *Power-sharing and International Mediation in Ethnic Conflicts*, Washington, DC: United States Institute of Peace Press, 1996.

2   Kjetil Tronvoll, *Ethiopia: a New Start?*, London: Minority Rights Group International, 2000.

3   William Wahlforth and Tyler Felgenhauer, "Self-determination and the Stability of the Russian Federation," in Wolfgang Danspeckgruber, ed., *The Self-determination of Peoples: Community, Nation, and State in an Interdependent World*, Boulder, CO: Lynne Rienner Publishers, 2002, 227–52.

4   The elements of autonomy that are of particular interest to ethnic communities are education and culture, including language choice. Other powers commonly reserved for regional units are independent taxing authority, police and law enforcement, local public works, and social welfare. See Michael Burgess and Alain G. Gagnon, *Comparative Federalism and Federation*, Toronto: University of Toronto Press, 1993; and Graham Smith, *Federalism: the Multiethnic Challenge*, New York: Longmans, 1995.

5   Arend Lijphart, *Democracy in Plural Societies*, New Haven: Yale University Press, 1977.

6   This is contrary to the celebrated assertion of John Stuart Mill that democracy and representative government are not possible in ethnically divided societies. See J. S. Mill, *Considerations on Representative Government*, New York: Liberal Arts Press, 1958 [1861], p. 230.

7   Alvin Rabushka and Kenneth A. Shepsle, *Politics in Plural Societies: a Theory of Democratic Instability*, Columbus, OH: Merrill, 1972.

8   Kris Deschouwer, "Causes and Effects of Constitutional Changes in Multilingual Belgium," in Stephen Brooks, ed., *The Challenge of Cultural Pluralism*, Westport, CT: Praeger, 2002, pp. 121–40.

9   Ibid.

10 Viranjini Munasinghe, *Callaloo or Tossed Salad: East Indians and the Cultural Politics of Identity in Trinidad*, Ithaca, NY: Cornell University Press, 2001.

11 Donald Rothchild and Michael W. Foley, "African States and the Politics of Inclusive Coalitions," in Rothchild and Naomi Chazan, eds, *The Precarious Balance: State and Society in Africa*, Boulder, CO: Westview Press, 1988, cited in Sisk, *Power-sharing*, p. 28.

Chapter 8 Patterns of Pluralism III: Integration

1 Milton J. Esman, *Ethnic Politics*, Ithaca, NY: Cornell University Press, 1994.
2 For an authoritative analysis and evaluation of American pluralism, see Lawrence H. Fuchs, *The American Kaleidoscope: Race, Ethnicity, and the Civic Culture*, Hanover, NH: The University Press of New England, 1990.
3 On the American mainstream, see John Higham, *Hanging Together: Unity and Diversity in American Culture*, New Haven: Yale University Press, 2001. Also Richard Alba and Victor Nee, *Remaking the American Mainstream: Assimilation and the New Immigration*, Cambridge, MA: Harvard University Press, 2003. G. Pascal Zachary's *The Diversity Advantage: Multicultural Identity in the New World Economy*, Boulder, CO: Westview Press, 2003, is a panegyric to ethnic diversity and "mongrelization" as a beneficial reality in the United States and a prescription for the rest of the world.
4 Michael Novak, *The Rise of the Unmeltable Ethnics*, New York: Macmillans, 1972.
5 Krisztina Zita Tohanyi, "The Future Generation of Reconciliation: Young South Africans' Views and Experiences of the Reconciliation Process," Ithaca, NY: Cornell University Peace Studies Program, unpublished MS, 2002.
6 Gary Rotstein, "Ethnic Neighborhoods Becoming Thing of Past," *Pittsburgh Post-Gazette*, May 25, 2003, p. A1.
7 An expression of this fear can be found in the polemic by Peter Brimelow, *Alien Nation*, New York: Random House, 1995.
8 In the United States and Canada, the long-standing policy of excluding Asians was reversed during the 1960s and immigrants from various Asian countries, notably Chinese, Koreans, and Indians are now integrating rapidly into their host societies.
9 A plea for the maintenance and invigoration of indigenous nations can be found in Taiaiake Alfred's *Peace, Power and Righteousness: an Indigenous Manifesto*, Don Mills, Ontario: Oxford University Press, 1999.
10 Harold Troper and Morton Weinfeld, *Old Wounds: Jews, Ukrainians, and the Hunt for Nazi War Criminals in Canada*, Chapel Hill: University of North Carolina Press, 1989.

Chapter 9   The Management of Ethnic Conflict

1   The perpetrators of the coup invaded the Parliament building and took 31 hostages, including the Fijian President and the Indian prime minister, and threatened to kill them unless their demands were met. The Constitution of 1997 had incorporated many power-sharing features which were intended to provide equitable representation in government for representatives of the two main ethnic communities that are nearly equal in numbers. Many Fijians, however, continue to distrust Indians, regarding them as foreigners bent on dominating government as they already dominated the economy and reducing Fijians to second-class status in their own homeland. They would be satisfied with nothing less than assured Fijian control of the state apparatus. Ralph R. Premdas, "Seizure of Power: Indigenous Rights and Crafting Democratic Governance in Fiji," *Nationalism and Ethnic Politics*, 8/4, Winter 2002, pp. 16–35.

2   Kemal Karpat, "The Ottoman Ethnic and Confessional Legacy in the Middle East," in Esman and Rabinovich, eds, *Ethnicity, Pluralism*, pp. 35–53. In the Ottoman Empire, Turks were officials, warriors, and peasants. The commercial economy and skilled trades were operated by members of the Christian and Jewish minorities.

3   From 1861 to 1865 the United States suffered a costly and devastating civil war over whether its southern, slave-holding states had the right to secede from the federal union. President Lincoln and his associates were willing to sustain heavy losses of lives and property to preserve the federal union.

4   The Kurdish region in northern Iraq has achieved a large measure of autonomy because the United States, after the 1991 Gulf War, prevented the Iraqi regime from reasserting control over this area.

5   Atul Kohli, "Can Democracies Accommodate Ethnic Nationalism: the Rise and Decline of Self-determination Movements in India," in Wolfgang Danspeckgruber, *Self-determination of Peoples*, pp. 287–314. India's failure to pacify Kashmiri nationalism is the result of unaccommodating Indian national leadership combined with active external (Pakistani) intervention.

6   In Iraq there are also much smaller but politically significant communities, including Turkmen and Christians, which demand official recognition.

7   This position has been argued by Donald Horowitz and Timothy Sisk. It is most fully elaborated by Benjamin Reilly in

Democracy in Divided Societies, Cambridge, UK: Cambridge University Press, 2001.

8   There is a vast technical and polemical literature on bilingual education. Among the more balanced treatments are Kenji Hakuta, *Mirror of Language: the Debate on Bilingualism*, New York: Basic Books, 1986; and James Crawford, *Bilingual Education: History, Politics, Theory, and Practice*, Trenton, NJ: Crane Publications, 1989.

9   A minority of African-Americans oppose affirmative action, objecting that their success due to individual achievement is stigmatized by the suspicion that it was gained only by racial preferences.

10   In favor of affirmative action, see Stephen L. Carter, *Confessions of an Affirmative Action Baby*, New York: Basic Books, 1991; opposed, see Thomas Sowell, *Preferential Policies: an International Perspective*, New York: W. Morrow, 1990.

11   Stephanie Larson, "The Creation of Singapore's Apolitical Culture," *Nationalism* and *Ethnic Politics*, 7/1, Spring 2001, 63–84.

12   President Franklin D. Roosevelt once reminded his Jewish friend, neighbor, and treasury secretary, Henry Morgenthau Jr, that the United States "is a Protestant country and the Catholics and Jews are here under sufferance." Therefore, "it is up to you" to "go along with anything I want" (Michael Bechloss, *The Conquerors: Roosevelt, Truman and the Destruction of Hitler's Germany*, New York: Simon and Schuster, 2000, p. 51). Ironically, Catholics and Jews were Roosevelt's most enthusiastic and consistent supporters.

Chapter 10   What of the Future?

1   Zachary, *The Diversity Advantage*.

2   Weiner, *Modernization*; also Black, *The Dynamics of Modernization*.

3   Islamic societies for centuries surpassed the West in economic, scientific, and artistic achievement and in military prowess. During the past two centuries, however, they have experienced military weakness, scientific and technological backwardness, and economic stagnation.

4   Alison Brysk, "Indian Market: the Ethnic Face of Adjustment in Ecuador," in Esman and Herring, *Carrots, Sticks, and Ethnic Conflict*, pp. 210–34.

5   This point is emphasized by Bose in *Bosnia after Dayton*, esp. chap. 6, pp. 253–82.

6 US Census Bureau data reported in the *New York Times*, October 10, 2003, p. A22.

7 US Census Bureau, *Statistical Abstract of the United States, 2000: the National Data Book*, Washington, DC, 2001, p. 47.

8 Writing in 1975, Nathan Glazer and Daniel Patrick Moynihan (eds, *Ethnicity: Theory and Experience*, Cambridge, MA: Harvard University Press) observed (p. 25) that "little in this field [ethnic conflict] has been resolved. We are all beginners here." That statement would no longer be valid.

Index

CPSIA information can be obtained at www.ICGtesting.com
Printed in the USA
BVOW06s1349220716

456443BV00010B/19/P

9 780745 631172